Capitalizing Religion

ALSO AVAILABLE FROM BLOOMSBURY

Capitalizing Religion

Ideology and the opiate of the bourgeoisie

CRAIG MARTIN

Bloomsbury Academic
An imprint of Bloomsbury Publishing Plc

B L O O M S B U R Y

LONDON · OXFORD · NEW YORK · NEW DELHI · SYDNEY

Bloomsbury Academic
An imprint of Bloomsbury Publishing Plc

50 Bedford Square
London
WC1B 3DP
UK

1385 Broadway
New York
NY 10018
USA

www.bloomsbury.com

**BLOOMSBURY and the Diana logo are trademarks of
Bloomsbury Publishing Plc**

First published 2014
Reprinted by Bloomsbury Academic 2015, 2016

British Library Cataloguing-in-Publication Data
A catalogue record for this book is available from the British Library.

ISBN: PB: 978-1-47252-744-8
      HB: 978-1-47252-164-4
      ePDF: 978-1-47253-337-1
      ePub: 978-1-47253-036-3

Library of Congress Cataloging-in-Publication Data
Martin, Craig, 1976- author.
Capitalizing religion : ideology and the opiate of the bourgeoisie / Craig Martin.
pages cm
Includes bibliographical references (pages).
ISBN 978-1-4725-2164-4 (hardback) – ISBN 978-1-4725-2744-8 (paperback) –
ISBN 978-1-4725-3337-1 (ePDF) – ISBN 978-1-4725-3036-3 (ePub) 1. Religion.
2. Spirituality. 3. Individualism–Religious aspects. 4. Capitalism–Religious aspects.
I. Title.
BL51.M354 2014
204—dc23
                                          2014003690

Typeset by Newgen Knowledge Works (P) Ltd., Chennai, India
Printed and bound in Great Britain

In memory of my dad

In the social production of their life, men enter into definite relations that are indispensable and independent of their will, relations of production that correspond to a definite stage of development of their material productive forces.

KARL MARX (MARX AND ENGELS), 1978, 4

[Individuals] always turn out on inspection to be social, and indeed historically specific.

STEVEN LUKES, 1973b, 75

The game of liberalism—not interfering, allowing free movement, letting things follow their course . . . . [T]his ideology of freedom really was one of the conditions of development of modern or, if you like, capitalist forms of the economy. . . . [T]his freedom, both ideology and technique of government, should in fact be understood within the mutations and transformations of technologies of power.

MICHEL FOUCAULT, 2007, 48

The disciplined study of any subject is, among other things, an assault on self-evidence, on matters taken for granted.

JONATHAN Z. SMITH, 2004, 389

Contents

Acknowledgments

I have had an incredible amount of support from colleagues while working on this book over the last couple of years.

I'm grateful for the support I've received from the St. Thomas Aquinas College community. First, thanks to Neerja Chaturvedi and C. J. Churchill for organizing the annual faculty research retreat, at which I experimented with some of the ideas in this book. Thanks go to the administration of the college for permitting me a course release during the 2012–2013 school year while working on this book. I would also like to thank the students in a number of my courses who suffered through lectures on some of this material or drafts of some of the chapters, in particular the students in my Religion and Capitalism, Evolution of Jesus, and Religions of the East courses. Last, I often rely upon my friends on the faculty for their moral support and solidarity, both of which are conditions for successful teaching and research.

Since I work at a small liberal arts institution with only one other faculty member in religious studies, I often rely upon the network of scholars on Facebook for a great deal of intellectual stimulation, discussion, book suggestions, help locating difficult-to-find articles, offers to read rough drafts of chapters, and so on. I've found Facebook to be an incredible tool for such scholarly purposes, and my online friends have been essential to the development of this book. I would especially like to mention junior scholars Dennis LoRusso, Brad Stoddard, Stephen Young, and Chris Zeichmann for their ongoing conversations and reading suggestions regarding critical theory, religious studies, capitalism, and so on.

Thanks also go to faculty and students at the University of Regina, the University of Alberta, and the University of South Africa for inviting me to speak (and funding my travels) on this research while it was ongoing. Much of what I originally presented there ended up in this book, and helpful feedback was provided on each visit.

My intellectual debts are innumerable, but a few in particular are worth noting. The research on the politics of the word "religion" by Russ McCutcheon (1997, 2001, 2003, 2005) and Tim Fitzgerald (1999, 2007, 2011) has been essential to my project; the arguments of Chapters 2 and 3 of the present book depend heavily on their work. When it comes to analyses of religion and capitalism, I've seen few works that model the critical approach

I've attempted here. Kathryn Lofton's book on *Oprah* (2011), Kimberly Lau's book on *New Age Capitalism* (2000), Matthew Wood's book on *Possession, Power, and the New Age* (2007), Bill Arnal's essay on Disneyland (republished in Arnal and McCutcheon 2012), and Jeremy Carrette and Richard King's *Selling Spirituality* (2005) are notable exceptions. Much of what follows attempts to walk further down the road in the same critical direction taken by Carrette and King in *Selling Spirituality*; in particular, most of part two of this book merely extends the analysis begun by Carrette and King. I hope that this book might be considered a sequel of sorts to their fine work. Last, I would like to acknowledge my doctoral advisor, Gail Hamner, who first encouraged my exploration of the work of Marx and Foucault in a graduate seminar long ago.

My colleagues have been very generous with their willingness to read rough drafts of one or more these chapters at various points. I have benefited from the guidance of Bill Arnal, Tara Baldrick-Morrone, Willi Braun, Leslie Dorrough Smith, Savannah Finver, Naomi Goldenberg, Sean McCloud, Russ McCutcheon, Aldea Mulhern, Brent Nongbri, Kevin Schilbrack, Jeremy Vecchi, Chris Zeichmann, and the reviewers for Bloomsbury. Savannah Finver deserves special mention, as she kindly read and commented on the entire manuscript when it was near completion. Above all others I must thank Bill Arnal for his continual encouragement and tireless reading and rereading of drafts of some of these chapters. Bill's prodding, motivation, and assistance in completing this project were invaluable, and I am greatly in his debt.

As always, the views expressed in this book may not reflect the views of those who helped me in the writing process.

Some of the material in the following chapters has previously appeared in print. Parts of Chapter 2 originally appeared in "Neoliberal mythmaking: On 'well-being' as the new protestant work ethic," *Religion & Theology* 19 (2012): 2014–2218. In addition, a few sentences from Chapter 2 originally appeared in "On the totems of science and capitalism," *Implicit Religion* 15(1) (2012): 25–35. Most of Chapter 3 previously appeared in "William James and Jesus Christ in late capitalism: Our religion of the status quo," *Studies in Religion/Sciences Religieuses* 42(4) (2012), which was also excerpted in *Religious Experience: A Reader* (2012), edited by Craig Martin and Russell T. McCutcheon.

Introduction

My father was at one time a poster child for capitalist success narratives. Growing up in a blue-collar family, he was one of the first in his family to get a college education. He moved around the United States following job opportunities, often working two or more jobs, and finally landed a position as a dock worker at a General Motors factory in Mississippi. He worked his way up the ladder within the company—eventually into a white collar position—via a series of promotions that he apparently "deserved" as a result of his choices, merit, and hard work, such that when I was an adolescent my family enjoyed a middle-class lifestyle, good health care, a nice middle-class home, new automobiles, disposable income for things like go-carts and motorcycles—and all of these (relatively) free of worries about money.

Responsibility for his success could be assigned in different ways. From the perspective of the ideology of individualism, we could assign responsibility for success to my dad, as his success was the result of his "choices." From a structural perspective, however, we might alternatively assign responsibility for his success to the Protestant work ethic he internalized as a child, to a waxing economy, or to the fact that a white man in the state of Mississippi might have been afforded a competitive advantage over minorities—none of which would have had anything to do with my father's individual "choices."

The 1990s and early 2000s saw increasing competition between American and foreign automobile industries, the export of US factories to countries with cheaper labor and fewer labor regulations, and a financial crisis brought about in General Motors and its subsidiaries resulting from pensions and health care formerly promised to baby boomers who were beginning to retire *en masse* (see Lowenstein 2008). My father eventually had to choose between early retirement and being laid off without any pension benefits, as the factory at which he worked in middle management was closing. He chose early retirement, but soon thereafter the company slashed pensions when it filed for bankruptcy. At that point my father reentered the job market, but finding work at a time with high unemployment—after the 2008 financial crisis—and having apparently failed to "choose" to develop job skills that seemed obviously transferable to new contexts, he was unable to find comparable work. After failing at a number of jobs as a salesman—it is difficult to get people to choose to buy one's products during a recession—he ended up choosing to become a "flexible" worker (practically a euphemism for "disposable" worker) stocking shelves at a retail store. Having always suffered from depression, this was a tough time for a man suffering the indignity of falling from a good middle-class, white-collar job to working part time as a stock boy, wondering if he was going to have to file for bankruptcy in the near future. A few days before his 61st birthday, he died from a brain hemorrhage that struck while he was taking a nap after a tiring day at work.

Responsibility for these relative failures at the end of his life could be assigned in different ways. We could of course say that since my father individually "chose" all of these things—chose a job in an industry with less than stable prospects, chose to retire, chose to work as a salesman during a recession—he as an individual is responsible for the effects of his "choices." From a structural perspective, however, we might say that my father was embedded in social and economic fields that limited his choices, rewarded some, and penalized others, so much so that, for instance, "choosing" early retirement over being laid off without benefits wasn't really a "choice" so much as something that any subject in his particular field would have done. Perhaps, as Stuart Ewan and Elizabeth Ewan write in *Channels of Desire*, "[c]loseted within all the choice is a gnawing sense of powerlessness" (Ewan and Ewan 1992, 201).

My father was saved from severe depression as the result of medication and self-help books that encouraged positive thinking. Like almost all mainstream self-help books, the literature he consumed taught that individuals are responsible for their own successes and failures, and that to succeed one must—as an individual—reflexively work on one's negative thought patterns. For instance, in *Unlimited Power: The New Science of Personal Achievement*, Anthony Robbins contends that "[t]he power to magically transform our lives into our greatest dreams lies waiting within us all. It's time to unleash it" (Robbins 1986, 4). Since the power lies within the individual to change his or her life, one must never blame someone else for the challenges that one faces, especially since challenges are always opportunities; rather, one must always transform oneself: "It's up to you to change your behavior" (76). There is no doubt that the "positive-thinking" ideology that my father incorporated into his own thought habits provided what I would call a form of psychological compensation, and for that I suppose I am grateful. However, no amount of "positive thinking" resulted in renewed career success. While I might have laid the responsibility for my father's indignities and financial frustrations at the feet of a capitalist system that supremely prioritizes profit, the ideology of the self-help books that he read taught that individuals and individuals alone were responsible for their fates. If, therefore, I am fascinated by capitalist mythmaking, it is in no small part due to watching my father consume the myths that blamed him as an individual for his failure even as they legitimated a system that arguably destroyed the life he had formerly enjoyed. This is, therefore, a book about the rhetoric of individualism.

* * *

Concerns about individualism have long been a part of the field of religious studies. "Sheilaism" was famously introduced almost 30 years ago in the very popular book, *Habits of the Heart* (Bellah et al. 1996, originally published 1985), a sociological study—arguably a nostalgic one—critical of the declining influence of institutional religion in modernity. According to the authors, a nurse named Sheila Larson had created an internal, private religion for herself—completely free of communal constraint—that was so individualistic that she had to invent a new, personalizing name for it: "Sheilaism." It was more or less deistic, having few tenets beyond the fact that her god exists and he "would want us to take care of each other" (221). As the authors of *Habits* assumed that communal religious institutions provide groups with social solidarity and authoritative altruistic moral norms that prevent democracies from collapsing back into Hobbes's state of nature—a war of all against all—they feared that the rise of Sheila's type of individual religion was a risk to democracy. Much like the seventeenth-century philosophers who argued—absurdly, in retrospect—that atheists aren't to be trusted to follow the law because they fear neither the gods nor the threat of hell, the authors of *Habits*—and others, such as Philip Hammond in *Religion and Personal Autonomy* (1992)—fear that subjects of individual religion are not beholden to any moral discourses that could help them negotiate competing individual and communal interests; Shelia apparently has no ultimate authority to provide her with a moral compass.

Habits was very influential and provoked a number of studies on how "individual religion" or "spirituality" is changing the face of religion in the modern world. However, unlike Bellah et al. and Hammond, other scholars were much more positive about the rise of spirituality—some even suggesting that it is a moral and political good. While Wade Clark Roof in *Spiritual Marketplace* (1999) is a bit ambivalent, others are downright laudatory, such as David Lyon in *Jesus in Disneyland* (2000) and Paul Heelas and Linda Woodhead in *The Spiritual Revolution* (2005). For Heelas in *Spiritualities of Life* (2008), freedom from external or communal social constraints is liberating, and the spread of individualism and spirituality is a good thing as it frees individuals from the "iron cage" of social control and organized religion. Heelas goes so far as to suggest that spirituality can be used to sacralize equality, dignity, and human rights (224ff).

Despite the fact that these two groups of scholars are divided on their evaluation of individual religion or spirituality, they both use the same vocabulary: organized religion vs. spirituality, communal vs. individual, social constraint vs. individual freedom, tradition vs. choice, and so on. *Habits* was remarkably successful in setting the terms of the debate. The work of Bellah et al. and Hammond was aligned with a rather conservative agenda reflecting worries about the declining influence of Christian institutions in the United States; however, this agenda doesn't particularly interest me as a scholar and is beyond the scope of this book. The appropriation of their vocabulary in support of the sacralization of "individual religion" is another matter.

When attempting to understand the pervasiveness of this vocabulary, it is worth noting that the scholars who evaluate "spirituality" positively use the same vocabulary that Ronald Reagan employed to distinguish between communism and democracy. For Reagan, communism is affiliated with totalitarianism, repression, orthodoxy, tyranny, controlling political forces, the subordination of the rights of individuals to the collective, and it stifles human freedom and muzzles self-expression—reasons for which communism is declining—while democracy is affiliated with diversity, tolerance, freedom, choice, self-determination, human rights, and is "responsive to the needs of their people"—reasons for which democracy is growing. Democracy must be helped along, of course, and Reagan recommended that we cultivate as widely as possible the ideology of individual choice. For Reagan, cultivating such an ideology "is not cultural imperialism; it is providing the means for genuine self-determination and protection for diversity" (see Reagan's "Evil Empire" speech, given to the British House of Commons in 1982). Similarly, Roof, Heelas, and Woodhead—all leading sociologists of religion—affiliate organized religion with obedience, deference to authority, collective conformity, and iron cages, while by contrast they affiliate individual religion or spirituality with openness, freedom, options, individual choice, self-determination, autonomy, independence, and individual rights—reasons for which spirituality is a growing force. The fact that these scholars unwittingly and unreflexively mirror Reagan's normative vocabulary is revealing.

Crucially, Roof, Lyon, Heelas, and Woodhead are—like Reagan—supremely uninterested in the conditions that limit, reward, and punish "individual choice"; they remain content to attribute "choices" to apparently autonomous subjects and thereby sacralize individual self-determination and freedom of choice. However, as Thomas Luckmann notes in his work on the function of "individual religion" in industrialized society, "[t]he discrepancy between the subjective autonomy' of the individual in modern society and the objective autonomy of the primary [economic and political] institutional domains strikes us as critical," as it appears that individual "autonomy" extends only to a very limited domain (Luckmann 1967, 115). For Luckmann, the sacralization of individual choice is coordinated with the ceding of political and economic power to institutions to which individuals must accommodate themselves. Thus, much like Reagan's rhetoric, these discourses on individual religion—which sacralize (a rather

limited) self-determination and freedom of choice—are capitalist ideologies.
First, they naturalize the emic vocabularies and discourses of capitalism by
suggesting that "the contemporary religious world resembles a supermarket,
in which customers are shopping for suitable commodities that are right for
them" (Lyon 2000, 76); on this view, the freely choosing *homo economicus* is
merely purchasing commodities to fill the apparently naturally occurring god-
shaped hole in her soul. Second, they naturalize or legitimate the surrender
of individuals to the capitalist mode of production by promoting quietism or
accommodationism through the characterization of any attempt to challenge
capitalism as extremist or fundamentalist, by encouraging consumption,
by emphasizing individual fulfillment or well-being as aligned with career
success, or by promoting increased worker productivity. The quietist or
accomomodationist elements of this ideology are so pervasive that when
I recently shared a satirical *Onion* article on Facebook titled "Finding a
Religion that Doesn't Disrupt Your Lifestyle," some of my colleagues did not
even realize it was a farce. Third, the discourses on individual religion tend
to envision individuals in isolation, rather than as subjects interpellated and
thereby brought into existence through ideologies and discourses; as such,
they block structural analysis by obfuscating the extent to which subjects in
a capitalist system are determined by social norms outside their control. Like
all rhetoric, the rhetoric of individualism has the effect of sanctioning some
social agendas over and against others, and the individualism inherent in these
discourses in particular functions—intentionally or not—to legitimate career
aspirations and consumer choice and, more importantly, to obfuscate the
extent to which capitalist social structures are constitutive of apparently free
individual choices. Indeed, the ideology of individual freedom is a technique
of liberal governmentality, in Michel Foucault's sense. Foucault writes,
"[t]he game of liberalism—not interfering, allowing free movement, letting
things follow their course . . . . [T]his ideology of freedom really was one of
the conditions of development of modern or, if you like, capitalist forms of the
economy. . . . [T]his freedom, both ideology and technique of government,
should in fact be understood within the mutations and transformations of
technologies of power" (Foucault 2007, 48).   → tribe.

Individualism has long been lamented by scholars in religious studies,
even prior to *Habits*. Individualism is a perennial concern—dating back to
Durkheim's work on anomie and suicide in modern society—because of the
fear that it dissolves communal bonds. This book argues, however, to put
it bluntly, that the problem with individualism is not that it is corrosive on
community or social solidarity, but that it doesn't exist. For reasons that
will become clear later, *there are no individuals*, even in societies where the
ideology of individualism prevails. The fact, for instance, that individualism
is often affiliated with fashion is a dead giveaway: a fashionable individual

fashion example

is one who conforms to a particular—fashionable—social code. As Steven Lukes suggests, individuals "always turn out on inspection to be social, and indeed historically specific" (1973b, 75), and, according to Karl Marx, "[i]n the social production of their life, men enter into definite relations that are indispensable and independent of their will, relations of production that correspond to a definite stage of development of their material productive forces" (Marx and Engels 1978, 4). From this perspective, the problem with the ideology of individualism is not that it dissolves community but that *it obscures how "individuals" are constituted by their communities.* Telling people that they are free to consume commodities or cultures in whatever way they wish does not make them autonomous; rather it obfuscates how their apparently free choices are determined by the social fields that limit, reward, and penalize their "choices." While individualism is not corrosive of community, *the ideology of individualism* is corrosive of the ability to intuit how ideologies and social structures interpellate subjects—and capitalism thrives relatively unimpeded in contexts where, for instance, fashionable individuals fail to see that their fashion choices are constituted by the social fields in which they reside.

true individual does not even exist

To lay my cards on the table, then, this book first argues that the ideology of individualism does not make people more individualistic, but rather masks the extent to which "individuals" are collectively constituted. Second, this book demonstrates that many of those forms of culture that scholars identify as "individual religion" or "spirituality" constitute individuals specifically as subjects of capitalism by encouraging consumerism, productivity, and quietism with respect to the economic and political structures. In addition, by all accounts "spirituality" does not appeal to the working class so much as the middle and upper middle classes, and I will argue that it serves as the opiate of the petty bourgeoisie, as it functions to help them accommodate or anesthetize themselves to all aspects of capitalism that might chafe—much as my father's turn to self-help books helped him adjust to unemployment.

Book Thesis

"cubicle people"

* * *

Part one of this book—"Religion, Capitalism, and Social Theory"—is primarily theoretical in nature. I attempt to show particular weaknesses in existing theories of "individual religion" and "spirituality," and propose an alternate theory that allows us to historicize the rhetoric of individual religion within a capitalist context.

In Chapter 1, I note that the specter of Émile Durkheim lies behind many of the theoretically impoverished accounts of "individual religion" or "spirituality." In *The Division of Labor in Society*, Durkheim made a distinction between mechanical solidarity and organic solidarity; societies bound together by organic solidarity produced individuals who were more free from society's collective conscience than in the so-called primitive societies bound by mechanical solidarity, for whom "individuality is zero." There is tension, however; Durkheim also argues in *Division of Labor* that none of us is really free, and that all individuals are slaves to social forces, from which we cannot escape. I argue that the determinist Durkheim is ultimately more persuasive, as it turns out that he brandishes the "we're more free" rhetoric only when he dubiously wants to insist on the relative spiritual superiority of industrialized moderns over "primitive savages." If the only mark in favor of the "we're free" rhetoric is ethnocentrism, then perhaps individuality is zero for *all* of us. I then point to those scholars who use the same determined/free distinction in order to imply the relative superiority of free "spirituality" over "institutional religion." This normative distinction is as objectionable in their works as in Durkheim's outdated evolutionary view of society, and we must therefore look for an alternative account. We need an analysis of what is commonly identified as "individual religion" without the language of "individuality."

In addition to their reliance on a problematic collective/individual dichotomy, almost all theorists of contemporary religion employ a (modified) secularization or privatization theory, according to which "religion" is increasingly displaced by the authority of secular institutions in the "public sphere" and therefore "privatized." In Chapter 2, I point out that such an account completely ignores the critiques of the concept of "religion" by scholars such as Russell McCutcheon, Timothy Fitzgerald, and others. In particular, what McCutcheon and Fitzgerald demonstrate is that discourses on "religion"—which present religion as an ontologically distinct part of culture or society—are invariably loaded and often appear to serve as legitimations for institutions or forms of power that are identified, by contrast, as "secular." Not only must Durkheim's latent normative rhetoric be abandoned, but we must also rethink contemporary "religious" culture without relying on the problematic concepts of "religion," "secularization," and "privatization." This chapter therefore proposes an alternate grid of classification with which we could bring into relief "individual religion" without "individuality" and without "religion." It proceeds by considering a series of social theorists who link the production of culture and subjectivity to the overall structure of society. In each case, I identify what is important for the theorist at hand, what is perhaps problematic, and what I want to borrow. By the end of this chapter, I assemble both a theory and a vocabulary that allow us to think about how the authority or reach of "religious" discourses is in part gerrymandered by their local identification as "religious" or "spiritual," and also how even those so-called private or individual religious discourses have a content and reach that is fundamentally determined by the division of labor in a capitalist society.

Yet another deficiency in the literature on "spirituality" is that many theorists rely on William James's distinction between "religious experience" and "institutional religion," which works similarly but not identically to Durkheim's distinction between individuality and collective conscience. Chapter 3 thus looks specifically at how James's normative vocabulary and his folk theory of religion are used in many contemporary discursive sites to sanction practices that conflict with consumerism. In short, James's rhetoric is used to suggest that any "religious" practice that interferes with one's work, one's fashion, or one's consumer habits is perhaps "fanatical," while the pursuit of consumer desires is presented as "spiritual" or even "common sense." This chapter concludes with a consideration of two accounts of the life of Jesus—Stephen Mitchell's in *The Gospel According to Jesus* and Thich Nhat Hanh's in *Living Buddha, Living Christ*—that utilize James's religious experience/institutional religion distinction in a way that domesticates Jesus for a bourgeois lifestyle.

Part two of this book—"The Opiate of the Bourgeoisie"—is devoted to a series of studies of what other scholars might call "individual religion" from the perspective of the theory elaborated in part one of this book. Contrary to the dominant scholarly narrative, according to which "individual religion" is the product of autonomous, private choices, these forms of culture look far more like capitalist ideologies that encourage quietism, consumerism, productivity, and accommodation to capitalism's workplace demands.

Chapter 4 provides a reading of Christopher Moore's *Lamb: The Gospel according to Biff, Christ's Childhood Pal*, a novel that advances a form of "religion" which recommends the pursuit of happiness coupled with political quietism. In this novel, Moore takes a young Son of God and his pal Biff on a journey from Nazareth to the "mystic East" and back again. Along the way, the messiah painstakingly learns the apparently universal truths of the world's great religions. At the end, Jesus is crucified because some of his followers wrongly assume that Jesus's mission involves overthrowing the Roman occupation of Israel. This book's more or less explicit message is that traditional religion is mostly nonsense; true religion requires us merely to enjoy life, be nice to others, and not to interfere with the state. In conclusion, I argue that the presentation of hedonism, social niceties, and political quietism as the universal essence of the great world religions is well-suited for privileged, bourgeois liberals who benefit from the existing social conditions but nevertheless want to feel "religious" or "spiritual," hence the appeal of this book to a middle-class audience.

Chapter 5 offers an analysis of Randa Abdel-Fattah's award winning novel, *Does My Head Look Big in This?* In this novel, Abdel-Fattah narrates the life of a young Muslim girl who chooses—to some extent against the wishes of her parents—to wear a hijab. The characters justify the action with the rhetoric of "individual choice," and even present freedom of choice (over slavery to tradition) as the very essence of Islam. However, the donning of the veil turns out to be little different than a fashion statement that functions to award social capital to the main character. While it's clear why such a nonthreatening construction of Islam might appeal to a middle-class audience, this chapter argues that Abdel-Fattah's construction is explicable only if historicized relative to capitalist discourses and particular consumer practices, and that the ideology of choice in the novel obscures the power of such social forces over consumers.

More than a century ago, Max Weber argued that Protestant ideology had the effect of making Protestants more productive than their Catholic counterparts, eventually resulting in an iron cage that worked to the detriment of everyone. Chapter 6 argues, through an analysis of Lewis Richmond's *Work as Spiritual Practice* and Matthew Fox's *The Reinvention of Work*, that modern "spirituality" or "self-help" discourses are in a sense the new Protestant work ethic, as they encourage individual workers to use reflexive "spiritual" practices to accommodate themselves to any feature of the workplace that chafes with their life. Richmond in particular draws from the Buddhist tradition, while Fox draws primarily from the *Bhagavad Gita*, yet both books teach the same lesson: teach yourself to desire what your corporation desires of you. As such, Richmond's and Fox's work is designed to produce happy and productive capitalist workers.

Chapter 7 considers Karen Berg's *God Wears Lipstick* and Eckhart Tolle's *The Power of Now* and suggests that their discourses function in a manner similar to Christian discourses on free will: they function to assign responsibility for suffering to individuals. Writing for middle- and upper middle-class readers dealing with family and work life, both Berg and Tolle suggest that the power to be happy is within everyone's reach, so that when individuals are suffering, it is their own fault. As such, individuals who are suffering have only themselves to blame, and must transform themselves— through a number of reflexive practices—rather than expect their social world to change. Just as appeals to free will protect the Christian god from being held responsible for evil in the world, so does Berg and Tolle's individualism function to protect capitalism from being held responsible for any suffering that workers might experience. The ideology of individualism is capitalism's theodicy.

*   *   *

I have intentionally chosen the term "ideology" for the purposes of this book, despite the fact that the term has recently fallen out of favor in scholarly circles. According to the common objection, the classical Marxist theory of ideology—as proposed by Louis Althusser in *Reading Capital* (Althusser and Balibar 1997), for instance—is problematic in that it contrasts a "distorted" view of reality with "objective," scientific knowledge of reality; however, poststructuralism has dissolved the claim to "objectivity" into, for example, a will-to-power, and hence there is no longer an "undistorted" view from which to critique "distortions." Knowledge, as Michel Foucault has rightly argued, is always necessarily tied up with power; there is no gods-eye-view independent of power relations from which to view or analyze the world. In addition, discourses serve a constitutive role in the creation of reality; as Althusser was later right to note in "Ideology and Ideological State Apparatuses" (Althusser 2008), identities interpellate subjects, bringing them into existence rather than naming a reality that already exists (these criticisms are surveyed succinctly in Therborn 1980). While I am completely in agreement with these critiques of "objective" knowledge, I do not want to let go of ideological criticism just yet.

Ideological critique need not be launched from a position of alleged "objectivity"; there are other positions from which one could make such a charge. First, *immanent critique* permits the charge of distortion. Sometimes, we can show that a claim distorts things for reasons that the claimant herself would accept. In *Masking Hegemony* (Martin 2010), I argued that John Locke distorted things when he claimed that church and state were two things infinitely distinct from one another; however, I did not argue that on the basis of some objective facts available only to me, but rather on the basis of claims Locke himself made in his *ouvre*—based on his own claims, it turns out, churches and states are interrelated in a variety of ways. Immanent critique permits charges of distortion not from some allegedly objective space but within a position that contradicts itself.

Second, ideological critique can be launched from a particular scholarly position. Given what we've learned about sexuality from Foucault and Judith Butler, it appears that sex or gender essentialism is a distortion. What's crucial is that this is not a distortion of "reality from a gods-eye-view," but rather "the world as constructed through Foucault's and Butler's discourses on sexuality." From where we stand in *this* position, *that* position looks like a distortion. Conceptual pluralism allows us to divide up the world in different ways using different discourses; interestingly, we can use multiple discourses at the same time, simultaneously noting how some discourses bring into relief what other discourses present differently, mask, or altogether obscure. I can accept, on the one hand, that the creation story in the Rig Veda about Parusha's body being divided into four different human classes perhaps played a role in creating a particular social reality, insofar as it interpellated priests, warriors, commoners, and servants—a process that did not "distort" their reality but rather partially ushered it into being. On the other hand, from the perspective of contemporary evolutionary theory, the claim that humans were created from the corpse of a god is certainly a distortion of how humans came to be. Such a claim is issued not from the point of view of "objective" scientific knowledge—rather, evolutionary theory is the product of peculiarly modern institutions—but nevertheless a charge of distortion is not nonsensical.

Therefore if in this book I argue that discourses on individualism distort the world, with such claims I do not insist I have insight into reality in and of itself—a *ding an sich*, in Hegel's sense, or fully present, in Derrida's sense—but rather that claims about individualism mask and distort what the social theory employed in this book brings into relief in an alternate, competing manner.

In addition to insisting that ideology critique can reasonably make claims about how ideology distorts, I also insist on an apparent priority of base over superstructure in the cases under consideration, although a *contingent* rather than necessary priority. Much of the ideology under analysis in part two of this book—"The opiate of the bourgeoisie"—could only have been created in a context in which late capitalist structures are already in place. This is not to say that capitalism directly caused these ideologies to come into existence, but that capitalism provides the conditions of possibility outside of which they could not likely have been imagined. In addition, it seems clear that capitalism permits a wide variety of forms of cultural production; capitalism makes possible—and perhaps necessary—both capitalist and anticapitalist discourses. However, I would argue that the infrastructure entails conditions in which procapitalist discourses are more likely to be received in a favorable light. If self-help ideologies recommending reflexive practices that encourage greater individual productivity are well-received, it is liable to be in part because such practices give individuals who adopt them a competitive edge in the social fields in which they compete. Such ideologies are thus well-received because they have a practical salience or an operational fit with the conditions of possibility that make them possible in the first place, yet they can serve a legitimating function at the same time, by presenting such conditions as natural. Over time such ideologies become widely accepted, taken for granted, and sedimented as established wisdom—*doxa*, as Pierre Bourdieu puts it—at which point they serve a constitutive role in limiting what can be thought and discouraging the development of discourses that do not have an operational fit with the existing structural conditions. In this way capitalist infrastructures can have an explanatory priority over the superstructures that legitimate them, yet without presuming a necessary, teleological relation from one to the other.

* * *

Although the social theory I assume in this book is perhaps radical—I reject, for example, the analytic usefulness of terms like "religion" or "individualism"—my interest in capitalism and consumerism is probably quite traditional. In *Capital*, Marx documents the conditions of the working class in England; he talks of workers laboring in dangerous and unsafe conditions, children working long hours without breaks—one boy reports having to be hand-fed by his mother because taking a break would mean stopping the machine on which he works. Sadly, many contemporary reports on factories in various parts of the globe report almost identical uses of humans and human labor: low wages, forced long hours and overtime, dangerous or even deadly working conditions, lack of worker's compensation in case of injury, uses of child labor, and so on. For instance, while I was writing this book, a factory building—whose owner had ignored warnings from inspectors suggesting the building was literally cracking apart—collapsed in Bangladesh, resulting in the death of more than a thousand workers. As I sympathize with workers laboring in such conditions, I am interested in rhetorics and discourses that naturalize or legitimate a capitalist system that makes such practices routine and apparently necessary. As Zygmunt Bauman notes in *Consuming Life*, these forms of so-called collateral damage may be unintentional, but "unintentional" is not at all the same as "impossible to intentionally avoid" (Bauman 2007, 118).

A second reason for my interest in this subject matter is of course the deteriorating effects of capitalist ideologies and practices on my own father's life. He was quite thoroughly interpellated—to his detriment, it seems to me—by an ideology that assigned to him responsibility for "his" failures. This book is dedicated to his memory.

PART ONE

Religion, capitalism, and social theory

1

"Individuality is zero"

We're all individuals.
MONTY PYTHON'S *Life of Brian*

In his commentary on Émile Durkheim's corpus, Steven Lukes notes at one point that Durkheim was not faithful to his own principles: "Here Durkheim was insufficiently Durkheimian" (Lukes 1973a, 177). In this chapter I argue similarly: in *The Division of Labor in Society*, Durkheim is not faithful to his own method and social theory, particularly in his discussion of individuality.

What would it mean for Durkheim to be faithful to himself? There are at least three points salient to my argument. First, Durkheim was a reductionist committed to rejecting emic explanations for social life: "We regard as fruitful this idea that social life must be explained, not by the conception of it held by those who participate in it, but by profound causes which escape consciousness" (quoted in Lukes 1973a, 231). Second, Durkheim's method requires a thoroughgoing determinism. "[H]uman behaviour . . . is capable of being reduced to relationships of cause and effect" (Durkheim 1982, 53). Third, and following from the second, Durkheim insisted that individuals are products of society; society always has a prior explanatory power. "Collective life did not arise from individual life; on the contrary, it is the latter that emerged from the former" (Durkheim 1984, 220–221).[1] Indeed, throughout his career he consistently opposed methodological individualism, the view that society is made up of previously existing individuals.

In *Domination and Power* (1987), Peter Miller identifies with clarity the differences between such a view, according to which social forces create subjects, and what I would call a liberal view of subjectivity, according to which a preexisting subjectivity is repressed rather than constituted by power:

> [P]ower and subjectivity have been conceived for too long as fundamentally opposed. Power has been viewed as operating exclusively through the

repression of an essential subjectivity. For power to operate it has been assumed that it must effect the crushing of subjectivity. . . . Foucault has suggested a directly opposed image of power, one which operates in precisely the other direction, not by repressing subjectivity, but by promoting it, cultivating it, and nurturing it. (1)

Miller attributes the theoretical shift from a liberal view of subjectivity (according to which subjectivity is opposed to power) to an antiliberal view (according to which subjectivity is constituted by power) to the work of Louis Althusser.[2] In his famous essay on "Ideology and Ideological State Apparatuses" (2008), Althusser argued that ideology does not constrain subjects so much as it interpellates them, thereby bringing them into existence. It is clear that this theoretical tradition did not originate with Althusser, as Durkheim, Marx, and other social theorists made similar claims decades prior (although arguably with less precision than Althusser and Foucault).[3] This is apparent, for instance, from claims Durkheim makes in *Rules of Sociological Method* regarding the positive effects of what is apparently constraining:

[I]t is patently obvious that all education consists of a continual effort to impose upon the child ways of seeing, thinking, and acting which he himself would not have arrived at spontaneously. From his earliest years we oblige him to eat, drink, and sleep at regular hours, and to observe cleanliness, calm, and obedience; later we force him to learn how to be mindful of others, to respect customs and conventions, and to work, etc. If this constraint in time ceases to be felt it is because it gradually gives rise to habits, to inner tendencies which render it superfluous; but they supplant the constraint only because they are derived from it. (Dukheim 1982, 53–54)

In addition, Durkheim states even more strongly in *Elementary Forms*: "collective force is not wholly external to us; it does not entirely move us from the outside. Indeed, since society can exist only in individual minds and through them, it must penetrate and become organized inside us; it becomes an integral part of our being" (Durkheim 2001, 157). This is a sort of Althusserianism *avant le lettre*—we become subjects as we are penetrated or interpellated by social forms outside of us. Power in this case is constitutive of subjectivity or individuality, not repressive of it.

In *The Division of Labor in Society*, Durkheim's central task is to explain why societies with a high division of labor do not disintegrate, despite their increasing heterogeneity. His explanation involved making a fundamental distinction between mechanical and organic solidarity. Briefly, Durkheim argues that subjects in a society with a low division of labor are relatively similar to one another and are penetrated by a homogeneous collective conscience; they are bound together by identical beliefs. Such a society exhibits mechanical solidarity. By contrast, in a society with a high division of labor we are no longer bound together by a collective conscience; on the contrary, our beliefs reflect an incredible degree of heterogeneity. Durkheim argues, however, that this does not mean that we are without any form of solidarity. We are held together by what he calls organic solidarity. "We as individuals are different from one another, but like different organs in a human body, we are bound together by our mutual interdependence upon one another." A heart, a lung, and a stomach are not the same, may not have the same collective conscience (metaphorically speaking), but are nevertheless bound together—with the help of the central nervous system—into an interdependent, organic whole. Modern societies do not disintegrate because, through organic solidarity, modern individuals have respect for differences, in part through our recognition of the necessity for difference in a society with interdependent organs."

All of this is, in principle, compatible with Durkheim's general method and social theory outlined earlier. Nevertheless, the argument in *Division* wavers between a liberal and an antiliberal theory of subjectivity. Of interest to me is the fact that *the liberal view generally appears when Durkheim is defending his most ethnocentrist claims.* In *Division of Labor,* Durkheim usually argues that individuals are effects of constitutive social forces; however, when he wants to demonstrate that modern individuals are more advanced than primitive savages, he draws upon the liberal theory of subjectivity, arguing that moderns are in some sense *freer* from repressive social forces.[4] This point is of more than historical interest because, as I will conclude, many contemporary sociologists make claims about "spirituality" and "individual religion" that are rhetorically homologous to Durkheim's most problematic claims in *Division of Labor.* For this reason, it may be worth revising how we think about "spirituality."

Before beginning my analysis of the arguments in *Division,* I would like to say a word about my own method. The sculptor Michelangelo is claimed to have said:

In every block of marble I see a statue as plain as though it stood before me, shaped, and perfect in attitude and action. I have only to hew away the rough walls that imprison the lovely apparition to reveal it to the other eyes as mine see it.

Scholarship is like sculpting, as Michelangelo describes it, in at least two ways. On the one hand, in what follows I will attempt to bring into relief for others what seems painfully obvious to me about *Division of Labor.* On the other hand, when we as scholars bring something into relief out of the stuff of the world, we often pretend—like Michelangelo—to have merely found what we bring into existence. By contrast, while scholarship doesn't create knowledge *ex nihilo*, scholarship is knowledge *production*. Something new is produced with every commentary. Or, as Derrida might put it, commentary is supplementary: the supplement both exceeds and produces what it claims to supplement. The (scholarly) sculptures we relieve from the stuff of the world—including this sculpture I'm relieving from *Division of Labor*—are not created *ex nihilo*, but they nevertheless create what they purport to describe. If Durkheim will not have understood himself as using two social theories at once, it is nonetheless quite possible that *my* Durkheim does. Nevertheless, if I quote Durkheim extensively later, it is because I do not want to be accused of creating my Durkheim *ex nihilo*.

Durkheim against Spencer

Durkheim uses what I am calling an antiliberal social theory when attempting to explain why, despite the increasing division of labor in society and apparent fragmentation of collective conscience, we have not yet centrifugally disintegrated. Durkheim's answer to this question is perhaps most clear when criticizing British philosopher and sociologist Herbert Spencer. The problem, for Durkheim, is that Spencer assumes the existence of individuals prior to the advent of society, and cannot explain what keeps these individuals bound together. Spencer uses a social contract theory to explain the origin of society; in a manner similar to Hobbes's or Locke's state of nature, Spencer alleges that individuals come together of their own free will and agree to cooperate to further their own, preexisting, individual interests (Durkheim 1984, 149). Contracts—the fundamental form of social interaction—are therefore made between free individuals for mutual benefit of some sort. On Spencer's view, according to Durkheim,

> Social solidarity would be nothing more than the spontaneous agreement between individual interests, an agreement of which contracts are the natural expression. The type of social relations would be the economic relationship, freed from all regulation, and as it emerges from the entirely free initiative of the parties concerned. (152)

This is, of course a social theory that naturalizes a *laissez faire* economic system; as Marshall Sahlins puts it, "The development from a Hobbesian state of nature is the origin myth of Western capitalism," so much so that "we make both a folklore and a science of the idea" (Sahlins 1976, 53). According to such a myth, which can only see a limiting rather than constitutive role of culture and society, the freedom of individuals would only be unnaturally and irresponsibly limited by social regulation. Since society is naturally founded on the cooperation of individuals coming together to serve their individual interests, individuals naturally become more free as social interventions *recede*; for Spencer, ideally "the sphere of social activity continues to diminish more and more in favour of that of the individual" (Durkheim 1984, 152).

Durkheim makes it clear that nothing could be more absurd. "[F]ar from decreasing, this mechanism [i.e., legal obligations and regulations imposed on individuals by society] is continuing to grow, becoming more complex" (153). Spencer distinguishes between positive and negative interventions; positive interventions tell an individual "*Do this*" and negative ones say "*Do not do that*" (153). Spencer allows that as society evolves or progresses, negative controls rightly increase but positive ones do not. Durkheim, however, does not allow the distinction as relevant:

> Whether positive or negative, this control is nevertheless social, and the main question is to know whether it is extended or contracted. But whether it is for decreeing something to happen or for prohibiting it, for saying *Do this* or *Do not do that*, if society intervenes more we have no right to say that individual spontaneity is increasingly adequate for all purposes. If the rules that determine conduct are multiplied, whether their commands are positive or negative, it is not true to say that they spring more and more completely from private initiative. (153)

Durkheim goes on to add that even if we allow the distinction, *both* negative *and* positive interventions are increasing. He considers two types of legal interventions at length: contract law and state administrative laws. Spencer thinks of contracts as spontaneous agreements between individuals, covering only what individuals freely agree to. Durkheim's riposte is that contract law, which increases in proportion to the division of labor in society, precisely covers what is *not* freely agreed to by individuals in a contract. That is, contract law determines the conditions for contracts, what one cannot contract, as well as things such as liabilities not expressly specified in contracts. Contract law is necessary because it would not be possible for free individuals to specify all such things every time they make a contract: "If therefore we had each time to launch ourselves afresh into these conflicts and negotiations necessary to establish clearly all the conditions of the agreement, for the present and the future, our actions would be paralysed" (161). Signing a contract for an mortgage might take an hour, and the contract might be several pages long, but the contract, the parties, and the courts that arbitrate disputes assume decades of jurisprudence—for example, legal rulings about the meaning of the terms of the contract, how far they can be extended, and so on. Were parties required to stipulate all of those things every time they entered into an agreement, no one would own a house. For Durkheim, then, contracts assume prior, constitutive social interventions: "As soon as we have taken the first step toward co-operation, we are committed and the regulatory action of society exerts itself upon us" (163).

In addition, staying on contract law for a moment, Durkheim points out that kinship relations are less and less contractual as society evolves. For instance, in industrial societies one can no longer purchase children (at least not legally). On the contrary, "domestic law . . . has become increasingly complex, that is, the different species of legal relationships that give rise to family life are much more numerous than formerly" (155). Contrary to Spencer, who sees society as nothing more than contracts between preexisting individuals, there is an increasing number of noncontractual regulations on familial relationships. In summary, we are seeing an expansion of contract law regulating what is in fact not in contracts, while at the same time the types of relationships one can contract are shrinking.

More importantly, and more obviously, is the expansion of state administrative law. For Durkheim, state administration is roughly analogous to the nervous system in "higher" animals: it regulates the interaction between organs in a way that makes their existence possible in the first place. Here he is talking about "the education of the young, protecting health generally, presiding over the functioning of the public assistance system or managing the transport and communications systems" (167). As the state takes over these administrative regulations, "the body develops" (168).

Contrary to Spencer, then, as the division of labor increases so must the number of necessary and constitutive social interventions increase—as it is the latter that makes cooperation between the various "organs" of society possible in the first place. "The division of labor gives rise to legal rules that determine the nature and relationships of the function thus divided up" (172). In addition, Durkheim is arguably more of a vulgar Marxist than Marx was: "Every people has its moral code that is determined by the conditions under which it is living" (184; on this point, see also Lehmann 1993, 33ff). Consequently, he sees a high division of labor as necessitating its own morality. To keep complicated societies running smoothly, the state sanctions legal transgressions not through repressive punishments but through restitutions— designed to restore prior states of cooperation between organs. In addition, "Where restitutory law is very developed, for each profession a professional morality exists" (Durkheim 1984, 172). Here Durkheim is referring not to legal codes but explicit and implicit professional codes:

With the same group of workers a public opinion exists, diffused throughout this limited body, which despite the lack of any legal sanctions, is nevertheless obeyed. There are customs and usages common to the same group of functionaries which none can infringe without incurring the reprimand of the corporation. Yet this morality is distinguished . . . [insofar as it is] localized within a limited area of society. (172)

However, alongside the morality of one's profession or one's organ, one experiences a sense of solidarity with all other organs in society as a whole:

Because no individual is sufficient unto himself, it is from society that he receives all that is needful, just as it is for society that he labors. Thus there is formed a very strong state of dependence in which he finds himself: he grows accustomed to valuing himself at his true worth, viz., to look upon himself only as a part of the whole, the organ of an organism. (173)

Consequently, individuals are nothing in themselves—they are "co-operating members, with whom it [the individual] cannot do without and towards whom it has duties" (173).

There are several things of interest here. First, this provides an answer for one of Durkheim's chief questions. As there is an increasing division of labor in society, what prevents it from centrifugal disintegration? We now have his answer: every society necessitates a morality, and societies with a high division of labor necessitate an organic sense of solidarity, according to which individuals do not see themselves as similar to others, but nevertheless as mutually interdependent upon others—as organs are interdependent upon other organs in a body.

Second, despite Spencer's claims to the contrary, individuals in a society with a high division of labor owe their existence to a nervous system— the state—that coordinates the cooperation between organs. Without such a nervous system, individuals could not become what they are. The state—including the legal system, contract law, administrative law, and so on—makes individuals' families, careers, and moralities possible. Individuals do not precede society, but are products of it.

Third, and most importantly for my purposes, Durkheim's critique of Spencer sheds light on what he means by "individual" and "individuality." Being an individual does not mean, as liberal social theories might have it, being autonomous from social constraints. On the contrary, society and social constraints are constitutive of what an individual is or becomes. Rather, what it means to be individual is only that one is increasingly *different* from other individuals. As this is fundamentally dependent on the increasing division of labor, presumably this means in part difference in terms of one's labor—hence there is a proliferation of diverse professions and professional moral codes. However, beyond this, Durkheim would add that as professional morality applies only or primarily in one's profession, one's "private life" (which is in scare quotes because Durkheim himself calls into question the public/private distinction; see 28) may be regulated by a further differentiated set of regulations. While at times he writes as if private life can, in a sense, be "more free" because one's professional morality does not apply there, this would be of course inconsistent with the immediate claims against Spencer. When arguing against Spencer, he notes that the regulation of education, health, families, communication, transportation, and so on via administrative law is actually increasing rather than decreasing. Here, at least, being individual does not mean not free from regulation, but that the regulations one is subject to are in many cases different from the regulations directed at one's fellow organs. This is why, when emphasizing the gap between "advanced" and "primitive" societies during his diatribe against Spencer, the most salient theoretical point is that "primitives" share a homogeneous collective conscience, as opposed to distinct, individual consciences.

His evolutionary model of social differentiation supports this. The "first step taken along the road to individualism" (143) is when the authority of a tribal chief is recognized. "In fact, the chiefs are the first individual personalities who have risen from the mass of society. Their exceptional position, which makes them unrivalled, imparts to them a *distinctive* presence and in consequence confers an individuality upon them" (emphasis mine; 143). What primarily makes a chief an individual is not that he is "free" but that he is distinctive. Whatever freedoms a chief might enjoy are, of course, consequent upon his position in the social system in which he is embedded—the constraints are constitutive, not repressive. Indeed, in *Division* Durkheim baldly states this point twice: "Liberty . . . is itself the product of a set of rules" (xxxiii); "Liberty itself is the product of regulation" (320). For Durkheim, at least when arguing against Spencer, *individuality is not freedom, but difference*.

There is an additional reason, not specified by Durkheim except in passing, for us to be suspicious of starting, as Spencer does, with individuals. Durkheim writes, "Collective life did not arise from individual life; on the contrary it is the latter that emerged from the former" (220–221). Indeed, "There is nothing antisocial about [the individual], because it is a product of society. It is not the absolute personality of the monad, sufficient unto itself" (221). Social theory at its best explains how individuals or individual choices are *products* of social forces. To explain things by pointing to individual choice is in fact not to explain them at all. Halting explanation by positing self-causing monads is to give up on our analytical task. Appeals to autonomy begin where scholarship throws up its hands in defeat; explanations that appeal to individual autonomy are, by definition, unscholarly. As Stephan Fuchs says in his critique of contemporary rational choice theory (RCT), "RCT stops asking further questions when it has reached the 'actor' with his tastes, beliefs, reasons, and actions. . . . RCT does not explain actors and actions, but celebrates them out of respect for the liberal self and private autonomy" (Fuchs 2001, 117). Social theory requires us to explain individuals rather than simply posit them as the ground of our explanations. To posit self-causing monads, even out of apparent respect for individuals, is to turn social theory into liberal ideology or, worse, theology—for what is more theological than self-causing agents, unmoved movers, which escape causal fields yet make effects in the world?

Durkheim's savages

To see the other Durkheim—the one who utilizes a liberal social theory—we will have to turn to where he deploys it most explicitly: his discussion of the difference between primitive savages and modern individuals. As I have noted so far, when attempting to explain why societies with a high division of labor do not fall apart, Durkheim posits an increasing number of constraints binding individuals into cooperation with one another. However, nothing much has been said about the gap between organic solidarity and its opposite, mechanical solidarity. What is it that makes individuals in a society with mechanical solidarity different from individuals in modern society? We already know that the former share a collective conscience, whereas the latter experience a greater diversity of consciences, which are required of necessity by the increased division of labor (which requires, e.g., variable professional standards).

Nothing about the distinction thus far seems particularly normative. However, like most social theorists of the late nineteenth century, Durkheim held that modern Europeans were clearly more advanced and superior to primitive savages in kinship societies. There is, then, more to the story: when advancing a claim of the relative superiority of moderns over savages, Durkheim resorts to a liberal account of modern individuality, according to which savages are slaves to social forces while moderns are more free.

The crucial passage explaining mechanical solidarity, collective conscience, and primitive inferiority argues that,

there is in the consciousness of each one of us two consciousnesses: one that we share in common with our group in its entirety, which is consequently not ourselves, but society living and acting within us; the other that, on the contrary, represents us alone in what is personal and distinctive about us, what makes us an individual. The solidarity that derives from similarities is at its *maximum* when the collective consciousness completely envelops our total consciousness, coinciding with it at every point. At that moment our individuality is zero. That individuality cannot arise until the community fills us less completely. . . . Moreover, at the very moment when this solidarity exerts its effect, our personality, it may be said by definition, disappears, for we are no longer ourselves, but collective being. (Durkheim 1984, 84)

In the following passages he also suggests that such savages are slaves or, worse, mere objects: "In societies where this solidarity is highly developed the individual . . . does not belong to himself; he is literally a thing at the disposal of society" (85). As Jennifer M. Lehmann puts it, for Durkheim here "[t]he individual does not belong to itself, the ego is not its own property . . . . The individual is one with society, and society totally, absolutely determines the individual's thought and behavior" (Lehmann 1993, 47–48).

Durkheim goes on to add that those in a society with a high division of labor and an organic form of solidarity are less penetrated by the collective. "[T]he collective conscience leaves uncovered a part of the individual consciousness, so that there may be established in it those special functions that it cannot regulate" (Durkheim 1984, 85). For moderns, our consciousness has more of a "free area," which leaves "more room for the free play of our initiative" (85). This makes us more like the "higher animals"—implying that the savages, those more constrained and less free, are more like the lower animals.

Thus far there is a slight ambiguity in Durkheim's account. We could ask the following question: are moderns more free of society in general or more free merely of a universal collective consciousness? Against Spencer, it would seem that Durkheim would agree with the latter but not the former: we are free from a homogeneous collective conscience—we need not believe all the same things—but we are not thereby free from social forces in general. In fact, contrary to Spencer, Durkheim insists that the social forces constraining us are actually increasing. This is presumably why, for instance, we see Durkheim make qualifications such as these when discussing freedom from collective conscience: for individuals in a society with high division of labor,

the activity of each one of us is correspondingly more specialized, the more personal it is. Doubtless, however circumscribed that activity may be, it is *never completely original. Even in the exercise of our profession we conform to usages and practices that are common to us all within our corporation.* (emphasis mine; 85)

Here, then, individuality looks less like "freedom" in the liberal sense, and more like differentiation. Perhaps moderns are not really more free; rather, it seems just that different professions are penetrated by different—local rather than universal—collective consciences. Perhaps it is not that moderns are no longer subject to a collective conscience, so much as there is a heterogeneous set of collective consciences.[5]

However, Durkheim goes far beyond noting the heterogeneity of professional consciences. There is, in addition to differentiation, a "freedom" offered to moderns when they are outside of work. "[T]he professional spirit can only have influence upon professional life. Beyond this sphere the individual enjoys that larger liberty whose origin we have just demonstrated" (243). In addition, Durkheim adds that because these professional standards are locally rather than universally accepted, they carry less authority, and as such "offer less resistance to change" (243).[6]

In addition, he alleges we are also more free—as opposed to merely more heterogeneous—by suggesting that movement from profession to profession is more flexible. He writes, quite romantically,

[a]s labor splits up even more, this flexibility and freedom become greater. We can see the same individual rise from the most humble occupations to the most important ones. The principle whereby all jobs are equally accessible to all citizens would not have become so general if it were not constantly being applied. (269)

A third way in which we are allegedly more free is by heredity and instinct. "In lower societies, where the [labor] functions are very general, these demand only aptitudes that are likewise general. . . . Each person receives at birth all that is essential to sustain his personality" (258). However, as societies become ever so slightly more complex, hereditary ability makes some races more suited to some jobs over others. "[P]rofessional ability was a quality of the race rather than the individual" (259). However, as the human race evolves, the relevance of heredity recedes as instincts recede. "[I]ntelligence and instinct always vary in inverse proportion to each other" (262). Durkheim assumed that heredity was cumulative: "A child does not inherit only from his parents, but from all his ancestors" (264). Thus both abilities and intelligence accumulate via heredity, and the further along a race or a species progresses, the more capacities an individual has inherited. With increased capacity comes increased flexibility, and thus heredity becomes less and less narrowly determining of individual capacity:

Not only is there an increasing number of things over which it has no hold, but the properties whose continuity it ensures become more plastic. Thus the individual is tied less strongly to his past; it is easier for him to adapt to new circumstances as they occur, and progress in the division of labour therefore becomes easier and swifter. (267)

It is worth noting that Durkheim uses a matter/spirit metaphor to make this point: "Progress may therefore have the effect of increasingly detaching the function from the organ . . . and life from *matter*, consequently *spiritualizing* it, rendering it more flexible and freer" (emphasis mine; 275).

So we have three reasons why moderns are not only more heterogeneous than savages, but also more free. First, although we are penetrated by the collective conscience of our professions, we are "free" when we leave work. Second, we are "free" to move from one profession to another. Third, we are "free" because we are biologically more plastic than savages, who are closer to nature and therefore more determined by instinct.[7]

Thus despite his insistence against Spencer that social regulation is increasing rather than declining, Durkheim does write as if moderns are not only free of a universal collective conscience but also more free of social forces in general—at least when compared to savages. Consider the following contrasts. First, he favorably cites Lubbock as saying, "No savage is free" (92). In addition, still quoting Lubbock, "every action of their lives is regulated by numerous rules" (92). By contrast, the modern "individual thus feels, and he is in reality, much less *acted upon*; he becomes more a source of spontaneous activity" (120). In addition, "local opinion weights less heavily with each one of us . . . . [B]oth social control and the common consciousness grow weaker" (241). Despite his diatribe against positing individuals as self-causing monads, Durkheim says in the conclusion, "[i]ndeed to be a person means to be an *autonomous source of action*" (emphasis mine; 225). Durkheim insists that by this he is not here invoking a "metaphysical attribute" (i.e., "free will"), but nevertheless goes on to call it a "faculty" (225). Last, this autonomous faculty, which moderns but not savages enjoy, "frees the individual consciousness in part . . . *from the social environment* that envelops it" (emphasis mine; 335).[8]

Taking sides

Two Durkheims, then. First there is Durkheim against Spencer, who insists that there is increasing differentiation in society but that we are no less subject to constitutive social forces—on the contrary, we are subject to an increasing number of constitutive social forces. Second there is the ethnocentric Durkheim, who insists that there is increasing freedom from constitutive social forces in societies with a high division of labor, when compared to savages, who are slaves to social forces.

The use of the term "ethnocentrist" might seem heavy-handed, but this is precisely what is at stake here. Without the use of the liberal theory of subjectivity and the appeal to freedom, the hierarchical difference between savages and moderns would be flattened. One group would be heterogeneous, the other homogeneous, but neither obviously better than the other. The primary justification for the superiority of one group over the other involves reaching into the liberal toolbox—ironically, the same one Spencer was using—and suggesting that one group of subjects is more constrained than the other. The reason why Durkheim could not fully admit that moderns are equally subject to social forces is precisely because to do so would be to flatten his social hierarchy.[9]

So should we take sides with one Durkheim over the other? If the liberal theory of subjectivity is removed as implausible—for all the reasons Durkheim gives when debating Spencer—the remaining empirical claims about modern freedom appear rather weak. First, Durkheim claims we are more free outside our professions. This is a weak argument, for reasons Durkheim himself provides. He offered empirical evidence that administrative law increasingly regulates not only professions, but also education, health, welfare, transportation, and communications. Second, Durkheim claims that we are more free because we can move from profession to profession. However, in the third section of the book, in which he discusses the "abnormal forms" of society, he freely admits that this is not the case. Due to heredity in the past and prejudices in the present, there is a forced division of labor. He is optimistic in that he hopes these conditions are receding. As prejudices are "gradually extinguished," "[e]mployment in the public sector is increasingly thrown open freely to everybody, with no stipulation as to wealth" (314). But he fully recognized that this was not the case at present, and—a century later—it appears that his optimism regarding this freedom was unwarranted. The third argument for modern freedom posited that moderns are, as a result of evolution and heredity, more free from instinct. Such arguments were perhaps plausible given the state of the biological sciences during Durkheim's generation—and they were useful for propping up racism and justifying colonialism—but are no longer tolerated in scholarly circles today.

While moderns still like to think of themselves as more free, the idea that people in kinship societies are identical automatons has become increasingly unpopular, and with good reason. Are we to believe, as Durkheim so easily did, that people in societies with a low division of labor were zombies controlled by a collective conscience, from the moment they awoke to the moment of falling sleep? In all stages and modes of their lives? Such a view is no longer an option for us.

If these arguments for "freedom" collapse under investigation, the normative hierarchy collapses as well. Consider all the following distinctions Durkheim makes, with the intrinsically normative ones marked with an asterisk:

labels → emphasis

Mechanical Solidarity/Organic Solidarity
Low Division of Labor/High Division of Labor
Homogeneous Collective Conscience/Heterogeneous Consciences

Universal Social Regulations/Variable Social Regulations
Less Free/More Free*
Closer to Instinct/Freer from Instinct*
Closer to Matter/Closer to Spirit*

The first few distinctions are rhetorically neutral; they suggest that different societies are ordered in different ways, but not that the latter are superior. Some societies are organized by these principles; other societies are organized by those principles. People in these societies have a low degree of differentiation; people in those societies have a high degree of differentiation. This all implies differentiation, but these claims so far are compatible with an antiliberal theory of subjectivity and Durkheim's general method. It is necessary to invoke the alternate, liberal theory of subjectivity only when Durkheim needs to justify the superiority of one type of society over another. These societies are not just different; some societies are better than others. How are moderns better? They are more free, less animal, more spiritual. "Freedom" appears to be the ideology of the colonizers, useful for othering or differentiating themselves from those they want to colonize. In this case, "words such as 'individual,' 'society,' 'personality,' [and] 'collective' [are] ideological weapons in the power struggles of various parties and states" (Elias 2001, 84).

Durkheim's vestiges

Criticizing Durkheim for his nineteenth-century ethnocentrism is neither groundbreaking nor particularly interesting. If I have dedicated such attention to Durkheim's contradictions, it is because I find contemporary social theorists making practically identical claims. Contemporary scholars in religious studies often make a distinction between organized or institutional religion and individual religion or spirituality; the former makes individuals slaves to the collective conscious, it seems, while the latter permits individual autonomy. Indeed, some even quote Durkheim on this point. Consider Paul Heelas and Linda Woodhead's *The Spiritual Revolution*, which argues that traditional, coercive, or controlling forms of institutional religion are now giving way to free spirituality:

> Some hundred years ago, Durkheim drew a distinction between 'a religion handed down by tradition' and 'a free, private, optional religion, fashioned according to one's own needs and understanding' . . . . William James, Simmel, Troeltsch, and others drew similar conclusions. They too thought that spiritualities of life were a growing force, so they would not be surprised by the extent to which the spiritual revolution has developed since their time. (Heelas and Woodhead 2005, 148–149)

TABLE 1.1 Heelas's and Woodhead's rhetorical vocabulary

Religion (−)	Spirituality (+)
"disruptive, undermining, and damaging" (4)	"true nature" (27)
"obeying these higher authorities" (23)	"nourish, cultivate, and enrich" (29)
"deference to 'higher authority'" (81)	"To thine own self be true" (85)
"straightjacket" (83)	*"freedom to be yourself"* (95)
"being told what to do" (95)	"personal autonomy, independence, and freedom" (120)
"conformity" (111)	"Individuals . . . making up their own minds" (120)
"externally laid down rules" (111)	"the *right* of every individual to work out his own philosophy of life" (125)
"conservative" (112)	
"impose" (112)	
"conformity" (114)	"freedom" (125)
"strict" (123)	"fulfilling" (125)
"forces of culture" (125)	
"immature religion" (125)	

Heelas and Woodhead seem to utilize the distinction in the same way that Durkheim did, that is, to justify one as superior to the other. Consequently, Heelas and Woodhead use the sorts of rhetorically loaded vocabulary in Table 1.1 to contrast traditional religion and spirituality.

In addition, consider Heelas's claims in his *Spiritualities of Life*. According to Heelas, organized or institutional religion—much like Ronald Reagan's "evil empire"—suffocates individuality (Heelas 2008, 2), requires conformity (28), and subordinates individuals to tradition (55), while individual spirituality allows for uniqueness, autonomy, and freedom (28). Heelas writes,

> Whether it be the personal life of subjective experience, the personal life of the "familiar" world of daily activities, or the cultivation of humanity, it seems as though holistic spirituality has a great deal to offer. We might well want to conclude that if it continues to become more popular, it will provide a worthy successor to Christianity in western settings; and, in the longer term, to exclusivistic, iron-cage forms of Islam (for example) in countries like Pakistan. (6)

All of this clearly reproduces the distinction Durkheim made: one group is repressive; one group is spiritual. Similarly, in *Spiritual Marketplace* Wade Clarke Roof makes a distinction between organized religion, which is "cut and dried, encrusted, and culturally bound," and spirituality, which is "truly the individual's own" (Roof 1999, 81). The former is institutional, but the latter is more open and tolerant (42), more personal (64), more individual (66), and "bound not by cultural conformity but . . . [encourages] being true to oneself" (67).

> [W]hen spirituality is recast in strictly psychological terms, it is often loosened from its traditional moorings—from historic creeds and doctrines, from broad symbolic universes, from religious community. There is narrative enmeshment, but in its specificity and inward focus the communal dimension so important historically to cultivating spirituality is weakened. The autonomous, often instrumentally-minded individual can be left alone. (109)

This too reproduces Durkheim's distinctions: one group is moored and collective, and the other group is autonomous and individualized. Such views have become sufficiently hegemonic that David Lyon can say,

> it has become a truism that religious activity is, increasingly, subject to personal choice, or volunteerism, and that, increasingly, for many in the advanced societies, religious identities are assembled to create a bricolage of beliefs and practices. (Lyon 2000, 76)
>
> . . . [W]here we once would have identified ourselves in terms of the villages or clans we came from, and located ourselves within a social hierarchy stretching down from prince or president to pauper, now nothing is fixed. . . . The realm of choice has opened up tremendously for most people in the affluent societies, giving us unprecedented opportunities to choose lifestyles and beliefs from a range of options. (91)

Adjusted for tone, this could almost have come out of *Division of Labor*. The vocabularies activated here are homologous to those Durkheim activated in defense of his ethnocentrism: some people are more free from community and tradition than others—and the implication is that the free people are better off for it.

Given the one Durkheim's criticism of Spencer—which I find persuasive—and the normative baggage that hangs on the other Durkheim, it might be useful to suspend the problematic distinction between collective conscience and autonomous individuality. In fact, it is quite possible that the distinction obscures more than it reveals. In his criticism of the scholarship of Heelas, Woodhead, Roof, Lyon, and others, Matthew Wood notes,

> Without acknowledging that they are doing so, scholars slip from asserting that self-authority is emphasized in New Age discourses to asserting that the exercise of self-authority marks the New Age. These views leave

the self and authority peculiarly un-theorized, given the prominence of sociological approaches that have directly addressed how the self is constituted or formed through social contexts and the authorities within these. (Wood 2007, 38)

The epigram for this chapter, "We're all individuals," is a famous line from Monty Python's *Life of Brian*. The line appears in a scene where a number of followers have gathered under their new leader's window—the eponymous figure Brian—and invite him to teach them. He refuses to do so and asks them to think for themselves, saying "You're *all* individuals." They reply, *in unison*, "Yes! We're all individuals." The joke is similarly made by Jenny Lawson in her humorous memoir, *Let's Pretend This Never Happened*; Lawson reflects on the irony of her and her high school friend's rebellion: "We both had complete contempt for everyone else in the town who followed the herd mentality and was afraid to be unique and individualistic like us, the two Goth chicks *who were dressed exactly alike*" (original emphasis; 2012, 75). It is as if Heelas, Woodhead, Roof, and Lyon are not in on the joke—the increasing popularity (and, arguably, homogeneity) of something called "individual spirituality" belies both the uniqueness and distinction implied by the qualifier "individual." As Bennett M. Berger notes of the coauthored *Habits of the Heart* volume that, in a sense, started this genre of scholarship,

> There is a lot of culture described, evoked, interpreted, and even moralized in *Habits of the Heart*, but there is very little social structure in it; little systematic effort to connect the webs of social structure in which its interviewees are caught (even stuck) to the probabilities of them choosing this or that cultural strategy from the toolkit of culture that is structurally available to them. (Berger 1995, 108)

Matthew Wood is correct: "These views leave the self and authority peculiarly un-theorized" (Wood 2007, 38).[10]

Durkheim is right that societies are different in ways that relate to the increasing division of labor. In the following chapters, I will attempt to account for some of these differences, while attempting to avoid the rhetorical slippage from "they claim they are free individuals" to "they are free individuals," which Wood quite rightly puts his finger on.[11] In addition, we must resist characterizing subjectivity as falling on a continuum stretching from "free" to "constrained." As Foucault suggests in his critique of liberal conceptions of freedom, "we should not think of freedom as a universal which is gradually realized over time, or which undergoes qualitative variations, greater or lesser drastic reductions, or more or less important periods of eclipse" (Foucault 2008, 63). Durkheim suggested that for savages, "individuality is zero." If we are to set aside the liberal theory of subjectivity and the normativity embedded in it, then *perhaps even modern individuality is zero.*[12] If moderns are not more free, but simply different in our differences, constrained in different ways, conditioned by different structures and discourses, then the rhetoric of "individuality" must be an explandum, not an explanans. As Durkheim said, "We regard as fruitful this idea that social life must be explained, not by the conception of it held by those who participate in it, but by profound causes which escape consciousness" (quoted in Lukes 1973a, 231).

2

Theorizing "individual re

The sense of autonomy which characterizes the typical individual
in modern industrial societies is closely linked to a pervasive
consumer orientation.
THOMAS LUCKMANN, 1967, 98

As Paul Heelas and Linda Woodhead point out in *The Spiritual Revolution: Why Religion Is Giving Way to Spirituality* (2005), a growing number of people identify as "spiritual," claim to be uninterested in "institutional religion," and seem to be attracted to the sort of writings that recommend, for example, "becoming yourself," "self-realization," or "finding the Kingdom of God within." This is a relatively new phenomenon, and as such there is also a growing body of scholarship that seeks to understand or explain the shift from "institutional religion" to "individual spirituality."

Unfortunately, theorists such as Heelas and Woodhead directly appropriate Durkheim's normative rhetoric (although putting it to a different use) and in doing so undertheorize "individualism." Their discussion of individualism more or less repeats insiders' accounts—in fact, the usual rhetorical qualifications one might expect in ethnographic reports, such as "according to practitioners," or "practitioners reported that," are almost entirely absent from their book. Arguably—as Jonathan Z. Smith puts it—"[t]he disciplined study of any subject is, among other things, an assault on self-evidence, on matters taken for granted" (2004, 389). Instead, Heelas in general recommends a hermeneutic of generosity: "it is best to take participants seriously," and "it is appropriate to take their *word*" (original emphasis; Heelas 2008, 93). To take first-order claims about individualism at face value, however, would be as problematic as uncritically absorbing Durkheim's criticism of primitive savages.

Another problem with their approach is that it completely ignores and fails to take into account a quarter century of research on the invention of religion" by scholars such as J. Z. Smith (1982, 2004), Talal Asad (1993), Daniel Dubuisson (2003), Russell McCutcheon (1997, 2001, 2003, 2005), Timothy Fitzgerald (1999, 2007, 2011), Tomoko Masuzawa (2005), Brent Nongbri (2013), and others. Oddly, this research has been ignored by all of the central figures in sociology of religion writing on individualization and secularization, including Peter Berger, Robert Bellah, Robert Wuthnow, Wade Clark Roof, Steve Bruce, Rodney Stark, Roger Finke, and Laurence R. Iannaccone.[1] The modified secularist narrative they usually tell—according to which "religion" is not exactly disappearing but is perhaps becoming a private, individual matter[2]—unreflexively employs a sacred/profane or spiritual/temporal distinction. Indeed, Heelas and Woodhead overtly reify a "sphere of the sacred" (2005, 9). This is problematic, not least of which, because the terms "religion," "nonreligious," and "secular" serve as first-order terms in discursive battles, or weapons in rhetorical wars. For instance, talk of "secularism" often seems tied up with the legitimation of nation-state action, as Timothy Fitzgerald (2007, 2011) and William Cavanaugh (2009) have convincingly argued, and as I'll argue in Chapter 4 (see also McCutcheon 2005, Arnal and McCutcheon 2012). As Cavanaugh puts it, "In the West, revulsion toward killing and dying in the name of one's religion is one of the principle means by which we become convinced that killing and dying in the name of the nation-state is laudable and proper" (2009, 4–5). If this is the case, drawing lines between religion and nonreligion—both of which, upon reflection, turn out to be contested, floating signifiers—is perhaps an ideological rather than a scholarly endeavor.

By contrast, I take it for granted that all institutions or practices are temporal institutions; if this is the case, there is perhaps no analytical traction to be gained by separating out some civil institutions as "religious," as if they were fundamentally distinct from other types of civil institutions. Of course it is clear that "religion," "nonreligious," and "secular" remain emic categories regularly used by social actors. As William Arnal and Russell McCutcheon write,

> they will continue to be useful in our scholarly description of some people's world-making activities—activities taking place in the very groups that we in the modern world inhabit (where people use these terms in acts of self-identification), as well as in those who, for whatever reason, have adopted (or have possibly been forced to adopt) these social techniques. However, without careful retooling, they are *not* analytic categories helpful in accounting for the creation, the successful reproduction, and the export of the worlds that their use has made possible. (Arnal and McCutcheon 2012, 120)

On this view, to take up "religion" and "secular" as academic tools would be as problematic as using "orthodoxy" and "heresy" as analytical tools to describe the rise of Christendom: like "primitive" and "savages," they are tools of war, useful for drawing lines in the sand, for gerrymandering social space, or for scoring points against opponents—they are insufficient for reflexive attempts to theorize how groups imagine themselves into existence.

In order to explain what insiders call "spirituality," we need a classificatory scheme that eschews all of these folk taxa: individualism, autonomy, religion, individual religion, spirituality, secularism, and privatization. By drawing upon a number of social theorists whose work does not hinge on these terms, this chapter attempts to provide a grid of classification that better brings into relief how what is usually called "religion" has changed under late capitalism. Durkheim's analysis of the division of labor will continue to be central to my analysis; while the dominant "mode of production" may not be determining in the last instance, it nevertheless has a considerable bearing on the production of culture. Much of what others call "individual religion," I will argue, is a specific strand of capitalist ideology, a strand that obscures the causes of "individual choice" while encouraging "individuals" to produce, consume, and accommodate themselves to the regnant mode of production.

Bruce Lincoln provides us with a way of thinking about how the structure of society is tied to the reach of regnant ideologies; those ideologies labeled as "religious" will be unable to attain an uncontested hegemonic status in societies where capitalist ideologies and practices are dominant, particularly because economic empires function through the inclusion of diverse ideologies only on the condition that such ideologies remain subordinate to the central economic functions of the empire. Thomas Luckmann offers a plausible account—closely following Durkheim's argument in *Division of Labor*—of how such an economic regime works: as roles in a complex capitalist society become increasingly differentiated, local ideologies proliferate, yet no local ideology appears as universally persuasive across all structural spheres; those ideologies which are a part of the so-called religious sphere cease to appear relevant in other "spheres." Richard Fenn extends Luckman's argument, suggesting that there isn't an intrinsically "religious sphere," but that what counts as "religious" or "not religious" is the product of turf wars between structurally divided institutions. Sociologist James Beckford takes Fenn's point to its logical conclusion: "religion" and "not religion" are merely emic claims to be tracked by scholars, and lack analytic usefulness. Despite its promise, one problem with Luckmann's account is that he appears to suggest that individuals gain freedom for themselves in their private spheres, and make their own individual religions with a pick-and-choose process; this looks precisely like the individualism I seek to avoid. To some extent Luckmann saves himself by suggesting that "individual choices" reflect socioeconomic status, but insufficiently develops this claim. In order to develop it further, I will turn to Georg Simmel and Jean Baudrillard, both of whom argue that in consumer capitalism we make individual choices that are not autonomous but which reflect our class location.

On the reach and integration of "religion"

Bruce Lincoln provides us with a means of reflecting on the relative scope or reach of what are identified as "religious" ideologies or cultures, as well as the extent to which they are integrated with the dominant culture or dominant institution in any given society.

In *Holy Terrors*, Bruce Lincoln makes a distinction between "maximalist" and "minimalist" religion in order to account for some of the changes that came about in the Western world during the modern period. In Europe prior to this period, Christianity was the "central domain of culture" (Lincoln 2006, 59). The social world was ordered, legitimated, sustained, and contested through the use of Christian vocabulary, Christian stories, Christian institutions, and so on. Lincoln uses the term "maximalist" to identify this state of affairs—during this period religion had a "maximal" relation to social order.

Lincoln suggests that after the rise of capitalism the economy becomes the "central domain of culture" (59). The world at large becomes ordered, legitimated, sustained, and contested by economic rationalities, discourses, and practices, rather than religious ones. When this happens, economics in a sense becomes "maximalist," while religion is moved to a "minimalist" position.

When religious minimalism becomes hegemonic, "cultural preferences [are] constituted largely as fashion and open to market fluctuations"; in addition, religious maximalism is "experienced in two ways: a quaint, seductive diversion for some, and as a resentful atavism, capable of reactionary counterattacks" (59). By this I take Lincoln to mean, for instance, that for people who adopt religious minimalism, those who do not—like the American Amish or al Qaeda—are taken to be either "quaint" (interesting for sightseers) or dangerous "fanatics."

While Lincoln has identified something fundamental—the fact that the reach of ideologies waxes and wanes, in particular in relation to the regnant mode of production—there are problems with the language of maximal/minimal religion. The minimalist/maximalist distinction ultimately breaks down for three reasons. First, it implicitly clings to the idea that "religion" is a distinct or special form of culture. Second, it can implicitly carry a judgment of orthodoxy: although I don't think Lincoln intends it, it might be taken to imply that maximalist Christianity, for instance, is true Christianity, and that minimalist Christianity is an inauthentic deviation.

Third, and more importantly, using Lincoln's terms one could argue that Christian maximalism (i.e., in the European middle ages) has been replaced by capitalist maximalism today: capitalism orders the lives of minimalist Christians more than Christianity does. However, insofar as minimalist Christianity has been domesticated by capitalism, in a sense this version of Christianity is actually maximalist: minimalist Christianity is ultimately maximalist *if it does order the lives of minimalist Christians*. To put it otherwise, minimalist Christianity is implicitly capitalist Christianity, and minimalist Christians may very well have their entire lives organized in ways that are complicit with capitalist Christianity. The idea of "minimalist religion" is subtly seductive, like the discourse of individualism: it organizes the social sphere as a whole while pretending to organize only a part of it. It prevents us from thinking about how the so-called minimalist religion has social effects far beyond the so-called religious sphere: if minimalist Christianity legitimates capitalism, its reach actually extends into the economic realm—in which case it ceases to be strictly "minimalist." What is useful, however, about the minimalist/maximalist distinction is the fact that it draws attention to the *relative reach* of ideologies, but we need more sophisticated terms.

In *Gods and Demons, Priests and Scholars*, Lincoln offers another insight that could shed light on how we might think about the relative scope or reach of "religious" ideology or culture in society. In his chapter on "Ancient and Post-Ancient Religions," he suggests,

> In the ancient, religion was a shared concern of groups existing at familial, civic, ethnic, and national levels of integration. The collective identity of such groups, moreover, was strongly overdetermined, being based simultaneously on territory, language, polity, kinship, and laws, as well as the religion that members held in common and that, in turn, held them. (Lincoln 2012, 79)

However,

> the post-ancient, by contrast, saw the emergence of communities based primarily—also most explicitly and emphatically—on religious considerations, integrating persons who might well be divided by geography, language, culture, and/or citizenship. (79)

We could of course drop the term "religion"; what is central here is that some communities—the ones Durkheim calls "primitive"—have a society in which the shared culture or ideology is integrated into or coterminous with all aspects of society, while other communities—those with a high division of labor, perhaps—segment groups on the basis of various ideologies that are not coterminous with all of society. The shift from one to the other was likely brought about in part as a result of empire (and we could add, arguably, changes in technology, especially transportation technology). According to Lincoln, empires "brought disparate populations into single political entity and tax structure, but left subject peoples only very imperfectly integrated in terms of religion and culture" (80). Sometimes those colonized would fit their local ideologies to the empire's idiom, and sometimes the empire would "introduce aspects of their native religion to the provinces, or at least to the elite strata therein" (80). Lincoln summarizes:

> as ancient religion gave way to post-ancient, one could observe . . . deterritorialized elective communities constructed on the basis of religious adherence displacing multi-stranded groups, within which ties of geography, politics, kinship, culture, and religion were isomorphic and mutually reinforcing. (82)

Perhaps, then, what might be of interest to us is how societies in which kinship, politics, culture, and ideology *are isomorphic* are distinct from societies in which kinship, politics, culture, and ideology *are divided* and cross cut one another. We might end up with a scale that looks something like this:

Isomorphic ←—→ Heteromorphic

kinship societies—medieval Europe—Roman empire—Western modernity

On such a scale, it would be irrelevant how minimal or maximal a "religion" is; rather, what would be important is whether a society has any ideology or culture that is maximal and which isomorphically orders all other ideologies and practices in line with it. For instance, Amish communities would perhaps be relatively isomorphic—at least as imagined in popular culture—as the local ideology is isomorphic with the social structure as a whole. Similarly, monasteries, where the entire community is organized around a shared ideology or set of practices, would be on the isomorphic end of the spectrum. By contrast, the United States today would be far more heteromorphic. The state's ideology—for instance, with its emphasis on innate rights, the founding fathers, and the constitution—does not tend to organize the social structure of individual families or professions. Isomorphic and heteromorphic are, of course, structurally close to Durkheim's distinction between societies with "mechanical" and "organic solidarity," but without any implications regarding the question of "solidarity."[3]

What is crucial here, for my purposes, is that the relative reach of an ideology or culture is perhaps fundamentally related to the social structure, division of labor, and the diversity of culture within one religion or empire.

Toward the restriction of "religion"

Thomas Luckmann's *The Invisible Religion* provides us with some details that flesh out Lincoln's picture, as well as specification of the mechanisms by which the reach of an ideology shrinks as societies become more heteromorphic. For Luckmann—who follows Durkheim's emphasis on the relative division of labor in society—one key difference between types of societies is that in kinship systems, the "sacred cosmology" (i.e., the legitimating ideology) pervades the social system as a whole; in modern society, the reproduction of a sacred cosmology has become a specialization relatively independent of other institutions. The transition from one to the other apparently happens via a slow evolution. While the sacred cosmology was originally reproduced by everyone in society and tied to the maintenance of the social system as a whole, as the division of labor increases in a society, the social function of reinforcing the dominant ideology becomes a specialized task (e.g., for priests alone); like Durkheim's first chief to take a leadership role, so priests come into existence as individuals take on a distinct role previously nonexistent. Over time, cosmologies reinforced by specialized persons or institutions eventually earn a relative autonomy from the social order as a whole.

According to Luckmann, the division between the maintenance of a sacred cosmology and other types of labor can lead to a segregation of "religious" from "profane" affairs. With industrialization, "total life values become part-time norms" (Luckmann 1967, 39). Whereas the cosmology reinforced by a particular institution may have been designed to legitimate a wide variety of everyday behaviors, individuals internalizing the cosmology through a segregated institution may see the duties prescribed as applying only within a segmented part of life. Luckmann writes,

> Performance of [what come to be known as] the nonreligious roles is determined by the 'secular' norms which develop in the more or less autonomous economic and political institutions. The more the traces of the sacred cosmos are eliminated from the 'secular' norms, the weaker is the plausibility of the global claim of religious norms. The latter become attached in an increasingly exclusive manner to the 'part-time' religious roles. (85)
>
> . . . [T]he individual . . . tends to restrict the relevance of specifically religious norms to domains that are not yet pre-empted by the jurisdictional claims of 'secular' institutions. Thus religion becomes a 'private affair'. (86)

In a sense, what Luckmann is attempting to do here is to account for the "why" of the transition from maximalist religion to minimalist religion, or from ancient to postancient religion, to use Lincoln's terms. Or, why is it that we went from having a cosmology directing or legitimating all of social life to institutions that direct or legitimate activity only in a so-called religious sphere or private sphere? The source of the transition—which Lincoln suggests is related to the rise of modern capitalism, but on which he doesn't elaborate—Luckmann finds in the increasing division of labor in modern society. Of course, these terms overlap to the extent that they are practically the same thing; the choice for one over the other may depend on one's preference for Marx or Durkheim.

What replaces "traditional" religion in the function of reinforcing an overarching cosmology, by which and in which everyday behaviors, practices, and norms are legitimated and integrated? Does a new global sacred canopy replace the receding sacred cosmology as it becomes increasingly isolated? Luckmann suggests that nothing takes its overarching place. Subjects in a segmented world with a high division of labor find themselves at the intersection of a wide variety of fields; as such, they do not deeply internalize the ideologies or norms of any of the fields. Rather, they play the games or roles of each field, wearing each role lightly, metaphorically speaking. Since they are eminently replaceable in a world with a high division of labor—for reasons clearly elaborated by Marx—subjects are not motivated to offer allegiance to any one field or role in said field. As Luckmann puts it, "The functional rationality of segregated institutional norms tends to make them trivial from the point of view of the person" (96). As a result, although the "jurisdiction originally claimed by the 'official' model of religion is total," this totalizing claim is fundamentally undermined by the structural transformation of the social world (96).

Luckmann suggests a step-by-step model of how—over a few generations—increasingly isolated sacred cosmologies are internalized by religious practitioners. That is, he attempts to account for how sacred cosmologies move from having a global reach to being received as having a limited or "private" (or even nonexistent) reach. He claims (using patriarchal language) that "fathers" are likely to experience a unity between their official "religious" cosmology and their "nonreligious" behaviors and priorities. As society changes but while the official religious cosmology remains *unchanged*, "sons" socialized into the cosmology of their fathers may experience (although entirely unreflectively) a gap between their cosmology and their "nonreligious" behaviors and priorities—that is, there may be a performative contradiction between their sacred canopy and their "secular" life. Children's experience in the third generation will be even further removed:

> what fathers preach but do not practice will be internalized by the sons as a system of rhetoric rather than as a system of "ultimate" significance.

At the extreme point of such a development—supposing that the "official" [cosmological] model is not adjusted—we find a situation in which everybody is still socialized into the 'official' model of religion, but the model is not taken at face value by anybody. . . . [R]eligious beliefs will be compartmentalized into opinions . . . which will have no direct relation to the individuals' effective priorities and everyday conduct. (89)

This leads subjects to have a *sense* of autonomy: "the individual does escape the consciousness-shaping effect of institutional norms to a considerable extent" (96). However, this sense of autonomy may be merely "illusory" (97). Luckmann goes on to offer a prescient analysis:

The sense of autonomy which characterizes the typical individual in modern industrial societies is closely linked to a pervasive consumer orientation. Outside the areas that remain under direct performance control by the primary institutions, the subjective preferences of the individual, only minimally structured by definite norms, determine his conduct. To an immeasurably higher degree than in traditional social order, the individual is left to his own devices in choosing goods and services, friends, marriage partners, neighbors, hobbies, and . . . even "ultimate" meanings in a relatively autonomous fashion. In a manner of speaking, he is free to construct his own personal identity. The consumer orientation, in short, is not limited to economic products but characterizes the relation of the individual to the entire culture. The latter is no longer an obligatory structure of interpretive and evaluative schemes with a distinct hierarchy of significance. It is, rather, a rich heterogeneous assortment of possibilities which, in principle, are accessible to any individual consumer. . . .

The consumer orientation also pervades the relation of the "autonomous" individual to the sacred cosmos. . . . [W]ith the pervasiveness of the consumer orientation and the sense of autonomy, the individual is more likely to confront the culture and the sacred cosmos as a "buyer." (98–99)

Lest one think that for Luckmann we are all "individuals" when it comes to religion today, he goes on to insist that a buyer's "selection is based on consumer preference, *which is determined by the social biography of the individual, and similar social biographies will result in similar choices*" (emphasis mine; 105). This absolutely crucial point is, however, insufficiently developed; for this reason I will develop it with the work of other theorists later.

According to Luckmann, with the increasing division of labor and the bifurcation of fields and their coordinate ideologies in the modern world, no ideology can serve the function of a single, overarching justification for the entire social order—all ideologies begin to legitimate not from "above" the social system but "within" their own, individual jurisdiction (101). There is no universal "sacred canopy" in the modern world: "The assortment of religious representations—a sacred *cosmos* in the loose sense of the term only—is not internalized by any potential consumer as a whole. The 'autonomous' consumer selects, instead, certain religious themes from the available assortment and builds them into a somewhat precarious system" (102). Luckmann insists that no "secular" ideology replaces the role formerly fulfilled by "religion": "The effective social basis of the modern sacred cosmos is to be found neither in the churches nor the state nor the economic system" (103).

Because the jurisdiction of ideologies becomes necessarily local and relative, and because they will be individually adapted by individuals in consumer ways, "it is more likely that individuals will legitimate the situation-bound (primarily emotional and affective) priorities arising in their 'private spheres' by deriving, *ad hoc*, more or less appropriate rhetorical elements from the sacred cosmos" (105). As a result, what some scholars call "individual religion" "will consist of a loose and rather unstable hierarchy of 'opinions' legitimating the affectively determined priorities of 'private' life," perhaps created and recreated on an ad hoc basis (105).

Individuals can make or remake whatever religions they want, although only *privately* so for Luckmann. He imagines individuals in the modern world making a sort of Faustian bargain: they are free to make or remake religious ideologies for themselves, in order to legitimate for themselves their own private world, but at the cost of leaving be the primary social institutions (such as state and economic systems). "Because the individual's performances are controlled by the primary public institutions, he soon recognizes the limits of his 'autonomy' and learns to confine the quest for self-realization to the 'private sphere'" (110). In the "Postscript," Luckmann draws attention to the discrepancy between the liberty granted to individuals in their private sphere and the autonomy given to the primary social institutions in the public sphere. The latter realm becomes one of "dehumanization," in which people become things at the disposal of society, to use Durkheim's terms.

Again, for Luckmann there is no dominant ideology legitimating the entire social system from "above": "The modern sacred cosmos [only] appears to operate as a *total* ideology. It provides an encompassing assortment of plausible ideas which supports the functioning of modern industrial societies—but *without* explicitly legitimating them" (116). Rather, Luckmann seems to be arguing that the discourse of modernization, secularization, public and private, individualism, and so on, all work to *structure* modern society but without *legitimating* that structure. Thus "it is not particularly useful to call the new social form of religion an ideology in the ordinary sense" (116).

So what is an *invisible* religion for Luckmann? Luckmann's book began with a diatribe against those sociologists of religion who see a decline in church membership as a sign of secularization. For Luckmann however,

> [t]he new sociology of religion consists mainly of descriptions of the decline of ecclesiastic institutions—from a parochial viewpoint, at that. The definition of research problems and programs is, typically, determined by the institutional forms of traditional church organization. (18)

> The main assumption—which also has the most important consequences for research and theory in the sociology of religion—consists in the identification of church and religion. (22)

By contrast, Luckmann argues that religion *does* persist in the so-called secular world, although it cannot be judged by church attendance. Rather than religion in the churches—or similar institutional settings where "membership" is easily identified and counted—we are surrounded by invisible religions, individual religions cobbled together by consumers who pick and choose what suits them and what will justify their personal lifestyle, given the preferences that result from their social context and personal biography.

If the concept of "religion" lacks analytical usefulness, then "invisible religion" is unlikely to be of use. However, Luckmann is right to point out that under a capitalist division of labor, society is fragmented such that those ideologies fabricated and distributed by particular sectors, but which rarely seem of use in other sectors, are less likely to achieve a hegemony. That might not, of course, prevent those in particular sectors from *claiming* a universal reach, but such claims will be received as more and more hysterical the less relevant that sector appears to other sectors. The pope can claim that everyone should practice Catholicism, but such a claim will look more and more like special pleading.

Losing "religion"

One reason why the assertion of a universal reach of a particular sector is more likely to be dismissed is because of a popular narrative about "religion" and "secularism," which suggest that those institutions labeled as "religious" do not rightly have a claim outside a so-called private sphere in which they're allowed to operate. Thus, a number of theorists, some working in the wake of Luckmann, have argued that "religion" is not a thing in the world but a gerrymandering term with which we organize society.

Richard K. Fenn doesn't take this position exactly, but anticipates it in his *Toward a Theory of Secularization*. Following Durkheim and Luckmann, Fenn argues that with increasing diversity in society comes increasing dissension regarding the dominant legitimating or justifying discourse. Leaders may either draw on increasingly abstract discourses (which may be more generally acceptable but also have less traction as a result of their abstraction) or dig in and continue using the "thick" dominant discourse (like a vaguely Christian "civil religion" discourse). There may be an increasing distance or gap between the state's legitimating discourse and the discourse of "private" civil institutions. This needn't pose a problem for the state, as long as the discourses of civil institutions are in a complementary rather than chafing relationship.

> A religious group may require that religious beliefs and values inform an individual's decisions and actions in all areas of social life, in work, for instance, and voting as well as in the family and other primary relationships, but the wide scope thus assigned to the sacred in social life is still unlikely to precipitate conflict over the basis of social or political authority unless the religious group requires that organizations such as political parties and businesses, schools and civic associations reflect the religious beliefs and values of their members and constituents. . . .
>
> . . . The more a religious group narrows the scope of the sacred and reduces its demands for integration between corporate and personal values and standards, the more adapted is such a group to secular society. (emphasis removed; Fenn 1978, 65)

However, when there is a chafing relationship between the state's practices and the practices of a particular civil institution, the latter may cry foul on the grounds of "freedom of religion," if they can plausibly characterize their discourse as "religious." The discourse and practices of a civil institution are more likely to chafe to the extent to which the civil institution sees its scope as comprehensive or partial, unless the civil institution's interest are fully aligned with those of the state. If the state utilizes the discourse of one particular civil institution, that is liable to increase dissension from competing civil institutions. The characterization of some particular discourses as "secular" or "religious" is therefore designed to justify their general deployment (in the former case) or prohibit their general deployment (in the latter case). Also, the characterization of some discourses as "religious" may be designed to limit the scope of those discourses identified as a "secular" (as in: this is a private religious matter and the state should not intervene).

Fenn goes so far as to create a four-part grid of "religious culture," in which one axis relates to the scope claimed by a group (i.e., how far should religious values claim to apply in the secular sphere), while the second axis concerns the expectation that members of the group integrate their religious ideals with their behaviors in the institutions they inhabit. He suggests that Mormons, for instance, limit the scope of their claim of authority over society as a whole, but do expect members of their group to integrate Mormon values into all of their behaviors (whether in "religious" or "secular" institutions; 69).

Fenn extends the argument in *Liturgies and Trials: The Secularization of Religious Language*. There Fenn argues that discourses characterized as "religious" fail to hold as authoritative in, for instance, courtrooms. While those discourses we consider religious or liturgical might be taken as authoritative in churches, such "claims are more precarious in the courtroom" (Fenn 1982, 56).

> When institutions like the court or the university therefore develop their own rules of discourse, for asking questions and giving answers, for stating facts and drawing conclusions, those separate rules are likely to make religious language inappropriate, irrelevant, or disruptive. A defendant who gives prophetic commands to the legal professional within the courtroom has clearly violated the court's rules of discourse. (100)

For this reason,

> Religious witnessing becomes inappropriate in formal situations within a modern corporation or political organization, for instance, although religious witnessing is not unusual in informal settings or by businessmen and politicians outside their immediate occupational contexts. (121)

In addition, according to Fenn the US constitution "gives, with one hand, the right to the churches to be free of governmental transgressions across the line between church and state, *while giving to the courts the right to draw the line between the sacred and the secular wherever they see fit*" (emphasis added; 120). Due to this, Fenn looks at US court cases in which competing parties are contesting whether a discourse, ideology, or practice is "religious." He finds that the state, when attempting to regulate some practice found undesirable, is more likely to use a narrow definition of "religion," such that the practice in question falls outside the protection of the first amendment. By contrast, groups who find state interference undesirable are more likely to utilize an expansive definition of "religion," so that their practices will be protected from state interference under the first amendment. "Narrow constructions of the First Amendment are more easily based on relatively narrow definitions of religion. It appears that the state abandons more generous [functionalist definitions of religion] when it perceives a danger to its own clear and compelling interests" (160).[4]

Fenn does not follow his social constructionist approach all the way down. If he had, he would see that this does not lead toward a theory of secularization so much as away from one. If nothing is intrinsically religious, and if various cultural traditions are merely identified as religious if and when it is politically advantageous to do so, then both religion and its opposite would have only social or political rather than analytical usefulness. Theories of secularization should then dissolve into theories that account how and why social actors might identify something as religious or not. In *Religion and Advanced Industrial Society* (1989) and *Social Theory and Religion* (2003), James Beckford develops his account of modernity in part on the basis of Fenn's work, but takes Fenn's claims to their logical conclusion:

> Given the wide extent of uncertainty and disagreement about what counts as religion . . . , it would be unwise for social scientists to intuit or impose a definition of their own making . . . . A better strategy is to map the varieties of meaning attributed to religion in social settings, to discern the relative frequency of the prevailing meanings, and to monitor changes over time. . . . I agree, therefore, with Susan Budd that a good way forward is "to try to discover what is 'religious' and what is 'secular' for each society and each group." In short, the field or the topic of religion would follow the contours of existing usages but without making any assumption about the possibility that "real" or "essential" religion might be lurking inside or behind these usages. (Beckford 2003, 20)

For this reason, Beckford insists that scholars track first-order or emic uses of the term religion (22).

When it comes to considerations of "privatization" or "secularization," then, Beckford claims that it is not the case that "religion" is a thing that is "private" and whose privacy is respected by something called "the state." On the contrary, privacy is defined by the state "as the sphere of life from which public authorities choose to exclude themselves in certain conditions" (87). In addition, Beckford criticizes Peter Berger's theory of privatization for not seeing the extent to which state discourses are constitutive of "privacy."

> In jargon terms, private individuals are "interpellated" or called to account for themselves by the daily experience of being, for example, consumers of mass-media products and market goods, citizens of a State, employees of organisations, members of categories identified by age, ethnicity, gender, social class, "lifestyle," and so on. Moreover, individuals are capable of reflecting critically on their "privatised" identity and therefore of choosing to flaunt it, to flout it, to flee from it, or to fight it. (88)

Consequently, there is no simply autonomous or free individual in a private sphere; rather, there are global discourses that interpellate individuals in their privacy, or which constitute interiority from the exterior.

In summary, for Beckford, as scholars we should not track the advance or retreat of something called "religion" or "secularism" but, instead, the *use of* such terms in the advancement of group agendas that are neither inherently "religious" nor "secular," and are only variably classified as such in the advancement of such agendas. On this view what will be of interest is not what is religious or not, but why certain social actors might classify anything as such.[5]

Following and extending the insights of Lincoln, Luckmann, Fenn and Beckford, I want to propose a classification grid that could bring into relief the relative reach of a culture or ideology without using terms such as "secularization," "privatization," or "religion." I want to suggest that any ideology, discourse, or practice could be analyzed in terms of its *effect*, *function*, *jurisdiction*, and *behavioral scope*.

Effect. We can distinguish between the intended and actual effects of discourses or practices. They may have effects that those who use them intend, but they might also be completely ineffective, or may have actual effects that are different from the ones intended. Discourses and practices are inevitably taken out of context and used in new contexts to new purposes (in fact, one could argue—as Derrida has—that possibility is what makes them functional in the first place). For instance, in *The Protestant Ethic and the Spirit of Capitalism* (2002), Weber tracked what were unintended yet very real effects of certain Protestant ideologies.

Function. We can distinguish between *structuring* and *legitimating* functions, following Luckmann. Discourses and practices may structure society, that is, serve a constitutive function, without thereby legitimating that structure. For instance, Luckmann argues that capitalist practices are constitutive of the shape of modern Western society, yet no one ideology has risen to legitimate the structure that for all practical purposes runs itself. However, when such structures or practices are called into question, it may be the case that legitimating discourses or ideologies are called upon in their defense. These two functions could, of course, be two sides of the same coin.

Jurisdiction. We could distinguish between discourses and practices having a global reach, a local reach, or merely a gerrymandering reach within a particular structure. At a university, the faculty manual or guidelines likely have a global reach within the institution, while a particular professor's syllabus would have a local reach only across the spaces of her course. A gerrymandering reach, by contrast, is one that organizes spaces—sets up walls, metaphorically or literally speaking—but may not order the spaces thus divided. For instance, normative "secularization" discourses may be intended as gerrymandering: they may suggest that society should be divided up in certain ways (public and private), yet make no claims to what happens in the "private sphere," over which it claims only a gerrymandering jurisdiction. In that "private sphere," perhaps "individuals" theoretically have control over their own jurisdiction, apart from a few global prohibitions of the state (although, as I argue in Martin 2010, while this discourse may be "intended" in this fashion, the actual picture is rather different). Arguably, consumer practices and discourses, while neither demanding nor claiming any particular jurisdiction, may nevertheless have a global reach into all "spheres" in the modern world.

Behavioral scope. We could distinguish between a comprehensive or a partial behavioral scope of particular ideologies or discourses, with respect to the extent to which they inform a subject's activity. This is similar to jurisdiction—the question is how far a discourse or practice reaches. However, it is slightly different in that a discourse that has a universal reach, for example, the state's prohibition of murder across all segments of society, may only inform a small part of a person's behavior (or even none at all). This dictum probably does not direct or inform most people's behavior on a daily basis, while—by contrast—consumer practices might inform the behavior of a subject on an almost comprehensive level. Professors are subject to an ethic that regulates their behavior with students, and in the sphere of the university, it may regulate their behavior relatively comprehensively. By contrast, a professor who claims to be a devout Catholic, and whose Catholic ideology is said to inform her life comprehensively, may in fact find Catholic ideology or practices of little use when it comes to interacting with students. In this case, the local ethic (academic professional ethics regulating professor–student behavior) has a comprehensive effect in this sphere, while the discourse that alleges a global and comprehensive reach (Catholicism) may have only a partial or no behavioral scope in such a context.

Individualism and consumer conformity

Earlier I noted that, for Luckmann, in a capitalist society individuals are free to pick and choose their own personal ideology or religion, although "selection is based on consumer preference, *which is determined by the social biography of the individual, and similar social biographies will result in similar choices*" (emphasis mine; Luckmann 1967, 105). Similarly, as Martyn J. Lee writes, consumer action "is never voluntary, in the sense that all members of society are *required* to choose and use goods according to certain established social conventions and from within existing social divisions and cultural differences" (emphasis mine; Lee 1993, 29). Georg Simmel and Jean Baudrillard are useful in that they explicitly theorize in more detail the ways in which apparently free consumer choices are determined by class position.

For Georg Simmel, writing at the beginning of the twentieth century, fashion is simultaneously tied to conformity and differentiation. The fact that fashion is arbitrary yet can function to mark difference is fundamental to its usefulness: wearing the latest in fall fashions is significant precisely due to its difference from the previous year's fall fashions. It's not that this year's fall fashions are intrinsically better or more beautiful—if they were they would still be beautiful (rather than passé) next year. Similarly, my provost wears a suit every day not because it is intrinsically striking but because of a set of identifications and oppositions it carries:

Suit : Jeans and T-shirt :: Provost : Student :: Elite : Hoi Polloi

As Simmel writes, "Union and segregation are the two fundamental functions which are here inseparably united" (Simmel 1971, 297).

> It is peculiarly characteristic of fashion that it renders possible a *social obedience*, which at the same time is a form of individual differentiation. Fashion does this because in its very nature it presents a standard that can never be accepted by all. While fashion postulates a certain amount of general acceptance, it nevertheless is not without significance in the characterization of the individual, for it emphasizes his personality not only through omission *but through observance*. (emphasis mine; 305)

One may be individually distinct—relatively speaking—but distinction would be socially useless without some conformity to a class. Absolute distinction of fashion would be, for instance, indistinguishable from hermitage—in which case it would cease to function as fashion. For this reason, Simmel notes that even fashion leaders are still conformists: the leader "represents something distinctly individual, which consists in the quantitative intensification of such elements as are qualitatively common property of the given set of class. He leads the way, but they all travel the same road. . . . [A]s a matter of fact, the leader allows himself to be led" (305). Even those who claim to eschew fashion tend to conform to it by inverting fashion. "The man who consciously pays no heed to fashion accepts its form just as much as the dude does, only he embodies it in another category, the former in that of exaggeration, the other in that of negation" (307). Consequently, "conspicuousness primarily rests content with a mere inversion" (307). For Simmel, the behaviors of those who claim to be most individual—on either side of the fashion spectrum—are explicable only if we understand them as conformist.

In *The Consumer Society*, Jean Baudrillard concurs with Simmel: "conformity is not status equalization, the *conscious* homogenization of the group (each individual aligning himself with the others), but the fact of having the same code in common, of sharing the same signs which make all the members of that group different from a particular other group" (Baudrillard 1998, 92–93). Consequently, "individuals" might "personalize" consumer goods in ways that are distinct from the goods belonging to peers in same class or group, yet practices of personalization will follow the same structural logic of difference. Consumer goods are often functionally identical, but cosmetically conspicuous: while all of us might have the latest smartphone, perhaps mine is distinct by being blue while yours is distinct by being red. Automobiles are similarly marked by functional similarity but cosmetic differences, while different tiers of cars are available for different income levels; thus one can signal class difference while at the same time signaling distinction from peers in one's own class—all the while, everyone is conforming to the same social logic. As Stuart Ewan and Elizabeth Ewan bluntly put it, "[t]oday's freedom is molded and taut. . . . Individuals are identical, but come in colors" (Ewan and Ewan 1992, 75).[6]

Baudrillard takes his analysis further, arguing that in societies where we seek well-being, yet make "*well-being* measurable in terms of objects and signs" that mark relative social distinction (Baudrillard 1998, 49), we set in place a competition for distinction that tends toward *accelerating* consumption and necessary inequality. Why accelerating consumption? Distinction can only be had by standing out among one's peers, and as changes in technology make consumer goods available more and more quickly, so must consumption accelerate in order to maintain or turn over distinction. Why necessary inequality? Distinction is intrinsic to the system—the goal is not to be equal but to continually differentiate oneself from others. In addition, while we are greatly constrained by this vortex of consumption, subjects seeking distinction in such a system may not experience themselves as constrained by the system that determines their actions:

> In the very act of scoring his points in the order of differences, each individual maintains that order and therefore condemns himself only ever to occupy a relative position within it. Each individual experiences his differential social gains as absolute gains; he does not experience the structural constraint which means that positions change, but the order of differences remains. (61)

Consequently, "the system survives on disequilibrium and structural penury . . . The system only sustains itself by producing wealth and poverty, by producing as many dissatisfactions as satisfactions" (55).

All of this is to say: the freedom to choose allotted to Luckmann's individuals in their "private sphere" is perhaps guided by a logic of consumption and is therefore at best a conformist freedom, although, as Baudrillard notes, it may not be experienced as such by "individuals," from whose perspective a relative differential gain in relation to one's peers may feel like "freedom." Taking "individual religion" at face value as "autonomous"—like Heelas and Woodhead do—is perhaps premature.

Conclusion

Thus far I have argued the following points:

1   The relative scope or reach of an ideology is determined in part by the social structure.

2   No ideology is intrinsically religious or secular; rather, the *identification* of an ideology as religious or secular is asserted in order to gerrymander its scope or reach.

3   In a society with a high division of labor, no ideology may be hegemonic; thus "individuals" may be free to cobble their own "private" religious ideology (indeed, the characterization of such ideologies as "religious" is part and parcel of the protection of such freedom).

4   Apparently free individual "choices" are likely determined by conformity to a logic of distinction and consumption over which individuals have no control.

In the following chapters, I will argue that so-called individual religions are often remarkably linked to the regnant mode of production and predictably tied to class location. The myth that "we are free to choose" when it comes to "individual religion" or "spirituality" unfortunately has the effect of (1) obscuring those causes that direct our choices, (2) positively sanctioning or naturalizing consumer choices, and (3) reinforcing the system of consumption and distinction, and I aim at an analysis that avoids these pitfalls.

3

Our "religion" of the status quo

[T]ell me how you classify and I'll tell you who you are.
ROLAND BARTHES, 1972, 175

According to William James and the intellectual tradition of which he is a part, institutional religion is the "excrescence" (James 2004, 432) built on religious experience. While much has been written on "religious experience," there is less critical scholarship on the idea of "institutional religion" or "organized religion." However, both sets of terms belong together in a pervasive and broadly persuasive contemporary discourse—a discourse that, ironically, informs those very religious traditions it was designed in part to criticize—and a consideration of one should involve a consideration of the other. In this chapter I explain how this contemporary discourse operates, how it is partially constitutive of a number of contemporary reinventions of the figure of Jesus, and how it belongs to a dominant folk theory of religion that dovetails well with consumerism under late capitalism. In summary, the experience/institution distinction is a building block of a modern, domesticated ideology of the status quo, which has incarnations in both modern "spirituality" and liberal forms of Christianity. I do not claim that all uses of "religious experience" and "institutional religion" advance late capitalism, but that they are easily and often aligned with late capitalist norms.

On "spirituality"

Before turning to William James, it is important to note that the use of "spirituality" in the literature under consideration is distinctly modern. A systematic investigation into the history of the term "spirituality" is beyond the scope of this book, but I will attempt to highlight a few key points. As Jeremy Carrette and Richard King note in *Selling Spirituality*, there are a variety of uses of "spirit" and related words in the Greek and Latin speaking worlds to which

European modernity is heir, yet none of which fit the modern view of spirituality as concerning "an interior, psychological self" (Carrette and King 2005, 35).

In *Cosmology and Self in the Apostle Paul: The Material Spirit* (2010), Troels Engberg-Pedersen analyzes Paul's use of "spirit"—*pneuma* in Greek—in the early Christian writings now collected in the New Testament. According to Engberg-Pedersen, Paul appropriates a Stoic cosmology similar to that of Cicero. This Stoic cosmology was fundamentally materialist, as the world consists of a number of "elements," including earth, water, air, fire, and aether (19). The "heavenly bodies"—the gods and so on—were made out of the aether, a sort of brilliant fire, and that fire was also called *pneuma* (20). Humans are made up of the same elements, with some bit of the pneumatic material, which provides humans with their intelligence; upon death the other elements would dissipate, but the matter of the *pneuma* would ascend to the heavens (20–21). Engberg-Pederson points out that when Paul discusses resurrection of the dead in 1 Corinthians, it is the "pneumatic body" in the Stoic sense that is raised.

> A "psychic" body belongs *on earth* as exemplified by the "earthly bodies" mentioned in [1 Corinthians] 15:39; and a "pneumatic" one belongs *in heaven* as exemplified by the "heavenly bodies" mentioned in 15:41. Or to be even more precise: a "pneumatic body" *is* a heavenly body like the sun, moon, and stars. (28)   body & soul

This is, to modern readers, an alien idea; Engberg-Pederson notes that this cosmology is no longer a viable option: "The cosmology, say, of Stoicism just cannot be ours" (193).

Philip Sheldrake, in his *Spirituality: A Brief History*, similarly notes that the use of the terms "spirit" and "spirituality" changes over time, and starts his book by contrasting *pneuma* in Paul's letters with alternate, contemporary uses. Sheldrake notes that contemporary uses are, as Carrette and King suggest, associated with an inner self. In his section on "Contemporary Meaning" in the chapter titled "What Is Spirituality?," Sheldrake writes,

> many people no longer see traditional religion as an adequate channel for their spiritual quest and look for new sources of self-orientation. Thus "spirituality" has become an alternative way of exploring the deepest self and the ultimate purpose of life. Overall, the spiritual quest has increasingly moved away from outer-directed authority to inner-directed experience. (Sheldrake 2013, 5)

Despite this admission that the use of the term changes over time, Sheldrake oddly doesn't hesitate to find the origins of "Christian spirituality in general" in the past (24). In the next chapter, titled "Foundations: Scriptures and Early Church," he goes on to discuss "spirituality" in 1 Corinthians, including the spirituality of "postresurrection" salvation (30). In summary, Sheldrake is guilty of a rather naïve conceptual anachronism. Ignoring both the radical differences between Paul's cosmology and our own and the radical differences between the use of the term *pneuma* and spirit in these varying contexts, Sheldrake finds an unbroken tradition of spirituality from the first century to the present, from the New Testament to "Christian spirituality in general." Given that he explicitly states his normative agenda of recuperating "authentic" spirituality (19), the reasons for his anachronism seem clear: connecting contemporary practice to a pure origin lends authority or legitimation to whatever present "spiritual" projects he hopes to advance. However, rigorous academic standards forbid a lazy appeal to an anachronistic return-to-origins narrative conflating modern "spirituality" with Greek *pneuma*. What Brent Nongbri claims of the concept "religion" is true of the concept "spirituality": "we have to be honest about the category's origins and not pretend that it somehow organically and magically arises from our sources. If we fail to make this reflexive move, we turn our ancient sources into well-polished mirrors that show us only ourselves and our own institution" (Nongbri 2013, 153). Despite Sheldrake's narrative, there is no unbroken chain from the ancient to the modern world—"spirituality" as a so-called inner turn is a modern phenomenon, and Sheldrake has primarily found himself in the mirror he's fashioned.

The contemporary bifurcation of inner world and outer world has some superficial similarities to premodern thought, but the origin of the contemporary view dates back to around the time of the Protestant Reformation. First, just before the Reformation we see the enormous popularity of the works of Erasmus, such as "Handbook of the Militant Christian" (originally published in 1503). In this essay Erasmus makes a fundamental distinction between the "inner man" and the "outer man" and associates true piety with the invisible, inner man. "You will find that you can best maintain this piety if, turning away from visible things, which are for the most part either imperfect or of themselves indifferent, you seek the invisible" (Erasmus 1983, 61). According to Erasmus, true piety cannot be achieved if one attends rituals such as Mass without having the proper inner disposition; "Mass also takes place in their hearts" (65). Outward ceremony without inward disposition is ineffective. Playing off of Paul's distinction between faith and works, Erasmus writes,

> to place the whole of religion in external ceremonies is sublime stupidity. This amounts to a revolt against the spirit of the Gospel and is a reversion to the superstitions of Judaism. St. Paul was incessant in his attempt to remove the Jews from their faith in external works. I feel that the vast majority of Christians have sunk once again into this unhealthy situation. (68)

Erasmus's point is not that "external" matters are irrelevant; on the contrary, they're supremely important. Rather, he sees the *source* of external change in internal transformation. We must "Advance from the body to the spirit, from the visible world to the invisible" (71), but only because if we have our inner selves in order we will be less likely to fall prey to lust, avarice, more likely to be charitable, and so on. For Erasmus, inner transformation is necessary insofar as it leads to a desired outward transformation.

Soon thereafter we see Protestant reformers employing the same distinctions in order to justify tolerance for themselves as dissenting parties. In *On Secular Authority* (originally published 1523), Martin Luther insists that piety concerns inward matters that are in principle outside the reach of civil authorities. Using the same inward/outward distinction—yet putting it to new purposes—he writes,

> Secular government has laws that extend no further than the body, goods and outward earthly matters. But where the soul is concerned, God neither can nor will allow anyone but himself to rule. And so, where secular authority takes it upon itself to legislate for the soul, it trespasses on [what belongs to] God's government, and merely seduces and ruins souls. (Luther 1991, 23)

Luther goes on to argue that the sword of the state cannot compel the soul, as it is in some sense autonomous from outward matters. "Faith is free, and no one can be compelled to believe" (26). From this Luther draws the conclusion that states should leave Protestant dissenters alone; attempts at forceful conversion would necessarily be futile on this view. All of the early modern arguments for religious tolerance and—eventually—separation of church and state depended on this supernatural anthropology. The distinctly modern use of the term "spirituality" comes not from Plato's realm of the forms or Paul's *pneuma* but from this early modern political propaganda, with its distinction between an inner self and an outer self, and the assumption that the former is somehow—supernaturally—autonomous from the latter.

William James and spirituality

Experience vs. institution in James's varieties of religious experience

I want to set the stage for the following discussion of William James with a brief anecdote about teaching James's *Varieties of Religious Experience*, shared by J. Z. Smith in *Relating Religion*:

> What my college students derive from [James' *Varieties*] is their own take on religion read back to them: the priority of the individual, the centrality

of experience and feeling, a vague but palpable sense of transcendence, a distrust of thought about religion (especially from "afar"), and the necessity of raising questions of ethical implications. None of these are helpful to a science of religion. If Harvard is to be our guide in the construction of such a science, I far prefer the lectures of James's colleague and critic, Josiah Royce. In his *The Problem of Christianity* Royce privileged both a theory of language and of community—two essential elements in any theoretical proposal concerning religion. Both are lacking in James. (Smith 2004, 162)

What is it about James's approach that makes it so easily appropriated by contemporary students (as well as others—often those who enjoy publishing success in popular literature on religion, such as Karen Armstrong)? Of course Smith's students' "take on religion" is not simply the result of the vast influence of William James; it is not that his ideas have been so widely disseminated that their interest in him is merely the result of the "trickle-down" effect of his theories into popular culture. James is only one person in a long line of thinking about religion that utilizes an inward/outward dichotomy, opposing inward "spirituality" to "institutional religion." Talk of "institutional religion" has a long history that can be traced from Erasmus's inside/outside distinction, to appeals for tolerance following the Protestant Reformation, to anti-Catholic sentiment in general, to Protestant Pietism, to French anticlericalism, to James's focus on religious experience as at the core of religion, up to today's "I'm spiritual, but not religious" (SBNR) rhetoric.

James offers us an important example of this discourse in practice. Historically speaking, as a philosopher his writings on religion lent an air of authority and credibility to the experience/institution distinction. "James' stature as a 'highbrow' intellectual has cast an aura of respectability over the continuing public fascination" with religious experience (Fuller 2001, 58). "Academic departments of psychology, philosophy, and religious studies consider him one of the most influential thinkers in the history of their disciplines" (134). Indeed, James's *Varieties* is often hailed as a laudable classic within the academic study of religion, especially in teaching contexts. Both inside and outside of the discipline of religious studies, James is held up as an important theorist of religion. His work is therefore important both because his model for thinking about religion was widely influential and because he provides a particularly clear example of this broader experience/institution discursive tradition being put to work.

In this broader modern tradition—again, of which James is but a part—we can trace the following distinctions, each of which builds on the prior associations.

Primary Term/Secondary Term
Inside/Outside
Inward Religion/Outward Religion

Faith/Works
Inward Sincerity/Outward Dead Ritual
Christianity/Judaism
Protestantism/Catholicism
True Religion/False Religion
Soul/Body
Spiritual/Temporal
Invisible Church/Visible Church
Religion/Civil Society
Religion/Magic
Religious Experience/Institutional Religion
Personal Religion/Organized Religion
Religion/Fundamentalism
Spirituality/Religion[1]

Of course, the term "religion" appears on both sides of this set of homologies, but even when it swaps sides the same primary/secondary distinction is maintained: when people say "I'm spiritual, but not religious" they are playing off of the existing primary/secondary rhetorical associations, not reversing them.

This discursive tradition often depends upon a supernatural ontology and anthropology, according to which all humans have souls and bodies, and true religion (or spirituality) is linked to the soul stuff, not the body stuff. Getting caught up in the external, secondary, bodily stuff is ultimately to miss the authentic, inward experience of the divine. Thus Luther could call Judaism a religion of works righteousness disconnected from sincere faith in God, Protestants in general could say the same of Catholicism, James could consider all institutional religions secondary accretions built on personal religious experiences, and the SBNR groups can say that all organized religions are unnecessary diversions from authentic experiences of transcendence.

As a pragmatist, James tends to be wary of such supernaturalist ontologies, and we can see his suspicion in *Varieties of Religious Experience*. He makes it clear that he does not intend to give much "ontological umpf" to the distinction between "personal" and "institutional" religion. He writes:

Now in these lectures I propose to ignore the institutional branch entirely, to say nothing of the ecclesiastical organization, to consider as little as possible the systematic theology and the ideas about the gods themselves, and to confine myself as far as I can to personal religion pure and simple. To some of you personal religion, thus nakedly considered, will no doubt seem too incomplete a thing to wear the general name. . . .

But if you say this, it will only show the more plainly how much the question of definition tends to become a dispute about names. Rather than prolong such a dispute, I am willing to accept almost any name for the personal religion of which I propose to treat. Call it conscience or morality, if you yourselves prefer, and not religion—under either name it will be equally worthy of our study. (James 2004, 37–38)

This is a typical pragmatist (and nominalist) gesture. In summary, James is suggesting something like the following: "We are not talking about 'personal religion' in the sense of some Kantian 'noumena'—rather, I'm using the phrase 'personal religion' to pick out something in the world of interest to me. We could just as well divide the world up differently by using different words or by using the same words differently." This nominalist gesture is one with which I have a great deal of sympathy. However, in the following paragraph James goes on to put the "ontological umpf" back in:

In one sense at least the personal religion will prove itself more fundamental than either theology or ecclesiasticism. Churches, when once established, live at secondhand upon tradition; but the *founders* of every church owed their power originally to the fact of their direct personal communion with the divine. Not only the superhuman founders, the Christ, the Buddha, Mahomet [sic], but all the originators of Christian sects have been in this case—so personal religion should still seem the primordial thing, even to those who continue to esteem it incomplete. (38)

Later in the book he suggests that the religious experiences he has put his finger on are the "nucleus" (432) or the "essence" (433) of religion. He therefore reclaims the ontological ground he gave up in the previous paragraphs. This "personal religion" *is* primary or fundamental just as the soul is primary in the soul/body supernatural ontology. That is, James is making precisely the sort of ontological distinction he claims not to be making.

This ontologizing of the distinction leads to dehistoricization (and mystification) in two ways. First, because the distinction is ontologized, it is difficult for people to see that the very distinction is a social construction, the product of a history for which we can perform a genealogy. Much like the public/private distinction unique to modern Western thought (see McCutcheon 2003, 2005; Martin 2010), this distinction is taken for granted as if it were a feature of the universe, rather than a product of human thought. As such, it is taken to be "discovered" in the world rather than "created." Because of this, its social or ideological effects are underanalyzed—or, rather, they aren't analyzed at all. (I'll return to the consequences of this naïve empiricism later.)

Second, and more importantly, the ontologizing of this distinction prevents the historicization of what the distinction presumes to identify or discover in the world: both "religious experience" *and* "religious institutions." On the surface, it would seem to prevent the historicization of only the former: the distinction implies that religious experience is pure, direct, unmediated, outside the effects of time, space, and history, whereas institutions are precisely those things that are mediated, inside time, space, and history, and can be analyzed using the methods of history (unlike experience itself). That is, in a way that hearkens back to the spiritual/temporal distinction used in the sixteenth, seventeenth, and eighteenth centuries, what the latter term identifies is subject to history and therefore can in principle be historicized, while the former cannot. By contrast, I'm arguing that while it obviously renders "experience" outside the realm of history—for it is of "the transcendent"—it simultaneously renders "religious institutions" outside of history. By ontologizing "institutions" as opposite to "experiences," they are rendered unchanging and unalterable in key ways: institutions are universally *secondary and derivative*. Institutions are just as ahistorical as experiences here: no matter where one looks in time and space, religious institutions will be the same.

The SBNR discourse has displaced James's use of "religion"; for this discourse, "religion" is the second term rather than the first term in the dichotomy, and James's "religion" has been replaced with "spirituality." Hence we get the following (which I've taken from a discussion board on Facebook's SBNR group, and which I take to be a paradigmatic example of the discourse I'm examining [I've corrected capitalization, spelling, grammar, and punctuation, as well as smoothed the diction in a few places]):

> To me religion is a set of rules set down by man and it is man, through man, through God. Religion has always been the bane of man's existence. Look at Europe during the Reformation where Christian was killing Christian due to minor differences in religion: such as whether to baptize a baby or wait until adulthood, whether to pay for indulgences or not—let alone how many non-Christians were brutalized and killed during these times because of religious ideas.

> Look at the Middle East where Muslim is killing Muslim over who the successor of Mohammed is, when ultimately that shouldn't really matter. The words of the Prophet and the spirit of Islam are what matters, not the personal interpretations of particular individuals.

> Spiritualism, or faith, is something directly between you and your God or Gods. It is a pure set of ideas that come from your mind and heart, and not from the rules of a man-made church. It comes from your interpretations of your scriptures, not from taking the words of another man who is no better than you. It comes from you—and you alone—with your relationship with the spirit.

Religion empowers evil men to do evil things in the name of benevolent beings, for religion does not allow deviation from interpretation. Religion does not allow one to freely think, hence the term "heresy," which when broken down to its original etymology means "free thinker."

Spiritualism allows people to think for themselves and to make their own choices in faith, based off of their own observations. It is a pure and direct link to God, where one is governed by one's conscience—which is the voice of The One. With spiritualism, one is not governed by religions which are the voice of man.

Even the Bible will tell you we are self-guided, as we ate of the Tree of Knowledge of Good and Evil, whereby we are now born with the innate knowledge of both. The original sin is when we know naturally what is right or wrong and we choose wrong. You are more apt to choose wrong if you let others tell you what right is.

You are your own judge.

This author reproduces the elements we find in James's ontology (while adding some matters James would not) and essentializes each term in the dichotomy: on the one hand are spiritualism or faith, purity, individuality,[2] direct connection with divinity, freedom, thinking for oneself, innate knowledge (specifically of good and evil), rightness, and on the other hand are religion (i.e., institutional religion), violence, mediated connection with divinity (through "man" and man's "interpretation"), secondary knowledge, evil and wrongness, and the imposition of the group on the individual (possibly "groupthink" or "herd mentality"). There is no room for historical variability—the second term has essential features that are unchanging.

To reiterate: whereas one might think that James's distinction might lead to the historicization of "institutional religion" if not "religious experience," it seems that his legacy has been aligned with forbidding the historicization of either term: "institutional religion" is always and ever degraded, secondary, and imposing on human individuality and freedom. As a result of the ontologization of the experience/institution dichotomy, neither are truly subjected to historical analysis.[3] (This ahistorical essentialization is part of a teleological folk theory of religion, which I will discuss further later.)

"Institutional religion" as a naïve, crypto-normative rhetorical device

Because James's rhetoric and the SBNR discourse are ontological and essentialist, they lend themselves to naïve empiricism. In contemporary scholarship, positivist realism is out of fashion: the world is not simply "there" to be discovered; not only do we constitute the world through language, but we can also investigate what historical conditions led to us constituting the world the way that we do. By contrast, the naïve empiricism of the ontologized spirituality/institutional religion dichotomy results in subjects just "finding" spirituality and "finding" religion in the world, with nary a concern about how this way of dividing the world is historically constituted.

A by-product of this naïve empiricism is that it becomes that much easier to use the phrase "institutional religion" as a pejorative term. In fact, the phrase is used precisely because of the negative associations that have come to be connected to it. *This rhetoric is intrinsically polemical.* "Institutional religion" is inherently a *bad thing*, and as such it is deployed as an insult, like the word "cult." One need not show what is bad about a so-called cult—the mere application of the word calls forth a negative evaluation and a set of social prescriptions. In addition, outside of those rare occasions where "fundamentalism" is used to refer to early twentieth-century evangelical Christian movements that emphasized the "five fundamentals," the word "fundamentalism" is similarly pejorative. When people refer to a group as "fundamentalist," we need not inquire into how they might evaluate such a group—we already know they view such a group negatively. When words such as these are used, careful description is traded for what amounts to name-calling. One pretends to find institutional religion in the world, but one is in fact passing off one's own evaluations under the guise of description.

Together these two elements—that is, naïve empiricism and the crypto-normative nature of the phrase "institutional religion"—end up functioning much like conservative Christian hermeneutics. Conservative Christians sometimes "interpret" the world using a certain hermeneutic that, once it gets off the ground, is self-confirming and impregnable. We see this in analyses of their god's presence in the world. When something good happens, that is interpreted as the hand of their god. When something bad happens, that is interpreted as the work of the devil. This hermeneutic works through projection of a subject's assumptions onto the world: what makes something "God's hand" or "the devil's hand" is not some objective feature of an event or object in the world itself, but the subject's view of what is good or bad. Anything the subject sees as good could be God's hand; anything the subject views as bad could be the devil's hand. The hermeneutic turns not on the world but on the subject's background assumptions about what is good or bad. The hermeneutic doesn't evaluate evidence so much as merely sort evidence. As such, counterfactuals are simply unthinkable—once a subject internalizes this hermeneutic, it is possible that nothing could contradict it.

The "institutional religion" rhetoric is not identical, but it works similarly. What an individual takes to be "organized religion" as opposed to "true spirituality" will follow not from some objective features of things in the world but from the subject's background assumptions. As Roland Barthes suggested, "tell me how you classify and I'll tell you who you are" (Barthes 1972, 175). One might think that "organization" is the key for this distinction, but it is not—there are several SBNR organizations. This is not indicative of bald hypocrisy; here the word "organization" is used like a symbol. In fact, the colloquial meaning of the term is probably largely irrelevant; what chiefly matters is that the term carries pejorative connotations. We see the same thing with the way the term "Nazi" is applied to people or groups— even Jews—who have absolutely no connection with Nazism and whom the Nazis would have hated. Rather, the word "organized" in "organized religion" is emptied of its usual content; what makes some instance of religion "organized" is not its features, but rather the fact that the subject making the identification does not like it. If one likes zazen, it is likely a portal to pure, internal religious experience; if one doesn't like zazen, it is probably a secondary ritual performance utilized by religious practitioners who are just "going through the motions" in an institutional setting. In addition, not only is this process invisible to the subjects employing this hermeneutic—that is, the subjects think they are discovering something in the world rather than projecting themselves onto it—but also it is the fact that their background assumptions themselves are socially constituted will likely remain invisible.

Armed with an impervious hermeneutic, and one whose function is invisible, the author of the quotation earlier—from the SBNR Facebook page—can sort anything he doesn't like into the category "organized religion" and can sort anything he does like into the category "true spirituality." The fact that he is projecting a reality rather than discovering one is unlikely to be noticed, and the fact that his background assumptions about what is good or bad are products of his own social, cultural, and institutional context remains invisible. Ironically, his institutional context (which has given him his background assumptions as well as the rhetoric he uses to sort the world) manifests itself in his scheme as pure, inward spirituality: his institutionally and socially produced "common sense" is taken to be inward truth. That is, what he takes to be "inside" is precisely what is from the "outside."

Those who utilize the SBNR rhetoric are not the only ones unable to historicize their own common sense. In *The Scandal of the Evangelical Mind*, Mark A. Noll criticizes American evangelicals' almost complete inability to historicize their own position and their own hermeneutic. In part his criticism is directed at the fact that evangelical populism is heavily dependent on the projection of their own "common sense" as if it were universally common sense. Noll locates this in the American evangelicals' appropriation of Scottish enlightenment thought, which emphasized "that all humans possessed, by nature, a common set of capacities . . . through which they could grasp the basic realities of nature and morality" (Noll 1994, 85). This appeal to their own inner common sense as common sense *tout court* had the effect of authorizing their values as universal. Although evangelicals eventually broke with key aspects of this Scottish philosophy, they "did not challenge the older conceptions of self-justifying authority or the dictates of common sense" (105). The naïve empiricism of the SBNR discourse works much the same way, and therefore it is no surprise that the author quoted earlier appealed to a universal common sense in justification for his position:

> Even the Bible will tell you we are self-guided as we ate of the Tree of Knowledge of Good and Evil, whereby we are now born with the *innate knowledge of both*. The original sin is when *knowing naturally what is right or wrong* we choose wrong. You are more apt to choose wrong if you let others tell you what Right is. (emphasis mine)

For him, objective right and wrong are no different than what he discovers to be right and wrong when he turns to his own inner conscience—which he views as "pure" and as the direct result of thinking for oneself.[4] In addition, his inherited rhetoric is easily historically locatable in a particular social context, but it is precisely that which prevents him from seeing his institutional context. The ideology of individualism masks the fact that "individuals" are socially, culturally, and institutionally produced.

It is worthwhile returning to Noll's evangelicals at this point. He argues that their biblical hermeneutic in the first half of the twentieth century was linked to a certain form of creation science, which was obviously a historical response to the rise of evolutionary accounts of human origins. However, the historical location of their particular biblical hermeneutic was lost on them:

> The result is a . . . tragedy. . . . [M]illions of evangelicals think they are defending the Bible by defending creation science, but in reality they are giving ultimate authority to the merely temporal, situated, and contextualized interpretations of the Bible that arose from the mania for science of the nineteenth century. (Noll 1994, 199)

That is, they misrecognize their local hermeneutic as *the* hermeneutic of the Bible, and misunderstand the Bible as a result. I am arguing similarly: the application of the experience/institution distinction as ontologically built into the nature of the universe allows individuals to take their own local values and local hermeneutic (embedded of course in local interests and local battles), project them onto the world, or interpret the world in terms of them, and as such mistake their creation for reality itself. This is naïve empiricism at its best: "individuals" opposed to "institutions" are unable to see themselves and their world as historically constituted by particular institutions (discursive and otherwise). In addition, their crypto-normative evaluation of "institutional religion" passes as objective because they are incapable of seeing the extent to which their evaluation is the result of a projective hermeneutic—and one that is, ironically, relatively identical to the hermeneutic of the "religious" people— that is, Noll's evangelicals—to which they rhetorically oppose themselves.

One might argue that I've strayed too far from James; the SBNR discourse is not *The Varieties of Religious Experience*. But we find the same crypto-normative language passing itself off as a description of the facts of the matter in James's *Varieties*. He talks about "institutional religion" with the following normative rhetoric: "corporate ambitions," "the spirit of politics and the lust of dogmatic rule," "hypocrisy and tyranny and meanness and tenacity of superstition" (James 2004, 293), "baseness," "bigotries," and "the spirit of dogmatic dominion" (296), "corruption by excess" (297), and "fanaticism" (298). James goes on to note that religious wars are not caused by true religious experience but by xenophobic tribalism inherent in the human spirit but distinct from true piety:

> I beseech you never to confound the phenomena of mere tribal or corporate psychology which it presents with those manifestations of the purely interior life which are the exclusive object of our study. The baiting of Jews, the hunting of Albigenses and Waldenses, the stoning of Quakers and ducking of Methodists, the murdering of Mormons, and the massacring of Armenians express much rather that aboriginal human neophobia, that pugnacity of which we all share the vestiges, and that inborn hatred of the alien and of eccentric and nonconforming men as aliens, than they express the positive piety of the various perpetrators. Piety is the mask, the inner force is tribal instinct. (296)

How does one know that true piety has passed into corruption or excess? "Common sense must judge" (297). Little attempt is made to situate the social-cultural infrastructure that informs moral judgment and "common sense," and James does not take note of the fact that what he takes to be "common sense" might very well have been taken by others as "fanatical," and vice versa—and it is at this point that James's own ahistorical naïve empiricism shines through.[5]

A folk theory of religion

James's *Varieties* contains something else that should trouble us as scholars:

> Churches, when once established, live at secondhand upon tradition; but the *founders* of every church owed their power originally to the fact of their direct personal communion with the divine. Not only the superhuman founders, the Christ, the Buddha, Mahomet, but all the originators of Christian sects have been in this case. (38)

James's discourse encourages a return-to-origins narrative that distorts history and prevents useful analysis of religious traditions. James's theory of religion is perhaps the most superficial theory one could possibly have; it goes something like this: a divine power strikes like lightning, giving an individual a pure experience he then shares with others. His teachings are, however, degraded when they are taken up by followers interested merely in power. While elements of the original, pure message—derived from the experience—can be found in the teaching that is passed down by his followers, it is used—wrongly—to control others. The institutional religions that result from this degradation are extremely authoritarian and require strict obedience from all members. Religious practitioners are little different from automatons. The development of all religions follows this same trajectory.

Lest readers think I've distorted his view in *Varieties*, here is the evidence:

- All religions start with a "direct personal communication with the divine" (38);

- The experiences constitute the "essential" (433) "nucleus" (432) of religion;

- Institutional religion is a secondary thing created by "disciples" and "sympathizers" with a "lust for dogmatic rule" (293);

- Institutional religion "contaminate[s] the originally innocent thing," and becomes tied up with "hypocrisy and tyranny and meanness" (293);

- Institutional religion expresses a "tribal instinct," and all "fanaticism" produced by this is external to "the purely interior life" (296);

- Institutional religion requires "exclusive devotion" and "idealizes the devotion itself" (298);

- The excessiveness or fanatical nature of institutional religion can be judged by "common sense" (297); and

- Institutional religion is the same for "every church" (38), for these things are "almost always the same" (433).

But this is not a social theory of religion—it is an ahistorical teleology that presumes all religious traditions form in exactly the same way. It suffers from the teleological excesses for which Hegel's theory of religion is rightly rejected. On this theory, historical differences do not matter, since all institutional religions are essentially the same. As I noted earlier, the religious experience/institutional religion dichotomy contributes to the dehistoricization of both "experience" and "institutions." It is only through this dehistoricization that James can mention Jesus, the Buddha, and Muhammad in the same breath, as if they functionally had the same experiences that gave rise to essentially identical, secondhand, authoritarian institutions. This is a popular, folk theory of religion, and it is a superficial one. However, it persists in part due to its association with James, who is widely considered an authoritative scholar of religion; his authority lends warrant to this folk theory.

What this folk theory allows is for people to tell a narrative in which they can slot their own favorite "good guys" and "bad guys." If we don't like al Qaeda, we can articulate this story onto the group. Our story will go something like this: At the origin of Islam Muhammad had an experience with the divine, but his followers degraded that message and wrote things into the Qur'an about killing infidels. Al Qaeda has taken that degraded message and formed an extremist, authoritarian institution, according to which all who do not agree with their strict views should be killed. They are killing in the name of God because they misunderstand the true message of the Prophet.

This sort of popular folk narrative—which will likely be familiar to those who work with popular rhetoric about Islam[6]—provides an explanation for al Qaeda's actions that need not bear any relationship to historical or empirical research. Since all organized religions are more or less fundamentally identical, we need investigate neither what al Qaeda actually says nor the sociopolitical context in which it is situated; because organized religions unfold according to an identical teleology, contextualization is irrelevant. We need not think about all of the following matters, each of which I would argue is fundamental to a proper contextualization and explanation of al Qaeda's actions: the United States's alliances with Saudi Arabia from the end of World War II onward; the United States's military involvement in Saudi Arabia—an absolute monarchy with ongoing human rights violations—from the early 1990s to 2003; the United States's unwavering support of Israel despite its settlements in Palestine; the United States's alliance with the mujahedin and the use of Afghanistan to fight a proxy war with the USSR, a war that resulted in the deaths of hundreds of thousands of Afghani civilians; the United States's participation in sanctions against Iraq that resulted in estimated deaths of half a million Iraqi children, and so on. The social, cultural, and political context that might give rise to al Qaeda is irrelevant; an eternally recurring storyline is substituted for historical investigation.

If all organized religions are the same, the following contemporary blogger can negatively characterize al Qaeda, the IRA, and the medieval Catholic Church in the same breath:

War is an obvious effect of organized religion, and there are many examples of this. The Catholic Protestant war in Ireland is a perfect example of this.

The crusades are another fine example of organized religion creating havoc. The most recent example is the World Trade Center and the Iraq war. It is supposedly because of religion.[7] . . . [O]ur government makes it seem like something new when it is not. Organized religion is meant to unite people, but in many cases it has only accomplished separation, stereotypes, and war amongst peoples. (Ganly 2007)

Al Qaeda, the IRA, and the medieval Catholic Church go together because the story of "organized religion" is not new; on the contrary, here we are dealing with the eternal recurrence of "good guys vs. bad guys." And James's view is little different; as I noted earlier, for James these things are "almost always the same."

This superficial theory is understandable when it comes from novices uninitiated in the methodologies and theories of those in religious studies or the social sciences generally, but it is unacceptable from a Harvard scholar with access to an Ivy League university library—leafing through the stacks for an hour or two would reveal that one must do a great deal of data manipulation to get all those traditions we call religious to fit into this straightjacket.

"Institutional religion," late capitalism, and consumerism

How is this dehistoricizing discourse easily aligned with late capitalism? If this rhetoric masks the source of social norms by positing them as springing from the soul or from common sense, from where do those norms come? What follows is a tentative attempt to address these questions.

I want to begin by situating James's view and the SBNR discourse alongside what are usually identified as liberal religious traditions. Liberal forms of Western religions are distinct from premodern forms in a way that is not well understood with the popular public/private rhetoric. It is not that at the dawn of the Enlightenment more liberal religious practitioners began making their religion a "private matter." For reasons I've discussed elsewhere (see Martin 2010), there is nothing "private" about what we colloquially call religions, and as a result the public/private rhetoric obscures more than it reveals.

Rather, as I argued in the previous chapter, identifying an ideology or a form of culture as "religious" may be part of a strategy designed to gerrymander whatever is identified in some way. Those institutions we colloquially call religions have been gerrymandered into a role subordinate to modern Western capitalism, at least at any point at which chafing might take place. For most of us in the modern Western world, our lives are ordered more by our jobs, our taxes, our retirement savings, our mortgages, our car payments, and our credit card debts—all in pursuit of social distinction tied to class difference—than we are by our identities as Jewish, Christian, or Muslim. However, this need not imply that there is something "private" about Judaism, Christianity, or Islam. For instance, evangelical Christians are highly active politically—to call their form of Christianity a "private matter" is to say something relatively nonsensical and devoid of analytical import. Indeed, evangelical Christian ideology might encourage practitioners to work and consume, in which case there would be very "public" consequences.

As capitalism becomes the dominant discourse and set of practices that order modern Western life, we see the development of forms of these traditions that fit to capitalism. We see an increase in "religious" institutions that make fewer and fewer demands on the lives of its practitioners that might conflict with capitalism. Any group that would demand that adherents actually *adhere* to a habitus at odds with Western consumerism is almost by definition "fanatical." According to Terry Eagleton—in a discussion of the rise of the popularity of atheism—more and more people are paying attention to religion, "even in England, where religion is in general a rather moderate, discreet, slightly shamefaced affair—and . . . where people are likely to believe that when religion starts interfering with your everyday life that it's time to give it up. In that sense it resembles alcohol, I suppose."[8] As long as one can hold a job and remain a consumer—thereby responsibly contributing to the economy—religion and alcohol are acceptable; once they begin interrupting one's responsible contributions to the economy, that is when people start to raise eyebrows. As capitalism and consumerism have achieved a hegemonic status, most contemporary Americans spend more time in shopping malls than in church, more time watching commercials than reading the Bible.

Christian Smith and Melinda Lundquist Denton demonstrate in *Soul Searching: The Religious and Spiritual Lives of American Teenagers* that the majority of contemporary teenagers in the United States—from many different religious traditions—are for all practical purposes, deists. They do not reject the religious traditions of their parents—they are neither anticlerical nor do they identify as "spiritual but not religious"—but when asked to describe their religion, it amounts to the belief that God exists, he wants everyone to be happy and good, and if we are good he will reward us by sending us to heaven. Smith and Denton call this "moralistic, therapeutic deism" (MTD) because of its thin content about the nature of the god identified and the emphasis on morality and happiness.

MTD makes no demands other than be good and be happy. Smith and Denton write,

[w]e talked with the teens we interviewed about what they get enthusiastic about, what pressing issues they are dealing with, and what forces and experiences and routines seem to them most important and central to their

lives. Most teenagers talk about friends, school, sports, television, music, movies, romantic interests, family relationships, dealing with issues of drugs and alcohol, various organized activities with which they're involved, and specific fun or formative events they have experienced. (Smith and Denton 2005, 130)

That is, they paint a picture of what life is like for a teenager in a late capitalist consumer society. "What rarely arises in such conversations are teens' religious identities, beliefs, experiences, or practices. Religion just does not naturally seem to appear much on most teenagers' open-ended lists of what really matters in their lives" (130). This is precisely what one would expect where consumer capitalism has become hegemonic—one's Christian, Jewish, or Muslim identity necessarily becomes subordinate. "[M]ost teens seem content to live with a low-visibility religion that operates somewhere in the mental background of their lives" (137). It is therefore no surprise that the teenagers interviewed do not find "religion" to be a point of conflict in their lives (cf. 122ff); one's religious identity would only be a point of conflict if it informed one's behavior in a way that caused friction with the behavior of others. If one's religious identity makes no demands on one's behavior that might interfere with the behavior of others, then "religious conflict" would be relatively inconceivable.

Although most of these teens often explicitly said their religious tradition was really important to them, it appeared not to be when they were pressed for examples. What they understood as their religious identities were so irrelevant that it was almost impossible for teens to articulate *any* practical consequence for their lives. One girl suggested that her faith prevents her from hanging out with Satanists, and another boy suggested that his religion teaches important moral prohibitions, "like murder or something" (139). Smith and Denton comment: "perhaps this boy does struggle with murderous tendencies, but more probably, this explanation merely establishes religious influences in a way that is not too demanding or threatening to his routine life" (139). If their religious identity *does* make demands on them, those demands are noticeable due to the way they conflict with consumerism. "One 16-year-old Seventh Day Adventist girl, for instance, explained the difference her faith makes in this way: 'Well, without my faith, my life would be different, um, I'd go shopping on Saturday 'cause they always have sales on Saturdays'" (139). Smith and Denton conclude, "our impression is that . . . the teens are simply groping for something, anything that might confirm their claim that religion is indeed important in their lives. And sometimes they seem to have to grope hard *because it actually is not very important*" (140).

For many of the teens, MTD was paired with a rejection of any practice that made demands at odds with consumerism—such practices were dismissed through the rhetoric of "fanaticism" or "extremism." An important category for these teens was the category of people who are "too religious" (141). When describing those "religious" traditions that made demands that could interfere with their "lifestyle," these teens started using the following pejorative vocabulary, phrases, and comparisons: holier than thou, sanctimonious, holy roller, Ned Flanders, weird, church-y, following everything to a T, fanatic, annoying, Jesus freak, overboard, extreme (141–143). According to one teen, "Sometimes people that are more religious take it to an extreme, like sure, but after a point, when are you going to finally live your life?" (143). I take it that "live your life" implies living life as a consumer in late capitalism— anything else would amount to *not* living one's life. As argued in the previous chapter, calling a cultural practice or tradition "religious" may be designed to gerrymander its scope or attenuate its effects. This seems to be precisely what these teens are doing; they have a "normal" life, and when something called "religion" interferes with their life, it has exceeded its appropriate bounds.

If religion is tied up with morality, what is moral?

One of the key teenage assumptions in this religion-morality equation is that right and wrong are simply common sense, something everyone just knows. For most teens, morality is not something that requires much thought or discernment. Everyone knows it . . . . They are just things that any reasonable person knows. (155)

The fact that "common sense" is both variable and a product of socialization is nowhere recognized. As a result, the local social and moral norms pass as if they were universal. Although these teens are socialized by a capitalist and consumerist social, cultural, and institutional context—all of which informs their ideas of what is morally right and wrong—they misidentify the moral norms they accept as springing from deep within the self.

In one particularly telling interview, a "14-year-old conservative Protestant girl" reveals how God's goodness is tied up with modern capitalist life:

[Interviewer]:   When you think of God, what image do you have of God?

[Teenager]:   [yawning]

I: What is God like?

T: Um, good. Powerful.

I: Okay, anything else?

T: Tall.

I: Tall?

T: Big.

I: Do you think God is active in people's lives or not?

T: Ah, I don't know.

I: You're not sure?

T: Different people have different views of him.

I: What about your view?

T: What do you mean?

I: Do you think God is active in your life?

T: In my life? Yeah.

I: Yeah, hmmm. Would you say you feel close to God or not really?

T: Yeah, I feel close. [yawns]

I: Where do you get your ideas about God?

T: The Bible, my mom, church. Experience.

I: What kind of experience?

T: He's just done a lot of good in my life, so.

I: Like, what are examples of that?

T: I don't know.

I: Well, I'd love to hear. What good has God done in your life?

T: I, well, I have a house, parents, I have the Internet, I have a phone, I have cable. (Smith 2005, 135)

In summary, this teenager's god is active insofar as he provides the amenities of bourgeois life in late capitalism. Apparently "good" means "middle class." What is taken to be good is not derived from Protestantism but invisibly comes from late capitalist middle-class norms—but the latter are passed off as what God wants for us.

Unlike the SBNR discourse, this MTD does not have a substantial anticlerical strain to it (i.e., of the sort we see associated with talk of "institutional religion"). I would suggest that this deism need not have one, as these teenagers' "clerics" make few if any demands on their behavior that conflict with their consumer lifestyle. The anticlericalism of the SBNR discourse is perhaps initiated only when clerics make demands that compete with adherents' lifestyle. Indeed, Robert C. Fuller notes that one thing that makes the SBNR discourse so appealing to its adherents is the fact that it makes no demands. "[A]lthough [spiritual] phenomena are intriguing, they don't affect the way most people go about their daily lives. . . . [T]he paranormal doesn't impose any religious demands" (Fuller 2001, 68).[9] Smith and Denton's teenagers' MTD versions of Christianity, Judaism, and Islam rarely make any substantial demands. If Christianity has taken a form that is so easily articulated onto late capitalism that clerics make no demands that would conflict with it, then there would be no call for anticlericalism. In addition, as Smith and Denton note, as soon as the teenagers are presented with forms of religious traditions where substantial demands are in fact made on adherents, they do begin to use the language of fanaticism and extremism. These teenagers, it seems, implicitly deploy a mainstream/extremist distinction that performs the same rhetorical function that the spirituality/religion distinction does for the SBNR groups. These religious teenagers are not anticlerical, but they are just as opposed as the SBNR crowd to religious groups that demand anything onerous from adherents. It appears that what they identify as their "religion" has been completely domesticated by the norms or practices of consumer life in late capitalism.

What perhaps distinguishes MTD from the SBNR discourse is that MTD suggests that one's values are derived from one's religious tradition: Smith's study shows that the teenagers interviewed—whether Jewish, Christian, Muslim, and so on—seemed to believe that their values and morals were derived from their traditions and sacred texts, although they also believed that the moral norms found, for instance, in the Bible were identical to the universal moral norms of common sense (Smith and Denton 2005, 155). In a sense, the following equation is at work, with the terms on the left taking priority:

modern consumerist culture = common sense = what it says in the Bible

As a result, anything in the Bible that conflicts with consumerist culture or capitalist values must be a fanatical, secondary degradation or insertion. As a student once told me, Jesus *would never* say that one should hate one's family (cf. Luke 14; Matthew 10); when asked how he could justify such a claim, he told me it was because the "hate" comments conflicted with the Jesus he simply *knew.* Apparently "Jesus" was the variable term that turned on his own, local common sense.[10]

By contrast, the SBNR discourse jettisons even this minimal appeal to (or projection upon) tradition or scripture: values come from direct, pure experience with the divine or with spirits, not from degraded historical messages; we can all have the experiences of God that Jesus or Muhammad had, for instance, without having to pass through the Christian or Muslim institution. In the end, however, it appears that the values of both the SBNR discourse and MTD are the values of late capitalism. In addition, most contemporary participants in the SBNR discourse are college-educated and hold white-collar jobs (see Fuller 2001, 7); the SBNR discourse is distinctly a *middle-class discourse.*

MTD and the SBNR discourse clearly do not have a causal relation to the rise of capitalism—they arrived much too late for that. In addition, MTD and SBNR do not even directly legitimate capitalism—that is, they do not offer some sort of narrative according to which capitalism or class difference is divine (as did John Withrop in his "Model of Christian Charity" sermon, or Henry Ward Beecher in his "Individual Responsibility" sermon [cf. McCloud 2007, 109ff]).

MTD and the SBNR discourse have nevertheless *become aligned with capitalism* insofar as they use the spirituality/institutional religion dichotomy (or some variant) in order to sanction any religious tradition that makes demands on practitioners that conflict with late capitalism: any form of "institutional religion" that makes demands on subjects is fanatical or extremist. In the end, these discourses *indirectly* legitimate late capitalist norms and sanction what falls outside of them—all the while mystifying those values by making it seem as if they spring from one's soul or common sense. That is, these discourses take consumerist desires, produced within a capitalist regime, and present them as divine in origin. The religious experience/institutional religion and spiritual/religious distinctions are perfect for this because they are more or less intrinsically ahistorical; they lend themselves to passing off the local as the universal and preventing one from historicizing the local. Late capitalism provides people with their values, but the spirituality/religion discourse makes it seem as if those values sprang directly from the soul.

It is worth noting that this discourse could arguably be used to justify the status quo in *any* type of economic regime. For example, in a socialist context one could use this rhetoric to say that capitalist forms of Christianity are institutional, degraded, and inauthentic. Since they are floating signifiers, "spirituality" and "institutional religion" could be used to sanction just about anything. However, currently in the United States this rhetoric has taken a form whereby these signifiers float over capitalist and consumerist norms.

It is for these reasons that the religious experience/institutional religion distinction can have the effect of maintaining the status quo in late capitalism. What better way to legitimate capitalism than to suggest that its values are universal, and spring from deep within one's pure soul—and that anyone who challenges late capitalism is obviously an extremist or dogmatist? Again, I do not mean to suggest that William James was a propagandist for late capitalism. However, his experience/institution distinction and the coordinate folk theory of religion is a convenient one for sanctioning any religious practices that create friction when they rub up against contemporary consumerism.

Summary

In summary, the experience/institution distinction is both ontologized as inherent in the world and made to carry negative associations; as such it is perfect for a naïve empiricism that is simultaneously polemical—it allows people to criticize "religious" matters they do not like by normatively applying the label "organized religion" while pretending to discover such "institutions" as a matter of fact. This rhetoric is often tied up with a teleological folk theory of religion, according to which there is necessarily a universally pure origin at the root of all religious traditions, a root that is necessarily degraded over time by followers of a founder—followers who are more interested in social control than true religious experience. This rhetoric fits well with late capitalism because it allows consumers to pretend to discover their social norms and common sense within a pure, inner intuition—which allows them to clothe or mask local late capitalist consumerist social norms with the trappings of universalism. In addition, the rhetoric provides them with an easy way of criticizing or sanctioning "religious" norms that might conflict with late capitalist consumerism: those norms are "fanatical" deviations from the religious morality or common sense intuitively available to all.

Jesus in late capitalism

What is the place of this rhetoric in contemporary reinventions of Jesus? There are, of course, a wide variety of Jesuses today: Gustavo Gutierrez's quasi-Marxist Jesus, Joseph Ratzinger's rather conventional Catholic Jesus, John Dominic Crossan's anti-empire Jesus, and so on. There is one, however, that I would call the late capitalist Jesus. This Jesus fits nicely with MTD: Jesus vaguely wants us all to be moral and happy, where "morality" and "happiness" are apparently saturated with the norms of late capitalism. In addition, Jesus tells us that the Kingdom of God is within us, for any "outward religion"—the demanding sort—is secondary or unnecessary (perhaps because it would cause friction with the more pressing demands of late capitalism). I could choose a wide variety of examples, but I'll limit myself to two: Stephen Mitchell's Jesus in *The Gospel According to Jesus* and Thich Nhat Hanh's Jesus in *Living Buddha, Living Christ*. Mitchell and Hanh provide us with perfect examples because of how obviously they utilize the rhetoric discussed thus far.

The Gospel According to Jesus

Thomas Jefferson, the third president of the United States of America, famously took a razor to the New Testament in order to cut out the parts he liked. Scientific naturalism seemed to be one of his guiding principles; the supernatural bits were among the first to go. As Jefferson fancied Jesus a great ethical teacher, most of what remained consisted of the moral comments Jefferson found nonobjectionable, such as the imperative to love one's neighbor (see Prothero 2003). Stephen Mitchell begins *The Gospel According to Jesus* by characterizing himself as a modern-day Thomas Jefferson: "In this book I have followed Jefferson's example. I have selected . . . only those passages that seem to me authentic accounts and sayings of Jesus. . . . And

I have eliminated every passage and, even within authentic passages, every verse or phrase that seemed like a later theological or polemical or legendary accretion" (Mitchell 1991, 5–6). What criteria does he use to determine which are authentic? He claims to follow in part the "scholarship of the past seventy-five years" (6). But more important is Jefferson's original criteria (which Mitchell quotes in part):

> But there are no scholarly criteria for spiritual value. Ultimately my decisions were based on what Jefferson called "internal evidence": the evidence provided by the words themselves. The authentic passages are marked by "sublime ideas of the Supreme Being, aphorisms, and precepts of the purest morality and benevolence . . . , humility, innocence, and simplicity of manners . . . , with an eloquence and persuasiveness which have not been surpassed. (6–7)

Mitchell goes on: "It is *easy* to recognize these qualities in the authentic sayings" (emphasis mine; 7). Since there is no recognition of the fact that the delimitation of "humility" or "pure morality" varies depending on one's social location, his approach is consistent with the naïve hermeneutic described earlier: whether or not some passage is identified as authentic turns not on what is in the text but on Mitchell's own preferences. He all but explicitly says as much: "For me, then, Jesus's words are authentic when scholarship indicates that they probably or possibly originated from him and when at the same time they speak with the voice that I hear in the essential sayings. This may seem like circular reasoning. But it isn't reasoning at all; it is a mode of listening" (8). Whether we call it reasoning, circular reasoning, or listening, it is a naïve hermeneutic—in effect Mitchell is saying the following: whatever *I think* was the voice of Jesus *is* the voice of Jesus. Mitchell is more honest than most who employ this naïve hermeneutic; at least he avoids masking his own contribution to the task of interpretation. However, he leaves unstated what criterion is at work for him—what implicit process of selection is at work in determining which sayings ring true to him and which do not?

Following the schema found in James's folk theory of religion, he believes Jesus's original spiritual insights to have been corrupted by his followers. The authentic message will be easy to distinguish from the latter accretions, Mitchell claims—utilizing, of course, an obvious return-to-origins narrative—because the latter are "the direct antitheses to the authentic teachings that were put into Jesus' mouth" (8). For Mitchell, the apocalyptic material and the portrayal of Jesus-the-judge are necessarily among the number of projections foisted upon Jesus by others; Jesus "teaches us, in his sayings and by his actions, not to judge" (8). While it is clear why one might think Jesus-the-judge and Jesus's command not to judge could possibly (although not necessarily) be at odds with one another, it is less clear why the latter is necessarily authentic rather than the former. One presumes it is because the latter is what Mitchell *wants* Jesus to be. According to James, common sense shows us that all else is fanatical, dogmatic, tribal, or meanness, and the same is apparently true for Mitchell. "No reader of the Gospels can fail to be struck" by the fact that anything "polemical" or that might involve "vituperation and contempt" (8), or anything "narrow-hearted" or "sectarian" is necessarily the result of passages "put into the mouth" of Jesus by others (9). Mitchell finds that when he strips out the materials that are not authentic—let us no longer hedge: when he strips out the material that doesn't dovetail with his own values—"we can find that Jesus speaks in harmony with the supreme teachings of all the great religions . . . . [W]hen words arise from the deepest kind of spiritual experience, from a heart pure of doctrines and beliefs, they transcend religious boundaries" (9). At the origin of Christianity lies a root experience common to all religions, as is clear from reading James's *Varieties* (in which Jesus's experience was the same as the Buddha's and Muhammad's).

For Mitchell, Jesus's message centers around love, and primarily an inner experience of love (as opposed to love as an action toward others). "What *is* the gospel according to Jesus? Simply this: that the love we all long for in our innermost heart is already present" (10). He immediately goes on to talk about love as an experience of joy, and it is this experience of joy that Jesus was talking about when discussing the kingdom of God. Mitchell insists that Jesus's message about the kingdom could not have been apocalyptic—he could not have been talking about a future state of affairs (12). It is *fundamentally apolitical*. "The kingdom of God is not something that will happen, because it isn't something that *can* happen. It can't appear in a world or nation" (13). The kingdom of God is not something one can bring about, but something one can find if one turns inward. "The portrait of Jesus that emerges from the authentic passages in the Gospels is of a man who has emptied himself of desires, doctrines, rules—all the mental claptrap and spiritual baggage that separate us from true life—and has been filled with the vivid reality of the Unnamable" (13).

Just about everything that follows in this book is a psychologization of Jesus's teachings—each has some meaning not for one's religious identity, economic identity, gender identity, or national identity, for his teachings "transcend religious boundaries, and can speak to all people, male and female, bond and free, Greek and Jew" (9). Jesus has *nothing* to say that has any bearing on one's social context or station in life—he merely wants everyone, no matter what their context or station, to find joy. Again, this is *fundamentally apolitical*.

One of Mitchell's most revealing moments is in his consideration of Jesus's talk of hating one's family and of letting the dead bury the dead. "Jesus' point here is that we have to be ready to give up everything if we want to enter the kingdom of God. That is quite true" (44). What is interesting to me about this material is that it is obviously grist for the mill if one is using Jesus as a part of a religion of revolution—this passage suggests that the social and material world as it is can and should be abandoned in favor of something superior, more godly, or more just. However, Mitchell argues that these were immature sentiments for Jesus (51), and that once one is truly adjusted to the kingdom of God within oneself, one can return to the social and material world as it is and be at peace with it.

> At this later stage, detachment and filial piety aren't mutually exclusive. When someone has found freedom in his heart, everything that was once an obstacle—parents, money, sex—becomes an opportunity for a further degree of surrender. . . . And we feel that someone as largehearted and compassionate as he would surely have been able to fulfill both the commandment to love God with all his heart and the commandment to honor his mother. (53)

Presumably the same is true of one's economic and sexual commitments. A self-transformed can be joyful in any context—the religion of Mitchell's Jesus is apparently well-suited, like Stoicism, to both emperors and slaves. Thus this set of passages, which could be used (and has been) to challenge the status quo, is in fact domesticated through careful interpretation such that any sharp edges that could possibly cause friction with the status quo are trimmed off.

While Mitchell accepts Jesus's command to the rich man to sell all of his possessions as among the "authentic" sayings, Mitchell considers this "radical" and by implication unnecessary. Mitchell provides a "just-so" story to explain away the literal meaning:

> We can't know what quality in the man prompted Jesus to make this radical response. Perhaps, noticing his rich clothing, Jesus intuited that the man's only attachment was to his wealth, and that if he could give it up he would step right into the kingdom of God. . . .
>
> "Sell everything" was a teaching for this particular man at this particular moment. (234)

That is, Mitchell refuses to extrapolate out such a teaching for others—Jesus's message to the man must have been *for this man only*, because *this particular* man must have had undue attachments to wealth. Jesus's command does not apply to rich men who have found the kingdom of God within themselves—they can hold onto their wealth. "Most religious traditions make a distinction between the path of the householder and the path of the renunciate. . . . [T]he two are equal, and each has its advantages and pitfalls" (238). At every turn Mitchell trims the gospels of anything that might remotely cause friction with life in late capitalism.

Similarly, Mitchell considers Jesus's teachings about "justice and compassion" in the Sermon on the Mount (164), but his emphasis is not on the social structures that organize family relationship, economics, or sexual relations, but on the attitudes of those individuals in such relationships. Thus he talks about dealing with anger: suppressing anger is misguided, but we should avoid nursing anger (165). And lust: desire is not in and of itself bad, but "misdirected" desire "leads to dangerous actions, actions that can cause great misery to a man's wife and children and to himself" (167). Again of interest is the fact that Mitchell takes for granted the existing social structures and only seeks to transform the mental states of the individuals in such structures.

This desire to transform individuals rather than the social structure in which they are embedded is called the "miracle motif" by Michael O. Emerson and Christian Smith in *Divided by Faith: Evangelical Religion and the Problem of Race in America* (2000). They write,

> The miracle motif is the theologically rooted idea that as more individuals become Christians, social and personal problems will be solved automatically. What is the solution to violent crime? Convert people to Christianity, because Christians do not commit violent crimes. What is the solution to divorce? Convert people to Christianity, because Christians are less likely to get divorced? (117)

"Miracle motif" is clearly a pejorative phrase; for sociologists such as Emerson and Smith, individualist solutions to structural problems are inherently misguided. "[W]hen problems are at least in part structural, they must be addressed at least in part by structural solutions. If a building is on the verge of collapse due to an inadequate design, improving the quality of the bricks without improving the design is not a solution" (130). I find myself in agreement with Emerson and Smith: the most racist people I know are also among the *kindest* people I know—even to people of other races. Focusing on individual dispositions is fundamentally misguided because it "substitutes emotional and personal vocabularies for political ones in formulating solutions to political problems. . . . A justice project is replaced with a therapeutic or behavioral one" (Brown 2006, 16; see also Carrette and King 2005, 54ff).[11] Mitchell's therapeutic Jesus is fundamentally accommodationist toward whatever social structure is regnant: his Jesus demands nothing other than a transformation of our internal dispositions. Like those forms of Western Buddhism that demand acceptance of the world as it is—for example, "If Zen is to become integrated into Western culture, it requires a Western idiom: 'Chop wood, carry water' must somehow become, 'Make love, drive freeway'" (Smith 1989, v)—Mitchell's Christianity is an ideology of the status quo.

Living Buddha, Living Christ

Even more than Stephen Mitchell, Thich Nhat Hanh draws on Buddhism in his recreation of Jesus. Hanh assumes a certain Buddhist ontology and soteriology, and projects those onto the figure of Jesus. In addition, like Mitchell he draws on a folk theory of religion similar to James's in his presentation of both Buddhism and Christianity, and inadvertently strips his Jesus's message of anything that could cause friction with life in late capitalism.

Hanh's ontology and soteriology center around a twentieth-century interpretation of Mahayana concepts. In summary, according to Hanh the *suchness* of the world is *impermanent* but *interconnected* (Hanh uses the word interbeing), but we *suffer* from *illusions*, according to which we see permanence and disconnectedness where none exists. We become *attached* to those things we wrongly perceive to be impermanent, and we suffer as a result. "It is our delusion that causes us to suffer. Regarding something that is impermanent as permanent, . . . we suffer" (Hanh 1995, 183). To overcome our individual suffering we must therefore become *enlightened* or *awake* by consciously *realizing* the impermanence of suchness. "When you touch the reality of the non-self [the impermanence of all things], you touch at the same time nirvana, the ultimate dimension of being, and become free from fear, attachment, illusion, and craving" (185). The potential for such awakening is already within us; we only need to turn within—through meditation, for instance—in order to realize it. Thus Hanh says that *nirvana*, which he equates with the kingdom of God, is within individual consciousness. "Buddhists and Christians know that nirvana or the Kingdom of God is within their hearts." (167). Once we are awake, or once we discover the kingdom of God within ourselves, we can become *bodhisattvas*—beings devoted to helping others end their suffering. For Hanh this can mean either helping others become enlightened *or* helping alleviate material suffering. For instance, he writes, "Monks and nuns participated in the work of helping refugees, orphans, and the wounded. In the situation of war, a monk cannot just sit in the meditation hall while bombs are being dropped all around" (174).

Hanh reinvents Jesus to fit this ontology and soteriology. To begin with, he identifies the Holy Spirit with mindfulness of suchness and interbeing.

According to Hanh, when the gospels say that the Holy Spirit descended on Jesus like a dove, this means something like Jesus achieving mindfulness of the interconnectedness of all beings: "He went into the wilderness and practiced for forty days to strengthen the Spirit in Himself. When mindfulness is born in us, we need to continue to practice if we want it to become solid. Really hearing a bird sing or really seeing a blue sky, we touch the seed of the Holy Spirit within us" (21). In addition, Hanh goes on to talk about God in pantheistic ways, where God *is* the impermanent suchness or interbeing we all participate in. "The body of Christ is the body of God, the body of ultimate reality, the ground of all existence" (31). Thus when Hanh talks about "Living in the Presence of God" as a Jewish tradition, it has pantheistic implications rather than monotheistic ones: "When you stand up and your feet touch the ground, you know the earth belongs to God. When you wash your face, you know that the water *is* God" (emphasis mine; 29). Similarly, Hanh reinterprets the institution of the Eucharist in pantheistic terms—if Jesus and God are one and God is the suchness, then by eating communion bread Christians are literally eating Jesus. Jesus's purpose was to "awaken His disciples" to "life eternal," where life eternal amounts to the end of suffering through mindfulness or the realization of interbeing (30). Consequently, he laments the fact that "many congregants are not called to mindfulness"—they are instead merely "distracted," which is "exactly what Jesus was trying to overcome" by instituting this ritual (31).

Jesus had the kingdom of God within him, by which Hanh seems to mean that Jesus's consciousness was mindful or awake. It is through an investigation of Jesus's life that we learn the essentials of his teaching—"the life of Jesus is His most basic teaching, more important than even faith in the resurrection or faith in eternity" (36). Similar to Mitchell, Hanh's soteriology involves an inward turn: when we turn to the kingdom of God within us, in order to become like Jesus, *"we are in touch with the highest spirit in ourselves, we too are a Buddha, filled with the Holy Spirit, and we become very tolerant, very open, very deep, and very understanding"* (37–38). The miracle motif is doing a lot of the work here: social change begins not with social structure but with an attitudinal transformation of the individual. Dismantling bombs will do no good if "the roots of the bombs are still here, in our hearts and minds" (77). It is therefore not surprising that when comparing Christian "sin" to Buddhism's "negative seeds," it is again human *attitudes*, not social practices, that are mentioned: "hatred, anger, ignorance, intolerance, and so on" (44). By contrast, the best of Christianity is not its social practices but its positive *attitudes*: "When the church manifests understanding, tolerance, and loving-kindness, Jesus is there" (57). Despite the fact that he insists on living one's life differently to be a true follower of Jesus ("It has to be realized by the *way we live*" [emphasis mine; 57]), he clearly privileges the inward turn, even using the word "only" at one point: "The *only* place we can touch Jesus or the Kingdom of God is *within us*" (emphasis mine; 44). I assume that this is because he is torn: Hanh wants people to live their lives differently, but he thinks that behavior is always motivated from within, and specifically from philanthropic or misanthropic attitudes toward other human beings. This tension between transforming one's mind and transforming the world runs throughout this book, although the former appears to take precedence. As such, this book tends toward a recommendation of therapeutic solutions over social ones; the miracle motif functions centrally, making Hanh's Jesus implicitly more accomodationist than revolutionary.

The Jamesian folk theory of religion rears its head in the final chapter where Hanh launches his deepest criticisms of Catholicism—particularly its exclusivism. Hanh assumes his own religious universalism (i.e., he sees all religious traditions have having at their core his own Buddhist ontology and soteriology, which he projects onto them), and because Catholicism officially denies that Buddhism offers a path to "salvation" (I use scare quotes here because it seems clear to me that Catholic doctrine and Hanh mean something rather different by the term), Catholicism is therefore a degraded form of Christianity. We must therefore return to the origin, bypassing Catholic corruptions of Jesus's true message (so long as we understand that the latter is identical to Hanh's message).

The rhetoric of James's folk theory of religion is not applied consistently throughout this book, but this is not surprising since it is most applicable in polemical situations. This rhetoric is not particularly useful when Hanh is describing what he wants Buddhism or Christianity to look like, but it is extremely useful when he wants to criticize other forms of Christianity. Consequently, in the last chapter we get a great deal of normative rhetoric, where the positive terms apply to Hanh's Buddhism and Christianity, and where the negative terms apply to those forms of Christianity he dislikes, usually Catholicism (both implicitly and explicitly) (Table 3.1).

In summary, "we have to remind ourselves again and again of our original purpose, and the original teachings and intention of Buddha, Jesus, and other great sages and saints" (178), where the "original teaching" is apparently whatever Hanh likes in the New Testament or can project onto it.

Is Hanh's reinvention of Christianity an ideology of the status quo or a revolutionary ideology? For reasons discussed earlier, it seems that Hanh's Jesus is *less* accomodationist than Mitchell's Jesus—Hanh at least raises social issues, even if the miracle motif tends to override the recommendation of structural solutions to these social issues. Like Mitchell, in the end Hanh's Jesus wants us to transform our dispositions above all else. In addition, Hanh's

TABLE 3.1 Hanh's rhetorical vocabulary

Positive Terms	Negative Terms
"true religious experience" (158)	"notions and concepts" (159)
"freedom, joy, and faith" (158–159)	"superficial" practice (168)
"understanding, love, peace" (168)	"churches and temples" (168)
"incomprehensible, invisible, unknowable" (160)	"charity work and social work" (168)
"mystical" (161)	"chanting and liturgy" (168)
"truly deep realization" (162)	"dry and automatic" (168)
"interior recollection (166)	"align themselves with . . . power" (169)
"authentic" (169)	"political power" (169)
"original" (172)	"dangerous attitude" (169)
"compassion" (175)	"conflicts and war" (169)
"contemplative life" (175)	"intolerance" (169)
"true values" (178)	"secular business" (172)
"peace and happiness" (179)	"dogmas" (177)
"non-dogmatic" (180)	"suffering" (177)
"love and compassion" (180)	"notions, rituals" (177)
"mystical renewal" (185)	"outer forms of the practice" (177)
"liberated self" (186)	"narrow, fundamentalist, and dogmatic practices" (178)
"dialogue" (193)	"religious intolerance and discrimination" (193)
"authentic experience" (194)	"organized religions" (195)
"true tradition" (194)	
"true experience" (195)	
"open-minded, tolerant" (196)	
"values that transcend all dogma" (198)	

use of the Jamesian folk theory of religion prevents him from recommending structural solutions:

But I am afraid that many Christians and many Buddhists do not practice, or if they do . . . their practice may be superficial. They support churches and temples, organize ceremonies, convert people, do charity work or social work, or take up apostolic ministry, but do not practice mindfulness or pray while they act. They may devote an hour each day for chanting and liturgy, but after a while, the practice becomes dry and automatic, and they do not know how to refresh it. They may believe that they are serving the Buddha, the Dharma, the Sangha, or serving the Trinity and the church, but their practice does not touch the living Buddha or the living Christ. At the same time, these men and women do not hesitate to align themselves with those in power in order to strengthen the position of their church or community. They believe that political power is needed for the well-being of their church or community. . . . [They] dismiss all other spiritual traditions as false. This is a dangerous attitude; it always leads to conflicts and war. (168–169)

Hanh seems to want social change, but for him this can only happen via the miracle motif; anything else would fall under the mess of "organized religion," which—like James—"*always* leads to conflicts and war." Hanh does not want an ideology of the status quo, but his version of Jesus is one whose hands are tied—his Jesus cannot make any revolutionary demands without falling into institutional corruption.

Conclusion

The experience/institution distinction we find in James's *Varieties* and adapted by others is easily tailored for capitalist or consumerist social norms; while these discursive elements may not intrinsically or directly advance or legitimate consumerism, they are certainly made to dovetail with it. In addition, these discursive elements are fundamental to a number of contemporary reinventions of Jesus. I've discussed only Mitchell's and Hanh's Jesuses, but I could very well have considered others' (the next chapter will focus on Christopher Moore's *Lamb* [2002]).

It is ironic that those who prioritize personal, individual religion appear to adhere so strictly to a common script, but it is clear to see why they do so: the ahistorical universalism of the experience/institution and the coordinate folk theory of religion rhetoric require them to project unity where none exists, insofar as they take it for granted that these things are "almost always the same." My conclusion is therefore not different from Russell McCutcheon's, in his review of Karen Armstrong's *A History of God*:

> *A History of God* is yet another instance of the liberal attempt to unify diversity by glossing over concrete differences of culture, politics, economics, and so on, in favor of a presumably abstract, nonhistorical— and, in this case—so-called religious or spiritual sameness. Armstrong's best seller is not a history of the concept of God but is an unknowing history, and practical example, of the ongoing human effort to create social identity and homogeneity by means of the rhetorics of unity, a rhetoric that purchases social identity at the expense of those who do not quite fit the pattern. (McCutcheon 2001, 55)

Similarly, the popular schema James and others use is part and parcel of an ostensibly "minimalist" religion that is in fact "maximalist" insofar as it "purchases" a pervasively ordering "social identity at the expense of those who do not quite fit" the consumerism of late capitalism.

While it may be the case that there could be *something* of value in James's *Varieties* or James's legacy for religious studies in general, I propose that his canonical status be retired; given the ease with which his work is appropriated into what amounts to vulgar rhetoric, it should be relegated to the status of Hegel's philosophy of religion: a historical curiosity that is interesting insofar as it has informed the field of religious studies in the past, but—due to its embedded ideological assumptions—presently not of much use to critical scholarship on religion. The pseudo-scholarly accounts of Jesus that rely on James's vocabulary and teleology should be recognized for what they are: sophisticated propaganda.

PART TWO

The opiate of the bourgeoisie

As I argued in part one, explanations that appeal to individual autonomy are, by definition, unscholarly. To attribute a phenomenon to a faculty that escapes cause and effect is to tantamount to saying "we don't know why this happened"; at that point "explanation" ceases to be explanatory. Those social theorists who attempt to account for "individual religion" or "spirituality" by saying that individuals are autonomously constructing a religion for themselves have failed to follow through on the imperative to historicize. In fact, their work is profoundly antihistoricist.

The following chapters, by contrast, attempt to historicize some specific examples of "individual religion" or "spirituality" by situating them within the horizon of late capitalism. On one hand, we must try to show how "choices" are determined by constraints within a particular social field. As Bennett M. Berger writes,

> choices are made under a series of constraints and incentives set by social structures and more or less legitimated by internalized culture. The business of a generalizing sociology of culture is to understand . . . how a specific range of possible choices is presented to the consciousness of a potentially active agent, and how situational or intervening variables . . .

reinforce or undermine the predisposition to choose from among the range of possible choices. (1995, 136–137)

In addition, we must try to show why ideologies are produced, why they appeal to particular audiences, what they naturalize, justify, or legitimate, and what they obscure, mask, or protect from criticism.

I've chosen six texts for analysis: two are novels presenting authentic religion as an autonomous, inward matter and four are within the "self-help" or "spirituality" genre. There are several reasons for my selection. First, I've chosen books that are popular or easily available to middle-class consumers. Most of the texts were published by major presses, such as Random House or HarperCollins; all of them are the sort liable to be on the shelves at a store like Barnes & Noble. Second, I've chosen texts that are representative of a particular ideological strand, including the following key themes:

quietism or accommodationism: this ideology sanctions existing political or economic structures by encouraging individuals to accept and accommodate themselves to such structures, perhaps by naturalizing the latter or presenting them as inevitable.

consumerism: this ideology naturalizes social fields in which individuals compete for social distinction through the consumption of consumer goods that award distinction; this ideology sacralizes consumer choice while simultaneously obscuring what might motivate individual consumer choices.

promotion of productivity: this ideology encourages individuals to reflexively work on their "self" in order to accommodate themselves to work or career and to increase their productivity or success.

anti-structuralism or individualism: this ideology assigns responsibility to individuals rather than institutions or social structures; for instance, "poor people are poor because they are lazy"; often deployed alongside the miracle motif, according to which social problems can be corrected through individual transformation.[1]

Almost all of the texts utilize some form of the normative distinction between "organized religion" and "individual spirituality," and in most cases specifically in order to negatively sanction anything that might conflict with capitalism, career, work, or consumerism.

For each of the books I've selected, I summarize the contents of the text, show how it exhibits one or more of these ideological strands, and attempt to historicize the "choices" of the author—how the text or its appeal to a bourgeois audience makes sense only within the context of late capitalism.

Capitalism does not sustain itself, but requires ideology for its maintenance. The self-help and spirituality publishing industry is, arguably, one of the ideological apparatuses of late capitalism. I'll conclude each chapter with a consideration of how the data at hand conflicts with the dominant scholarly narrative about "spirituality" and "individual religion"—as exemplified by Heelas and Woodhead—according to which religion is increasingly private, individual, and autonomous from social forces. In addition, following the agenda set in Chapter 2, I'll show how these discourses often claim a universal or global authority, how they intend to gerrymander the relationship between the economy or the state and other civil institutions, how they intend a comprehensive rather than private behavioral transformation, and how they are tied to very particular social and economic circumstances and are not free-floating autonomous creations.

For the most part the ideological "opiates" discussed later are more likely to appeal to the petty bourgeoisie than the so-called masses. However, as with Marx, the use of the word "opiate" is intended ambivalently. The ideologies under consideration here arguably make individuals passive before the regnant mode of production, but they also arguably anesthetize individuals to the more painful effects of the mode of production. I've little doubt that self-help does, in fact, sometimes help people—like my father—accommodate themselves to work and career in ways that make their lives happier and less stressful. My aim is not to take away such opiates, but to historicize their appearance and to show why they might have been necessary.

4

Quietism: The empire's gospel

The discrepancy between the subjective 'autonomy' of the individual in modern society and the objective autonomy of the primary institutional domains strikes us as critical.
THOMAS LUCKMANN, 1967, 115

One does not have to be a vulgar Marxist to see that those cultural myths categorized as "religious" can sometimes be read as reflecting and reinforcing social, economic, political, and imperial forces. While "superstructure" may not always reflect the so-called base, it is clear that cultural myths often dovetail with the political and economic infrastructures that serve as their condition of possibility. Such structures do not maintain themselves, and late capitalism has produced its own disciplining practices and mythmaking strategies that naturalize capitalist institutions and the material means of reproducing them—in part including the creation of individual subjects seeking personal realization but political quietism through worker satisfaction and the pursuit of habits of consumption tied to meaningful social distinction.

One Jesus myth worth considering in this contemporary social and political context is provided by Christopher Moore in the irreverent novel, *Lamb: The Gospel According to Biff, Christ's Childhood Pal* (2002). In this story, Moore takes a young Son of God and his pal Biff on a journey from Nazareth to the "mystic East" and back again. Along the way, the messiah painstakingly learns the apparently universal truths of the world's great religions, while Biff passes the time with prostitutes and concubines. At the end, Jesus is crucified because some of his followers wrongly assume that Jesus's mission involves overthrowing the Roman occupation of Israel. Despite the fact that Moore claims in the afterword that he's "simply telling stories" (439) and that the novel is "not designed to change anyone's beliefs or worldview" (438), there is clearly a political ideology in the novel. In summary, the book's more or less explicit message is that traditional religion is mostly nonsense; true religion requires us merely to enjoy life, be nice to others, and not to interfere with the state. This chapter argues that the presentation of hedonism, social niceties, and political quietism as the universal essence of the great world religions is well-suited for privileged, bourgeois liberals who benefit from the existing social conditions, but nevertheless want to feel "religious" or "spiritual."

The Gospel According to Biff

The novel begins at the end of the twentieth century, as the angel Raziel raises Jesus's disciple Levi—also called "Biff"—from the dead. Raziel raises Biff so that he can write a narrative of the life of Jesus, whom Biff calls Joshua or simply Josh.[1] Raziel locks Biff up in a hotel room—the Hyatt Regency, St. Louis—and watches TV while Biff writes. Apart from the prologue recounting the act of raising Biff from the dead, written from the perspective of a third-person omniscient narrator, and the afterword, written from Moore's first-person perspective, the novel reads in Biff's first-person voice. Biff's story shuffles back and forth between the contemporary and ancient contexts, in some passages narrating his interactions with Raziel in the hotel room, but in most narrating his history with Joshua.

Biff begins his story with the first time he met Joshua. Much like the antics of Jesus as a child in *The Infancy Gospel of Thomas*, Joshua is inquisitively testing out his magical abilities: he is continually bringing back to life a lizard that his little brother repeatedly smashes with a rock. They become fast friends, and as Jesus and Biff grow up together we get a number of humorous exchanges such as the following:

> Many a morning I was still dripping and shivering from the bath when I met Joshua to go to work.
>
> "Spilled your seed upon the ground again?" he'd ask.
>
> "Yep."
>
> "You're unclean, you know."
>
> "Yeah, I'm getting all wrinkly from purifying myself."
>
> "You could stop."
>
> "I tried. I think I'm being vexed by a demon."
>
> "I could try to heal you."
>
> "No way, Josh, I'm having enough trouble with laying on of my own hands."
>
> "You don't want me to cast out your demon?"
>
> "I thought I'd try to exhaust him first." (64–65)

Moore uses the first section of the book to set up a triangular relation between Josh and his friends, the Jewish leaders and other groups (the Sadducees, Pharisees, Zealots, and Sicarii), and the Romans. Josh and his friends are presented sympathetically and therefore serve as the "good guys," the Jewish leaders are presented negatively and serve as the "bad guys," and the Romans are an ambivalent group, neither exactly good nor bad. Although the narrative vocabulary does not explicitly use a religion/state rhetorical binary, it's clear that this is precisely what is being reproduced with this three-way relation: Josh represents good, individual religion; the Jewish leaders and other groups represent bad, institutional religion; and the Romans represent the state. Indeed, one of the central messages of the book is that what makes the Jewish leaders bad is that they wrongly seek to mix up religious and political power. The kingdom of God, Joshua insists by the end of the book, is within you and has nothing to do with politics.

The first mention of the Pharisees takes place when they are discussing Mary, Joshua's mother, who is reported as having talked to angels and claims to have "borne the Son of God" (10). Biff's mother says that Mary "should be careful that the Pharisees not hear her ravings or we'd be picking stones for her punishment" (11). Indeed, the threat of stoning by the Pharisees is brought up continually throughout the book. The first actual appearance of the Jewish leaders is through Jakan, a Pharisee's son and later a Pharisee himself. Jakan is presented as a quintessential creep and bully, as well as leader of a local gang.[2] It is at this point in the narrative that Biff shares his summary of the Pharisees:

> There were perhaps a dozen Pharisees in Nazareth: learned men, working-class teachers, who spent much of their time at the synagogue debating the Law. They were often hired as judges and scribes, and this gave them great influence over the people of the village. So much influence, in fact, that the Romans often used them as mouthpieces to our people. With influence comes power, with power, abuse. Jakan was the only son of a Pharisee. He was only two years older than Joshua and me, but he was well on his way to mastering cruelty. (23)

By contrast, the Romans are presented far more ambivalently. Some individual Romans are presented as kind—some are even allies of Joshua—while others are presented as mean and cruel. Of course the Romans keep slaves, tax the Jews, and they use whips and other forms of punishment or torture that are regarded as excessive. Ultimately, however, the Romans keep the peace; they "are here to see that we [i.e., the Jews] don't revolt" (32). In Galilee they constantly appear in the background—always there, but usually at a distance unless the Jews get excited.[3] At one point a centurion leader banters in good humor with Joshua, Biff, and Mary Magdalene (called Maggie). When Joshua suddenly and brashly asks him, "Will you slay my people if we follow our God?" (35), the centurion, whose name significantly happens to be "Justus" (i.e., "just"), responds affably and apparently reasonably: "Whatever they tell you, boy, Rome has only two rules: pay your taxes and don't rebel. Follow those and you'll stay alive" (35). It's simply a matter of fact—apparently neither good nor bad—that "nothing can stand against Rome" (49).

The Zealots, Biff tells us, are expecting a messiah to liberate the Jews from this Roman rule:

[S]ince I could remember there was always talk of the coming of the Messiah, of the coming of the Kingdom of God, of the liberation of our people from the Romans—the hills were full of different factions of Zealots who skirmished with the Romans in hope that they could bring about the change. (36)

This hope for political change, however, is increasingly presented as misguided and wrongheaded.[4] At the end of the novel Joshua insists, quite pointedly, "The kingdom of God is upon us, but the Romans will remain in Israel. The kingdom of God has nothing to do with the kingdom of Israel" (392). Indeed, at one point Zealotry is called "bullshit" (420).

Before the journey to the "mystic East," Joshua notably meets Bartholomew, a local homeless Cynic (who later becomes a disciple), and the Rabbi Hillel. From each Josh learns a lesson. From Bartholomew, he learns that one should "Be simple" (39).[5] When Joshua visits Hillel's lectures in Jerusalem, the purpose of the meeting seems to be to denigrate the Jewish tradition and to present Pharisees as petty. Jakan, the future Pharisee, asks Hillel "if it would be a sin to eat an egg that had been laid on the Sabbath" (96). Hillel responds with vehemence: "What are you, stupid? The Lord doesn't give a damn what a chicken does on the Sabbath, you nimrod! It's a chicken. If a Jew lays an egg on the Sabbath, that's probably a sin, come see me then. Otherwise don't waste my friggin' time with that nonsense" (96). When discussing whether or not Joshua is the messiah—about which Josh is having a serious existential crisis—Hillel turns out to express a view that sounds much like deism.

I don't believe there will be a Messiah, and at this point, I'm not sure it would make a difference to me. Our people have spent more time in slavery or under the heels of foreign kings than we have spent free, so who is to say that it is God's will that we be free at all? Who is to say that God concerns himself with us in any way, beyond allowing us to be? I don't think that he does. So know this, little one. Whether you are the Messiah, or you become a rabbi, or even if you are nothing more than a farmer, here is the sum of all I can teach you, and all that I know: treat others as you would like to be treated. (98)

Hillel therefore dismisses the Torah and the Jewish tradition; nothing matters except the golden rule.[6] However, Hillel goes on to suggest that if Josh wants to find out if he really is a messiah, maybe he should seek out the three magi that visited him upon his birth. So Josh and Biff set out to meet and learn from Balthasar, Gaspar, and Melchior. This journey provides the story arc for the book as a whole; Josh and Biff spend several years with each magi in turn, before returning to Nazareth for the story's climax and denouement.

From Balthasar Josh learns that tradition must be changed. At one point, Biff and Josh reflect on a battle with some bandits they encountered on the way to Balthasar's place. Josh feels guilty that several of the bandits were killed, as well as the fact that he magically blinded one of the bandits in anger. Biff attempts to assuage Josh's guilty conscience:

"The Torah says, an eye for an eye, a tooth for a tooth. They were bandits."

. . . "But I didn't save them, and I blinded that bowman. That wasn't right."

"You were angry."

"That's no excuse."

"What do you mean, that's no excuse. You're God's Son. God wiped out everyone on earth with a flood because he was angry."

"I'm not sure that was right." (151)

The Jewish Law—which stands in for "organized religion," it seems—might not be correct, and God's actions might actually have been wrong. Later, after studying with Balthasar, Josh decides that Lao-tzu's teaching is superior to the Torah: "Recompense injury with kindness" (167).

Soon thereafter, the Jewish Law's prohibition of pork is brought up and rejected. Biff becomes quite excited about Joshua's suggestion that they eat some bacon: "Joshua, you're the Son of God. You're the Messiah. That implies—oh, I don't know—that you're a Jew! You can't eat bacon" (169). Josh shrugs it off: "God doesn't care if we eat bacon. I can just feel it" (169). Later Josh makes it clear that what he learned in this section of the book is that he must be an "agent of change" (305). "You have to let tradition fall sometime, you have to take action, you have to eat bacon. That's what Balthasar was trying to teach me" (202).

What remains obscure, however, are the criteria by which one would determine whether or not something is worth changing. Here, the change or overturning of the past seems rooted in affect: Joshua *feels* bad about the bandits, or *feels* that God doesn't care if he eats bacon. No principle is explicitly given, but perhaps the implicit one is that we should change the rules if and when we feel like it; the possible social sources of our feelings are left unconsidered and thereby obscured.

They depart from Balthasar's palace after learning the essentials of Confucianism and Taoism (and after battling a demon who tried to eat them). They find Gaspar at a Buddhist monastery in China, and they both become initiates. The details are not important here, but what they learn from Gaspar and the Buddhists is that one must practice compassion; Josh achieves enlightenment but decides that he will be a bodhisattva in order to help suffering beings.

After learning about compassion, Josh and Biff depart for India to study with Melchior and to learn about Hinduism. Upon arrival in India, however, and before finding Mechior, they are caught up in a drama involving the ritual sacrifice of untouchables to Kali. They immediately decide to save the untouchables from the imminent ritual and the "homicidal priest[s]" (278), and hatch a plan that involves dressing up like goddesses and creating bombs with gunpowder (which they learned how to make during their time with Gaspar and his concubines). They disrupt the ritual with their bombs and save the children who were slated to die.

The purpose of this section of the novel, in addition to the spectacle of the action sequences, is apparently for the reader to learn about the cruelty of social hierarchies imposed by "organized religion." One untouchable says that he is "the lowest of the low. The scum of the earth. None of the higher caste may acknowledge my existence. I am Untouchable" (264). Both Josh and Biff are horrified by this and the caste system in general. "The sacrifices to Kali, the way the Untouchables are treated. Whatever they might believe, in practice their religion is hideous" (280). The treatment of the untouchables invites comparison to the way the Jews treat their unclean (281), and Josh comes to believe that just as these social hierarchies are horrible, perhaps also are the social divisions between Jews and Samaritans, or between Jews and Romans. He eventually decides that the kingdom of god will include both Jews and gentiles alike. "Even sluts" (320).

One interesting experience they have with the untouchables takes place when one of the men is found, "stark naked, sprinkling salt on his erect member as a large humpbacked cow . . . licked the salt" (282). Despite the fact that Biff claims this is a "super-bonus abomination," Josh refuses to criticize it. "Go with God," is all Josh says to the man (282).

They then leave the untouchables to study with Melchior. Melchior has Josh read the Upanishads and the Bhagavad Gita and teaches him about the "Divine Spark" that is in all human beings (this section of the novel is called "Spirit"),[7] while Biff pays a prostitute to tutor him in the Kama Sutra, one page at a time, as well as in Tantric discipline. There's a brief squabble about Biff's extracurricular activities, but it's clear that Josh doesn't object to Biff visiting prostitutes, which he's been doing throughout the book: "They [the prostitutes] still don't bother me, it's just that you don't have any money" (290).

When they get back to Galilee, the rest of the novel follows the narrative in the canonical gospels. Joshua gathers disciples together, teaches them his new gospel, and as a group they travel, heal, and spread the good news—and the story concludes with the death of Josh after his betrayal by Judas.

Moore uses this section of the novel to escalate tensions between Josh and the mean, judgmental Pharisees on the one hand, and the angry, misguided Zealots and Sicarii on the other. The Pharisees (as well as the Sadducees and anyone on the Sanhedrin) are depicted as merely interested in power (318). Jakan is described, now an adult, as "a bully with power" (334). The Pharisees wrongly chastise Josh "for having fun, drinking wine, and feasting" (385). They quiz Joshua with petty questions about the law that sound like word problems in an elementary school math class (409).

The legitimate authority of the Roman Empire is reinforced. The Zealots (and sometimes even Biff) are portrayed as wrongly wanting to expel the Romans from the kingdom. John the Baptist is portrayed as wrongheaded for criticizing Herod the Great, who works with the Romans (322). When John is thrown in jail and later executed, the general view seems to be that it is sad, but that he got what was coming to him. Judas is presented as an irrationally angry, disaffected Zealot. He unreasonably threatens Romans and is filled with unjustified anger (370). His universal prejudice against the Romans—"No Roman is the friend of a Jew" (370)—is also unreasonable, as he misses the fact that Josh and Justus the Roman centurion are friends.

Moore builds toward Joshua's death by developing a sort of antisacrificial sacrificial theology. After having seen the sacrifice of members of the lower caste in India, Joshua is completely opposed to sacrifice. Joshua says, "no more sacrifices. No more" (395). Biff claims that because of this, "he's going to allow himself to be killed to show his father that things need to be changed" (395). Joshua's death is therefore redemptive in sending a message to God: Joshua is so kind, opposed to violence, and opposed to social prejudices, that rather than resist Roman rule or the Pharisee's persecution, he will willingly turn the other cheek and submit to punishment in order to demonstrate to God that the old "eye for an eye" thing will be no longer accepted. In the end, Joshua is crucified much as Jesus is in the canonical gospels, Biff kills

Judas, and then Biff kills himself. At that point the narrative returns to the present day, in the hotel room; Raziel brings Maggie to Biff, who also has been resurrected just as Biff had been so that she could write a gospel of her own, and Biff and Maggie set out on a new life together.

A true false story

In the afterword Moore writes: "The book you've just read is a story. I made it up" (438). In addition, "My sending Joshua and Biff to the East was motivated purely by story, not by basis in the Gospel or historical evidence" (443). There's no question: the story clearly is made up, often anachronistic, almost always farfetched, and clearly false. Nevertheless, there is a sense in which Moore manages to present it as a *true* false story. Yes, the story is made up; however:

> While there are indeed astounding similarities between the teachings of Jesus and those of Buddha (not to mention those of Lao-tzu, Confucius, and the Hindu religion, all of which seem to have included some version of the Golden Rule), it's more likely that these stem from what I believe to be logical and moral conclusions that any person in search of what is right would come to, e.g., that the preferable way to treat one another is with love and kindness; that the pursuit of material gain is ultimately empty when measured against eternity; and that somehow, as human beings, we are all connected spiritually. (443)

With this Moore sends the signal that while the story is made up, something like it must be true, because the teachings of Jesus presented in the novel are *logical and universal*. The story is false, but since Jesus taught universal truths that all great religious thinkers arrive at, in a more important sense *it has to be true*. In addition, Moore has done just enough research on historical Jesus scholarship, Confucianism, Taoism, Buddhism, and Hinduism to lend an air of authenticity to his narrative. Those readers with any prior familiarity with popular accounts of "world religions" will easily recognize some of the material in the novel as plausible. In addition, the fact that these truths are "religious" seems to be designed to award them a special authority; these truths are not only universal, but they're universal *spiritual* truths. Moore ultimately sends two messages to the reader: on the one hand, it's just a story; on the other hand, it's more than a story—it contains logical and universal religious truths. This rhetorical gesture in the afterword has the effect of quite seriously naturalizing or authorizing the morality of the novel; consequently, I believe that this apparently silly story warrants careful scrutiny.

Religion is mostly nonsense (or worse)

Along the way, Josh and Biff learn that most things affiliated with "institutional religion" are—as Hillel implied—mostly "nonsense" and perhaps—like Zealotry—"bullshit." Many of the apparently wise religious leaders they find perform illusions or sleight of hand to impression others.[8] Some figures secretly admit that they don't understand what they claim to understand.[9] Some apparently profound truths are revealed to be errors, misunderstandings, or jokes.[10] The Pharisees who take phylacteries seriously are presented as idiotic:

[The Pharisee] was white-bearded and wore his prayer shawl and phylacteries wrapped about his upper arms and forehead. (What a jamoke. Sure, we all had phylacteries, every man got them when he turned thirteen, but you pretended they were lost after a few weeks, you didn't wear them. You might as well wear a sign that said: "Hi, I'm a pious geek." The one he wore on his forehead was a little leather box, about the size of a fist, that held parchments inscribed with prayers and looked—well—as if someone had strapped a little leather box to his head. Need I say more?) (345)[11]

When Joshua and Biff pray to God, they typically discover nothing but silence in return: "As was his habit with me, God remained quiet, and I suddenly realized how frustrated Joshua must have been, asking for a path to follow, a course of action, and being answered by nothing but silence" (191). The lesson is that God doesn't really answer prayer, and certainly can't be counted on. The few times God does speak—when Joshua is baptized and at the so-called transfiguration—it is merely in approval of Joshua as his son, in whom he is well pleased (in these scenes Moore sticks close to the canonical gospels). Since, by the end of the book, Joshua overturns what God is said to have commanded in the Torah, God's pleasure in Joshua signals that God is pleased with overturning God.

Moore claims in the afterword to have gotten the description of the human sacrifice to Kali from an academic source, which suggests that readers should take the account of death here deadly seriously. There are baskets of goat heads, rivers of blood, and even priestesses that "mimed having intercourse with the corpse [of a beheaded man], then rubbing their genitalia against the bloody stump of its neck before dancing away, blood and ochre dripping down the insides of their thighs" (276). Biff's narration suggests, "The sheer magnitude of the carnage was all that was keeping me from vomiting. It was as if the atrocity of the whole scene couldn't fit in my mind all at once, so I could only see just enough for my sanity and my stomach to remain intact" (276). Joshua notes that the caste system and the claims about reincarnation are used to control the Untouchables, making them passive. "That's how the Brahmans keep them in line. If they do what they are told, then perhaps they will not be Untouchables next life" (281). As noted above, the characters agree that the Untouchables' religion is "hideous" (280).

In summary—and consistent with James's folk theory of religion—most of what is usually associated with "institutional religion" or the gods is presented in the novel as silly, sham, nonexistent, nonsense, petty, bullshit, manipulative, sickening, or evil.

Good religion: Be kind

If most of religion is nonsense or bullshit, is any of it worth saving? What would "good religion" look like? To begin with, Joshua's ideology is explicitly apolitical. As noted earlier, near the end of the novel Zealots and Sicarii are corrected by Josh for thinking that the kingdom of god had anything to do with the Roman Empire: "The kingdom of God is upon us, but the Romans will remain in Israel. The kingdom of God has nothing to do with the kingdom of Israel" (392). Upon overhearing Zealots talking about the need to take Israel back from the Romans by force, Josh spats, "That is a crock of rancid yak butter" (392). In addition, when Joshua apparently achieves enlightenment while studying at the Chinese Buddhist monastery, he claims to have "achieved perfect freedom" (228). However, when Biff suggests that he's obviously been "free" from the Romans since they had left Galilee, Joshua retorts:

"It's not the same. That's what I came to tell you, that I can't free our people from the rule of the Romans."

"Why not?"

"Because that's not true freedom. Any freedom that can be given can be taken away. Moses didn't need to ask Pharaoh to release our people, our people didn't need to be released from the Babylonians, and they don't need to be released from the Romans. I can't give them freedom. Freedom is in their hearts, they merely have to find it." (228)

As such, true religion is individual religion, to be found in one's heart.

What can we say about "good religion," other than that it is individual and not political? The positive moral code Moore seems to want to advance is largely embedded in the narrative's good guys and bad guys, and concerns attitudes and dispositions above all else. What makes the bad guys bad is that they are angry, mean, cruel, power seeking, or bullies. In addition, those bad guys who would defend any tradition or practice that interferes with unbridled hedonism are presented as petty or unreasonable. What makes the good guys good is that they are kind, and perhaps so kind as to return violence with kindness. Such a dispositional or attitudinal moral code is, significantly, conspicuously unconcerned with social structure. Despite the brief critique of the caste system, social structures are not criticized in the novel. People with good attitudes can be found at any point within the social structure, and it is just the same when it comes to people with bad attitudes. Whether one is rich or poor, high caste or low caste, Jew or Greek, slave or free, and so on, is largely irrelevant—what matters is simply whether one is nice or cruel.

In addition, Biff summarizes the "gist" of Joshua's sermons as follows:

You should be nice to people, even creeps.
And if you:

   (a) believed that Joshua was the Son of God (and)

   (b) he had come to save you from sin (and)

   (c) acknowledged the Holy Spirit within you (become as a little child, he would say) (and)

   (d) didn't blaspheme the Holy Ghost (see c),

then you would:

   (e) live forever

   (f) someplace nice

   (g) probably heaven.

However, if you:

   (h) sinned (and/or)

   (i) were a hypocrite (and/or)

   (j) valued things over people (and)

   (k) didn't do a, b, c, and d,

then you were:

   (l) fucked. (366)

The disposition or attitude of being "nice" is clearly placed first. In addition, despite the mention of "sin" here, it appears that throughout the novel "sin" means little more than "unkindness"—the "sinners" Josh opposes are those people who are angry, mean, or violent, or those who would in any way interfere with one's enjoyment of life. What many Jews might traditionally think of as sin, such as violations of the kosher laws, seem not to count as sin. Indeed, Joshua explicitly says the Jewish law should be overturned or changed. Despite Josh's condemnations of fornication as sinful, Biff and Josh are actually rather libertine in their sexual practices. Although Josh believes that as a messiah he cannot know a woman carnally, he is nevertheless quite curious—so much so that he gives Biff money to sleep with prostitutes and report on what it is like. However, Josh still does not seem able to understand sex. Biff writes,

> Much as I tried—and I did try—I didn't seem able to convey to Joshua what it was he wanted to know. I went through a half-dozen more harlots and a large portion of our traveling money over the next week, but he still didn't understand. . . . Truth be told, I'd developed a burning sensation when I peed and I was ready for a break from tutoring my friend in the fine art of sinning. (116)

This passage is representative of Josh and Biff's views of fornication: it's sort of sinful, but not really. Biff has sex with prostitutes, girlfriends, other people's girlfriends, and—it's hinted—an animal or two; in general, Josh encourages Biff's hedonism more than he disapproves. Indeed, Josh muses, "Why would the Lord make sin feel good, then condemn men for it?" (122). The unspoken answer to the question seems clear: he wouldn't.[12]

Morality therefore seems to be reduced to being kind, rather than harsh, mean, violent; apart from that, it appears that unbridled hedonism is the order of the day, while the social origins of one's desires are left unconsidered. Using a schema identical to James's, what Moore doesn't like is slotted into "outward religion" and what he does like is slotted into "inward religion."

How seriously should readers take the demand to be kind, even to repay evil with kindness? It is made clear that Josh, with his *unwavering* kindness, is in fact not a fit model for human action. In the middle of a discussion about the fact that men are "lying pigs," Josh quotes Confucius on virtue, saying, "the superior man does not, even for the space of a single meal, act contrary to virtue" (175). Biff's immediate retort is, "the superior man can get laid without lying. I'm talking about *the rest of us*" (emphasis mine; 175). The distinction between Josh's unrealizable model and Biff's "the rest of us" reappears throughout the book. Biff, more than Joshua, is apparently a more realistic model for the reader. At one point when Joshua is feeling guilty for having failed at saving someone, Biff tells Joshua "You can't save everyone" (363). When Josh responds that he's divine, so he *could* potentially save everyone, the unstated but implicit corollary is that "the rest of us" could not in fact follow Josh's ideal.[13] Consequently, it seems that Biff is more likely a fit model than Josh—in which case the call for unwavering kindness is of course asking for too much.

Imperial ideology for privileged liberals

When I taught this book a few years ago, my students loved it and vehemently resisted my attempts to render any critique. Arguably, my largely white and middle-class American students liked it not only because they found it funny, but also because it presents hedonistic pursuit of desire as divine in origin and recommends a moral code that fits with how they already imagine themselves—as nice.

The emphasis on morality as rooted in nothing more than mere disposition or attitude is perhaps what makes it so appealing to liberal-minded readers who *already* think of themselves as having the right attitudes and dispositions. In contemporary America, almost no one thinks of themselves as bigoted, mean, or a bully. In addition, narrowly focusing on dispositions and attitudes shifts attention away from any consideration of social structures. In *Divided by Faith*, Michael Emerson and Christian Smith (2000) discuss the fact that because white American evangelicals primarily think of racism in terms of overtly bigoted attitudes, which they do not personally hold, they are largely incapable of seeing white privilege or explaining the continuing gap between white and black wealth. Consequently, they tend to blame minorities for inequality—poor people must be poor because they're lazy—and do not see how their own white privilege might in some way contribute to and implicate them in inequality. Thinking of racism entirely in terms of bigoted attitudes or overtly racist statements washes them of any responsibility for inequality. As Wendy Brown makes clear in "Moralism as Anti-Politics," moralistic critiques of individuals and individual *attitudes* leaves aside or even actively masks the structural causes of inequality and asymmetrical social power:

> [M]oralistic reproaches to certain kinds of speech or argument kill critique . . . by configuring political injustice and political righteousness as a problem of remarks, attitude, and speech, rather than as a matter of historical, political-economic, and cultural transformations of power. Rather than offering analytically substantive accounts of the forces of injustice or injury, they condemn the manifestation of these forces in particular remarks or events. (Brown 2001, 35)

Thinking of good and bad in terms of attitudes or people rather than structures and institutions has the effect of masking and protecting the latter from criticism. Of course, those who benefit from the existing structures and institutions have little reason to want to call them into question.

Similarly, this story is a feel-good story for liberal readers in a rather literal sense: privileged liberal students who already think of themselves as nice—and who face few systematic structural constraints that might hinder their success in life—are of course pleased to read a story that says religion is mostly nonsense, enjoy life, just don't be mean to others. In addition, any fanatics from "organized religion" who might interfere with their pleasures are the bad guys, toward whom they can feel superior. They can feel good knowing that by enjoying their life they are doing exactly what Jesus—and every other great religious teacher, Moore suggests in the afterword—would want them to do. At bottom, they feel good because the story tells them what they want to hear, or—better yet—because it doesn't really tell them anything at all. This version of Jesus makes no substantial demands on them—readers are offered a picture according to which: one must not lie, except when it is required; one must not be mean, except when it is deserved; one must not be violent, except when it is necessary. In addition, no objective criteria are offered that would help readers sort out when to make such exceptions—it seems that one must go on one's "feeling."

By "believing" in this feel-good message, privileged liberals can consider themselves moral, righteous, and religious, or at least "spiritual"—and therefore remain confident that all is right with them and their place in the world. Or, if all is not right, it is because someone else is being mean, toward whom they can be righteously indignant. In addition, the moral code insists that state power is legitimate power, and presumably all challenges to state power are illegitimate grabs for power. Do *nothing* politically, and they are doing what's right. Critical questions about whether we are situated in structures or institutions that serve the interests of some more than others, as well as the social forces that bring such structures into place, are foreclosed in advance—and, in fact, raising such questions might make one look like a zealot.

Luckmann argued that along with the increasing division of labor under capitalism, there is an increasing privatization of ideologies identified as "religious," in the sense that the central legitimating social function of, for example, Christian ideology for the European middle ages has given way to a proliferation of ideologies, none of which can gain a hegemonic place in the so-called public sphere (although, arguably, a hodge podge of late capitalist ideologies and consumerist practices has done this). Luckmann suggests that there is a Faustian bargain of sorts: there is an increasing autonomy in the "private" sphere for individuals to make or remake their own religious ideology in unique and individual ways, but at the cost of ceding all power to state and economic institutions in the so-called public sphere. "The discrepancy between the subjective 'autonomy' of the individual in modern society and the objective autonomy of the primary institutional domains strikes us as critical" (Luckmann 1967, 115). The "liberation" of individuals from the complete control of the primary state and economic institutions "represents a historically unprecedented opportunity for the autonomy of personal life for 'everybody.' It also contains a serious danger—of motivating mass withdrawal into the 'private sphere' while 'Rome burns'" (117).[14]

In *The Sacred Is the Profane*, William Arnal and Russell T. McCutcheon argue similarly, that under late capitalism the desire for utopia is segregated to places like Disneyland or a so-called religious sphere:

> To some degree, this is an *intrinsic* function of those forms of social activity that are normally denominated "religious." Modernity's creation of the *category* "religion" was not necessary for those actual behaviors designated as "religious" (which have long predated "religion" itself) to serve, as Marx said, as a "fantastic realization of the human essence," as a "sigh of the oppressed creature, the sentiment of a heartless world" (1978: 54). Any projection of utopian desires onto a fantastic, imaginary, or otherwise segregated reality—including the individual, or home life, or romantic "love," or personal hobbies, or other restricted spheres of this sort—not only serves a compensatory function vis-à-vis grim reality, but also serves the specific ideological function of implying that all utopian resolutions are to be sought precisely in such segregated space and thus not in real social existence. The sociopolitical effect is ultimately conservative: There is no point in trying to change *this* world; such hopes and dreams are not proper to it; they belong in a misty realm that affects nothing and has legitimate claims on no one. (Arnal and McCutcheon 2012, 62)

This is precisely what Moore's Jesus asks of readers; using a vocabulary that's almost identical to Luther's in *On Secular Authority*, Joshua suggests we segregate our desire for freedom to the *inward life only*: "Moses didn't need to ask Pharaoh to release our people, our people didn't need to be released from the Babylonians, and they don't need to be released from the Romans. I can't give them freedom. Freedom is in their hearts, they merely have to find it." Or, as Luckmann notes, individuals are free to pursue whatever private or individual projects they wish, even as "Rome burns." Empires like Rome or the United States will tolerate a great deal of ideological diversity, provided that one's ideological diversity does not chafe against the empire itself. As Justus said to Joshua, "Whatever they tell you, boy, Rome has only two rules: pay your taxes and don't rebel." Cede political and economic control to the empire, and one is free to do what one wants with one's private "religion."

It seems clear that *The Gospel According to Biff* fits this thesis, with one rather significant qualification: if the central tenets of one's autonomously made, private religion are "be nice and don't disrupt the empire," it ceases to look particularly autonomous. Moore's Jesus invites readers to trade outward slavery for inward freedom—for even Israelite slaves could be "free" under Pharaoh. But if the substance of this "autonomous" religion is fundamentally designed legitimate empire, how "autonomous" is it?

Despite the dominant narrative about "individual religion" as something merely private and autonomous, Biff's gospel is a myth designed to gerrymander the institutional relationship between empires and civil institutions; primarily it legitimates the right of empires to regulate and oversee taxation, commerce, and social difference. In addition, insofar as it is presented as a universal teaching of all wise thinkers, the myth claims a global or universal rather than individual reach; despite the fact that the message is identified as a universal "spiritual" truth—a claim that gives it a special authority—the gerrymandering claim is presented as having a reach beyond the so-called individual sphere it segregates. Last, it also claims a comprehensive behavioral scope: it recommends that individuals be nice to others and accommodating to state power in all aspects of their lives. In summary, despite the fact that it presents religion as an inward manner, it is neither particularly private nor individual; this ideology offers an overarching legitimation for an entire social order, for a particular organization of institutions within that order, and for a certain type of behavior for individuals within those institutions. The gospel according to Biff is imperial myth, not an individual, private religion.

5

Consumerism:
The fashionable hijab

*Governing in a liberal-democratic way means government
through the freedom and aspirations of subjects rather than
in spite of them*
NIKOLAS ROSE, 1999, 155

Apparently free choices are always determined on the basis of a number
of social factors, not the least of which includes the range and limits to
choice offered in particular social contexts, as well as incentives that motivate
and reward some choices and sanctions that discourage and penalize others.
Responsible social theory demands that we never take choices or the individual
that chooses at face value; on the contrary, just as the theory of evolution
dissolved divine agency into a passive process of natural selection, so too
must social theorists dissolve individual agency into the passive product of
social selection. From this perspective, "determined" or "constrained" are
not pejorative terms; we are not contrasting constrained choices with free
ones. However, demonstrating that all choices are determined *is* a criticism
of ideologies that present determined choices as if they were free, as these
ideologies obfuscate—and thereby naturalize—the social constraints that
direct apparently free choices.

Arguably, nothing obscures the forces of consumer capitalism over our
lives more than the discourses that sacralize choice and freedom of choice.
From a sociological perspective, it is clear that consumer choices are
determined by internalized aspirations for social distinction that are often
very class-specific. Subjects compete for distinction in particular social
fields in which only certain consumer choices are rewarded. This operation
of power through individuals—including their internalized aspirations, the

rules of the field, incentives and disincentives, and so on—are obscured by ideologies that present choices as originating from deep within individuals, rather than from within the structured fields that reward and punish subjects' choices. As such, ideologies that sacralize individual choice mystify and naturalize this operation of power, protecting it from criticism. Subjects may experience their consumption habits as liberating when exercising their capacity to choose from an almost dizzying array of consumer goods, but may not notice that to succeed in almost any field in a postindustrial society, one must consume in very particular ways; one *cannot not consume*. From this critical perspective, consumption is the product of a demand rather than a choice.

In this chapter I briefly discuss some social theorists who help us to explain how acts of consumer choice are determined or demanded by social fields in which individuals compete, even as individuals in such fields experience their behavior as free. Then I turn to a close reading of Randa Abdel-Fattah's young adult novel, *Does My Head Look Big in This?* (2005), which tells the story of a young Muslim girl who chooses, to some extent against her parents' wishes, to wear the hijab. I demonstrate that the novel's ideology sacralizes individual choice, obscures the forms of power that direct apparently free choices, and presents the pursuit of happiness through successful career and consumer goods as the essence of Islam, and perhaps even all religions. Abdel-Fattah's novel offers readers a brilliant, if unwitting, capitalist ideology.

Determined "freedom"

How can apparently free choices be determined?[1] How might consumer freedom be a regulated freedom? According to Georg Simmel and Jean Baudrillard's account of fashion—discussed in passing in Chapter 2—fashionable "choices" are structurally determined. For Simmel, fashion permits one simultaneously to mark both identity with a class and difference from other classes, and—in addition—to mark relative distance from others within one's own class. Fashion choices are therefore determined by a social logic of differentiation. One's choices cannot simply parrot those of others, for in that case one could not gain relative distinction with respect to others within one's own class. However, one's choices can neither be random, as in that case relative distance too would be lost, for relative distinction requires that all play within the same general field and by the same general rules—an attempt to achieve distinction with random fashion would be like attempting to win at chess by declaring one has four aces. According to Simmel, even the so-called fashion leader "allows himself to be led" (Simmel 1971, 305), as his or her choices are inversely determined by the direction of those running behind; the direction and speed of those attempting to run just ahead of the herd are determined by the herd itself.

Although such choices are determined, Baudrillard argues that they may be felt as free by subjects making them, insofar as they have internalized the social code they follow.

> The consumer experiences his distinctive behaviors as freedom, as aspiration, as choice. His experience is not one of being *forced to be different*, of obeying a code. . . . [However, i]n the very act of scoring points in the order of differences, each individual maintains that order and therefore condemns himself only to occupy a relative position within it. Each individual experiences his differential social gains as absolute gains; he does not experience the structural constraint which means that positions change, but the order of differences remains. (Baudrillard 1998, 61)

As such, "bureaucratic constraints" that permit the expansion or increased pace of consumerism (perhaps including banking and loan regulations, state manipulation of interest rates, interstate commerce regulations, tax laws designed to stimulate consumerism, etc.) may be celebrated as increasing the "realm of freedom" (84); social controls are legitimated under the guise of liberation.

Baudrillard suggests that the central role of the ideology of consumerism in such a context is to train subjects "*in the unconscious discipline of a code, and competitive cooperation at the level of that code; it is not by creating more creature comforts, but by getting them to play by the rules of the game*" (94). On this view, consumerism doesn't pacify or even repress subjects but rather motivates them. According to Baudrillard, ideology in the traditional sense—as something that mystifies reality and covers up what is "really going on"—is not necessarily present in such a system; once consumers internalize the "rules of the game," the game runs itself without anyone needing to mystify it or mask it. "[C]onsumption can on its own substitute for all ideologies and, in the long run, take over alone the role of integrating the whole of society, as hierarchical or religious rituals did in primitive societies" (94).[2]

Along the same lines, Nikolas Rose suggests, "Governing in a liberal-democratic way means government *through* the freedom and aspirations of subjects rather than in spite of them" (Rose 1999, 155). According to Rose, we are encouraged to pursue the creation of self-identity through consumer practices and the creation of "lifestyle":

> Become whole, become what you want, become yourself: the individual is to become, as it were, an entrepreneur of itself seeking to maximize its own powers, its own quality of life, though enhancing its autonomy and

then instrumentalizing its autonomous choices in the service of its life-style. (158)

This pursuit of the self-construction of individuality is aligned with consumer capitalism: subjects are in a circle of production and consumption, for one must work to consume. As such, "Consumer choice can be aligned with macroeconomic objectives and business advantage" (162).[3] As with Baudrillard, in such a system subjects do not experience themselves as repressed but, insofar as they have internalized the social codes by which they consume to construe their identities—in Rose's words, insofar as the system has produced "subjects of a certain form . . . with particular desires and aspirations" (114)—they likely experience their consumer choices as free. Indeed, the social and political regulations that make this late capitalist social organization possible are legitimated by the language of freedom and choice (79). What better way to regulate subjects than to socialize them with particular aspirations (e.g., for distinction), and then set them "free" to pursue those aspirations? Ideologies that sacralize choice serve a key legitimating function for this cycle of consumption.

How are apparently free consumer choices linked to the inheritance of culture? In *Shopping for Identity: The Marketing of Ethnicity*, Marilyn Halter argues that modern consumer societies do not become melting pots where cultural or ethnic differences disappear; rather, ethnicity is bought and sold as a mark of social distinction. Utilizing Herbert Gans's theory of "symbolic ethnicity" (Gans 1979), she suggests that ethnic identity becomes more or less symbolic, in the sense that people claim ethnic affiliations in ways that are relatively costless:

This is ethnicity-lite, a harmless form of ethnic identification that demands little and carries few costs. . . . Symbolic, or voluntary, ethnicity is, above all, comfortable and usually manifest as a form of leisure activity expressed in entertaining festivals and fairs; cultural spectacles or music, art, film, theater, and dance; and samplings of a smorgasbord of both traditional and nouvelle cuisines where diverse groups can coexist in harmony rather than put the focus on histories of social iniquities, interethnic tensions, entrenched notions of cultural superiority, and anti-immigrant bias. (Halter 2000, 78–79)

Much like "boutique multiculturalism" (Fish 1999), subjects pick and choose from those cultural traditions available to them those elements that can most easily be domesticated and consumed in the present context. In postindustrial societies, the inheritance of any cultural element that might chafe with the state or the productive capacity of self or society is liable to be sanded smooth before being put to use.

For Pierre Bourdieu, mastery of a cultural repertoire provides subjects with what he calls "cultural capital," insofar as demonstrating mastery of a cultural tradition can facilitate collusion, mark social status, or garner respect within a particular social field. Some scholars have used the term "religious capital" to refer to the accumulation of capital that comes with mastery of forms of culture colloquially called "religious." Along these lines, Bradford Verter has suggested the term "spiritual capital" for those forms of "religious" capital that fall outside the scope of "institutional religion" (Verter 2003, 158). In the United States, for instance, mastery of exotic or esoteric "Eastern religions" might award one "spiritual capital" among one's peers, although not likely among one's rabbi or (Catholic) priest. However, for Verter, the appeal of traditions such as Vedanta or Zen in the United states is in part due to their "scarcity":

> Vedanta is not as popular today as it once was. The value of particular varieties of spiritual capital is subject to the fluctuations of the market. . . . [P]ositional goods become devalued once they become congested . . . . If the symbolic value of positional spiritual goods, such as Vedanta or Zen or Scientology, depends on their real or perceived scarcity, then their worth declines as they become more accessible. This suggests an approach to understanding religious fads, which scholars of religion generally have been at a loss to explain: spiritual fads represent the social trajectory of estimations of religious value. (166)

Given the fact that these "extrainstitutional" or "individualistic" choices (158) reflect institutionalized social fields, I'm unpersuaded that "spiritual capital" is the right word for this, as it carries associations tied to the ideology of individualism that Bourdieu consistently disrupts. In addition, I would also suggest that these fads come and go at a pace where "mastery" of the cultural repertoire at hand cannot take place, a priori—by the time one would have mastered the cultural tradition, it would already be out of fashion. Consequently, I propose the alternate term "exotic capital" to denote these forms of social capital that come from the use of culture that appears exotic in a particular social context, but which is precisely *not* mastered by the user.

Why consume "ethnic" culture or utilize symbolic ethnicity or identification in the way Halter describes? Primarily because difference is often exotic, romantic, or tied to nostalgia, and as such confers social distinction or exotic capital. Halter quotes a Russian immigrant: "Those families who entered the United States 60, 70 years ago, what were they telling their kids? Study English, get rid of the accent, . . . blend in. Today it's not so. It's OK to be Polish-American, Russian-American, Japanese-American; it's okay to be a hyphenated American. *It's even sexier in some ways*" (emphasis mine;

Halter 2000, 80). Similarly, in *New Age Capitalism* Kimberly Lau analyzes the production and consumption of aromatherapy, macrobiotics, yoga, and t'ai chi in the 1990s: because of romanticized orientalist fantasies in modern Western culture, consuming what is advertised as the "mystic east" can garner cultural capital. "Difference becomes a highly marketable commodity, and this form of globalization has made it chic 'to eat fifteen different cuisines in any one week,' to wonder at pluralism while taking 'pleasure in the transgressive Other'" (Lau 2000, 11). However, for this to take place difference must be "commodified, sanitized, and thus *neutralized* for easy consumption" (12).[4] Not any difference will do; only those forms that can be easily appropriated, yet still award status or exotic capital (18).[5]

Last, it's worth noting that subjects not only consume commodities in this process, but also in a sense turn themselves into exotic commodities for others. As Stuart Ewan and Elizabeth Ewan note, consumption fundamentally depends on the internalization or expectation of the gaze of one's compatriots: "In a theater of perpetual quick judgment, one [is] encouraged to assemble an effective response to the judgment of others" (Ewan and Ewan 1992, 140). Zygmunt Bauman similarly argues that consumers must transform their own selves into commodities for others: "[t]hey are expected to make themselves available on the market and to seek, in competition with the rest of the members, their most favorable 'market value'" (Bauman 2007, 62). Adorned with just the right exotic cultural accessories, one might fetch a high price from other buyers.

Approaching an item of culture or the practice of consumption from the perspective of the theorists just discussed will require us to forego taking "freedom" and "choice" at face value. What we must do, rather, is attempt to historicize apparently free choices in particular contexts. These are the questions we face: How does the consumption of this or that element of culture make sense in a particular social field? How is the field constructed so as to reward or punish particular forms of consumption?[6] When an element of culture is appropriated and deployed in a new field, what is trimmed off and what is kept? To what extent is the element domesticated for the new context? And, most importantly for my purposes, how is the field or the mode of production mystified, naturalized, or legitimated by authoritative discourses that circulate in this context? These are the questions I wish to take to Abdel-Fattah's *Does My Head Look Big in This?*

Nonthreatening Islam, consumer muslims

Does My Head Look Big in This? (2005) is a young adult novel written by Randa Abdel-Fattah, an Australian Muslim woman with a Palestinian and

Egyptian heritage. Abdel-Fattah is a lawyer in Australia, identifies as a Muslim feminist, has written about the plight of Palestine, and has been involved in interfaith efforts in Australia. The novel is written from the first-person perspective of the main character, a teenager named Amal, whose upper-middle-class Muslim family lives in modern-day Melbourne, Australia; like Abdel-Fattah, Amal too has a Palestinian heritage. In the opening chapter Amal declares that she has decided to begin wearing the hijab full time, despite her parents' hesitations and warnings, and the remainder of the book follows the life of Amal, her family, and her friends for several months. The narrative is sprawling, including a series of events that are often only loosely connected to one another, but a majority of which relate in some way to her choice to don the veil. The reception Amal receives is of course mixed: some of her family and friends look favorably upon her choice, whereas some peers at her "snotty prep school" (14) tease or even bully her on the basis of the choice. Much of the story recounts the sort of often humorous teen drama one would expect from young adult fiction about a high school girl,[7] but the plot—what little there is of one—centers around moments where Amal makes and learns from mistakes and, in the end, triumphs over adversity. The novel was well-received by critics and won Australian Book of the Year for Older Children in 2006. While it originally appeared in Australian markets, it was soon after reissued in European and American markets, and has since been translated into Arabic. Its worldwide success reveals an appeal that makes the book worth serious consideration.

The novel first appeared in 2005, just a few years after the September 11 attacks, and it is therefore not surprising to see the author going to great lengths to present Muslims as "normal" to a predominantly non-Muslim Western audience, where "normal" implies that they live a petty bourgeois lifestyle and are surrounded by brand name consumer goods and media. The first chapter opens with Amal on her treadmill watching reruns of the television show *Friends*. We are told that Amal is wearing Adidas brand shorts and a Winnie-the-Pooh shirt. She attends a prep school. Her parents met at medical school—dad is a doctor and mom is a dentist. Although they were born in Bethlehem, "there are fifty-two years of Australian citizenship between them" (3), implying that they are not a threat to Australian state sovereignty. Amal says she "bonds" with her mother when they go shopping, although, apparently like all teens, she says "'you're ruining my life' to [her] mother at least four times a week" (4). Her mother is apparently obsessed with diet fads (4), and although she wears the veil she also wears "Gucci shades, and drives a car with an 'Islam means peace' bumper sticker" (10). Amal watches *Sex and the City* (4), reads *Glamour* (12), *Cosmo* (67), and *Teen Vogue* (14), and constantly drops pop culture references (e.g., to *Lord of the Rings* [15] or J. Lo [18]). Her family lives in "one of Melbourne's trendy suburbs. Beautiful treelined streets, Federation homes, manicured front lawns, and winding driveways" (5). It is clear that while she is Muslim, she is not a Palestinian terrorist, but rather a typical upper-middle-class teenager who consumes the same forms of popular culture as others in her class. Indeed, in the second chapter she makes it clear that although she will be wearing the hijab, "I'm not going to abandon my fashion sense—you'd better believe I'd never give up my shopping sprees" (8).

Much of the book takes great pains to separate out good Muslims from bad or false ones. Amal and her family, of course, are good Muslims: they might pray, fast at Ramadan, and wear the hijab, but they're certainly not affiliated with those things that capitalist societies find threatening. Amal's family does not associate with "terrorism, extremism, radicalism, any ism" (13), nor the Palestinian Liberation Organization (123), nor do they carry AK-47s (84). Bad Islam is satirized as a foil to good Islam throughout the book. Amal jokes that the Muslim school she attended at one point was one where "they indoctrinate students and teach them how to form Muslim ghettos, where they train with Al-Qaeda for school camp and sing national anthems from the Middle East. NOT!" (12). "[Y]ou can't be very holy if you're going around blowing people to smithereens" (156). The ones with bombs are "lunatics" (248) or "murderers" (252). In addition, they're not truly Muslim. It is inaccurate, Amal tells us, to imply that "these barbarians somehow belonging to my Muslim community. . . . It gives them legitimacy, this identity that they don't deserve. These people are aliens to our faith" (250). As I suggested in the previous chapter, this sort of discourse serves the ideological function of preserving the political status quo—only nation-states rightly have a monopoly on violence and all other communities or organizations must cede power to the state. Or, as William Cavanaugh puts it in *The Myth of Religious Violence*, "revulsion toward killing and dying in the name of one's religion is one of principal means by which we become convinced that killing and dying in the name of the nation-state is laudable and proper" (4–5).

As with symbolic ethnicity or boutique multiculturalism, much of what Amal identifies as authentic Muslim practice seems to be adapted or domesticated for a capitalist society with a high division of labor, in which individuals must be disciplined for education, work, or career. For instance, daily prayer is presented primarily as *useful*.

My dad wakes me up for the morning *fajr*, prayer. I'm not my best at dawn and sometimes I throw the pillow and tell him to go away. But most mornings I get up with them to pray. The walk to the bathroom is always a zombie-steps experience. Some mornings I manage to knock into a wall, but that's actually quite useful for waking me up. Then I perform the *wuduh*, the ablution, wetting my hands, face, arms, feet, and crown of my head. And then we pray. . . . I feel a strange sense of calm. I feel like nothing can hurt me, and nothing else matters. And that's when I know I'm ready. (29)

While Muslims in other contexts might emphasize prayer as for their god, Amal mentions her god only once in this section, and only in passing. The prayer seems to be not for her god but for herself, to wake her up in the morning and to help her feel calm and ready for the day. She explains an additional usefulness of prayer to Adam, the boy she has a crush on for most of the book:

Imagine you're playing one of your basketball games . . . . You're running up and down the course, doing your layups, shooting hoops, smashing your body into exhaustion. You've got nothing on your mind except the game. Nothing is distracting you from it. But when it's time out, you get this three or four minutes of calm. You get to drink your Gatorade, catch your breath, rethink your strategy . . . . That is how prayer is for me. It sounds corny, I know. But it's kind of . . . like that. Except there are five Gatorade breaks a day. (145–146)

In this case, her god is not even mentioned in passing; prayer is a time-out from daily stress—presumably so that when one returns to work one can be more effective at one's job.

Similarly, Ramadan is conceived as a ritual that apparently has little to do with the prophet Muhammad or Amal's god; rather, it too is transformed into a practice that is useful in a way that would appeal to many in a postindustrial society, not just those who identify as Muslim. First, it creates an opportunity for family bonding each night when the fast is broken—bonding that is presumably necessary because in a society with a high division of labor individuals in a family may be divided from one another on a daily basis by work and education. Second, Ramadan provides an opportunity for individuals to empathize with those who are hungry:

It took me some time to realize that Ramadan is not just about hunger and thirst. I guess that when we're a McValue Meal away from relieving a hunger pain in a world where millions of people are dying of starvation, empathy does more to your conscience than a news report. (335)

Despite the opportunity to empathize, at no point does Amal's empathy motivate her to do anything about world hunger. It seems that empathy is useful above all else in order to produce a bad conscience that is simultaneously a good conscience: she can feel good that she feels bad about hunger. Such empathy primarily serves a psychological function and appears to pacify rather than motivate.

In both cases—prayer and Ramadan—the practices at hand are transformed into something that almost anyone negotiating life in late capitalism could accept as useful. Who could object to a ritual that helps one wake up for work or school, or that helps one relax intermittently throughout the day? Who could object to occasionally reminding oneself that others go hungry, especially if it helps one feel good about oneself? Here these practices are appropriated and employed in new context in a way that is, by design, nonthreatening. As Lau noted earlier, cultural differences in consumer society are "sanitized [and] *neutralized* for easy consumption."

True Islam: Freedom of choice

After Amal begins wearing the hijab, there are a series of vignettes in which other characters—such as the principal at her school, her friends and other peers at school, her elderly neighbor, and so on—wrongly assume that Amal's parents have forced this practice upon her. In each case she insists that this was not forced on her, but was a matter of voluntary, individual choice. Characterizing this as a matter of her individual choice is designed to legitimate it to the other characters; it is implied that wearing the veil would be acceptable if it is her choice, but unacceptable if her parents were forcing her to wear it. When her parents point out that her prep school's dress code might prohibit the wearing of a veil, Amal insists, "How can they stop me? It's up to me whether I want to or not" (23). In addition, "the thought that somebody else might take that choice away from me is energizing something inside me" (23). The reader is repeatedly told this is a choice that Amal *wants* to make:

> Nobody has *made* me wear it, Ms. Walsh. It's my decision. (39)
>
> I've never felt so sure about what I wanted. (57)
>
> I'll wear what I want. (83)
>
> I'm going by what *I* feel is right. (92)
>
> I feel independent and I know I've got the choice to be whoever I want to be. (130)

In addition, Amal and other characters make it clear that wearing the veil is not required by Islam. Rather, true Islam permits freedom of choice. "[E]very girl is going to interpret the hijab differently. It depends on their culture or their fashion sense, you know? There's no one uniform for it . . . . [S]tricter women cover their face, but it's not required in Islam. It's their choice to go to that extent" (72). That Islam permits choice is nowhere made more clear than in an ongoing subplot involving Amal's friend Leila and Leila's more conservative mother, Gulchin. If Gulchin had her way, Leila would submit to an arranged marriage, drop out of school, begin bearing children for her husband, and take care of her husband's home. Amal's mom, however, makes it clear that Gulchin is simply ignorant, and that Leila "can be all she wants to be, not in spite of Islam, but because of it" (88). For Amal's mother, it appears that Islam requires nothing more than for individuals to pursue what they individually *want* to be or do. The lifestyle Gulchin wants for Leila would be fine, but only if Leila herself chose it (89). The problem is that Gulchin is *forcing* this way of life onto Leila (89).

The novel presents the source of individual desires, wants, or choices as random, unpredictable, or unexplainable. The first words of the book are "It hit me when I was power walking on the treadmill at home, watching a *Friends* rerun" (1). Amal explains that the *Friends* episode was one in which Jennifer Aniston's character considers singing a song at a friend's wedding; despite her fears and the fact that people "making fun of her" for wearing a "hideous bridesmaid's outfit," she "suddenly gets the guts to jump on stage and sing" (1). Amal claims she felt "this rush of absolute power and conviction" (1). The television scenario of someone successfully overcoming social fears sets an example Amal now felt empowered to follow, and she decides—despite fear of peer feedback—to begin wearing the hijab full time. While it's clear that the content of the *Friends* episode was related to her decision, the claim that "it hit me when I was power walking on the treadmill" makes it seem as if motivations or decisions—much like James's religious experience—strike at random like lightning.

The idea that choice or motivation springs from deep within the self—as opposed to without—is apparent not only from this choice that "hit" her on the first page, but at other points as well. When her Uncle Joe challenges her choice to wear the hijab, Amal claims, "some weird sensation starting raging through me. I don't know what it was. Defiance? Anger? Pride? I can't define it. Whether I choose to be an astronaut, a pilot, a lollipop lady, a scientist, or a Tupperware party host, this piece of material is coming with me" (107). At another point Amal and her friends were frustrated with some events taking place at school. She writes, "Then something comes over me," and suddenly she suggests they cut school (298). Choice and motivation strike, inexplicably—these things can't be explained. "[T]his decision, it's coming from my heart. I can't explain or rationalize it" (52).

By contrast, social theorists like Simmel and Baudrillard would suggest that such choices are in fact not random or inexplicable; while individual choices might not be predictable—presumably because of the complexity of the social system—they nevertheless typically abide by a social logic that is in many cases not at all difficult to discern. However, presenting the cause of choices as obscure or inexplicable mystifies and legitimates them. Social practices and expectations not seen as inevitable are often subject to revision; by contrast, if we can characterize choices as inexplicable there would be no more sense in challenging them than there would be sense in challenging the roulette wheel for not choosing one's number. When depicted as inexplicable, choices are protected from criticism.

True Islam: The pursuit of career

Around the discussion of Leila and Gulchin, Amal introduces a distinction between Islam and "culture," in this case the "village culture" that Gulchin grew up in: "Any moron would realize that [Gulchin is] following her village's culture, not Islam. So for her to go around and tell the world it's Islam when it's the exact opposite is so dumb" (89). According to Amal, Gulchin thinks that "guys should go to school and get to do what they want but girls have to stay home till they're ready to be married," but that this is a case where she doesn't understand her own religion (90). Leila wants a career, which in Gulchin's mind makes Leila a "bad Muslim" (91–92). However, as Amal points out, this is a "backward interpretation of Islam" (91). Presumably the reverse is true: true Islam would allow Leila to pursue a career. At a later point Leila concurs with Amal's assessment; "Mom's following her own customs more than Islam . . . . My relatives in Turkey are all educated about Islam. The girls pray and some of them wear the veil and they go to university and work, because they know it's their right to do that in Islam" (151–152).[8] This distinction between Islam and culture is clearly normative; the characters use it to positively sanction what they affiliate with Islam and to negatively sanction what they affiliate with culture. As always, however, such rhetorical distinctions are ad hoc and variably created to legitimate different agendas in different contexts.

The tension between Leila and her mother escalates when Leila and Amal lie to Leila's parents about a night out and go to the mall without permission; they're caught by Leila's brother, who grabs Leila and takes her home. At that point Leila's parents appear to isolate Leila, prevent her from going to school, and ramp up their efforts to arrange a marriage. The climax of this subplot comes when Leila runs away from home and disappears; at that point there are a number of tense engagements between Amal's and Leila's parents, as Gulchin suspects Amal knows where Leila is (although Amal does not).

Gulchin confronts Amal, saying that Leila turned away a "good man for engagement" (310). Amal responds, "Why couldn't you just leave her alone? . . . It's not time for her to marry!" (310). When Gulchin claims, "I know what's best for my daughter!," Amal's mother interrupts with what is presented as the voice of reason: "This is your daughter's life, Gulchin . . . . There is plenty of time for her to meet somebody and settle down, if she chooses to. She's still so young and her duty, Gulchin, her *Islamic* duty, is to gain an education, to seek knowledge" (311). True Islam is not only about choice, but also about education and career. At one point Amal insists, "I'm picking and choosing what I like and what I don't like. But Islam is where my rights come from, so if some crappy rule says I have to throw out my education or sit at home for life, then forget it" (331).

At the climax of the novel as a whole, just after a successful performance on her school's debate team (a debate for which Amal has been preparing for most of the book), Amal announces to her parents, "I want to be a scientist with a law degree or a lawyer with a science degree" (328). Her parents are extremely happy with the choice to pursue a prestigious career path: "They hear law and go absolutely ga-ga on me" (328). Leila reenters the story, admits to having stayed at a women's shelter, but says that she would return home if her mom allowed her to "go back and study and get what I want"; in that case, "I'd have choices" (345). Leila's mom agrees to allow her to come back home in order to pursue education and career.

The novel wraps up with a happy ending; Ramadan comes to an end, and the characters say "Happy *Eid*" to one another, and "May every year bring you happiness" (355). Happiness has indeed arrived for Amal, as she received an "A" grade on her exams at the same time. Happiness has also arrived for Leila because Gulchin has taken Leila back home, and even Gulchin, previously angry with Amal, kisses Amal and wishes her a Happy *Eid* (355). True Islam—permitting individuals to do what they want, that is, pursue education and career—brings about happiness.

Fashion

Islam is characterized as protecting choice, but why might Amal be motivated to choose the hijab? As already noted, Amal claims that her choice is motivated by something that can't be explained. Amal also explicitly denies that her choice is about fashion, saying "It's not a game or a fashion statement or a new fad" (32). In addition, three or four times throughout the book she insists that the hijab is just "a piece of material" (24, 113, 327), although she also claims that it is a "badge" (7) or "symbol" (24), and as such it displays her identity to others. This symbolic function even proves useful at one point when she visits the mall and is approached by two other women wearing the veil: "These girls are strangers to me but I know that we all felt an amazing connection, a sense that this cloth binds us in some kind of universal sisterhood" (28). Additionally, wearing a veil allows her to follow her god's command for women to "act and dress modestly" (8). Related to this is the fact that covering up will allow her to worry less about her body, her hair, and whether she has zits. However, these reasons for her choice are *absolutely dwarfed* by her and her friends' constant discussion of fashion concerns.

I'm not going to abandon my fashion sense—you'd better believe I'd never give up my shopping sprees. (8)

[T]his [decision] means we have to go shopping soon and get you a whole new wardrobe. Mix-and-match spree. (21)

If you're at my age and you're at Chadstone shopping mall on a Thursday night with your friends, you're not there for the sock sales. You're there to make an impression. . . . Chadstone means makeup, designer clothes, and great hair. So basically I've just got to replace great hair with great hijab in the equation and I'm all set. (26)

I still dressed to impress and I took ages to get my makeup, clothes, and hijab just right. But I didn't feel I was compromising myself by wanting to make an impression. (29)

It's going to be one of those mornings because now my hijab won't work. I want a perfect shape, a symmetrical arch to frame my face. That means no creases, no flops, no thread pulls. . . . It's taken me forty-five minutes. Not even moussing my hair takes this long. (32)

Do you not understand that if you wear eyeliner and eye shadow your eyes will be devastating with the scarf? . . . When Mom does her eyes up under her hijab she looks hot. (49)

Adam . . . thinks I look beautiful in the hijab because it accentuates my eyes. (56)

Work out what color scarves you've got so we can mix and match. Also, bags. Have to match your bags to your veil. Tell you what, write a list of all your scarf and bag colors. Shoes if you want as well, but I recommend a [shoe shopping spree] be conducted separately, to give it the full attention it deserves. (87)

How about my scarf? . . . Is the front curve OK? I mean, are there any dents in the shape? Is it too tight? Are my cheeks squashed up so my face looks fat? (139)

[When she is with family and could take off the hijab:] I can't be bothered. My hair's a mess. Bad hair day. I'll just leave it on. (182)

I've been in front of the mirror for three hours. No kidding. My entire wardrobe is on my bed and floor . . . . It takes me ages to finally look semi-decent. I've highlighted my eyes with eyeliner and mascara, applying some lip gloss and a touch of blush. . . . I decide on a baby-pink chiffon hijab with a white cotton headband underneath. I've draped the hijab loosely around my head so that the headband shows, flicking the tail ends over my shoulders and clasping them together with a brooch I bought from a funky jewelry shop on Bridge Road. I go for a long, straight black skirt, a soft pink fitted cashmere top, and pink heels. It's clearly all very centerfold. I still feel ugh, but if "I feel like a supermodel" is ten and "Even my mom would think I'm ugly is one, then I'm hovering on five. There's no way I'd enter Chapel Street [mall] on a Saturday night on a score of one to four. (288–289)

Amal knows that difference is "exotic" (20), and she craves the positive attention and exotic capital she is awarded as a result of her new fashion statement. In particular, she responds dramatically to the attention she gets from a boy she has a crush on. At first Adam is intrigued and asks a lot of questions (72–73), and reports being impressed with her because wearing the veil was "gutsy": "you've got more balls than any girl I've ever known" (96). Amal is so excited after this exchange that she says, "Somebody get me an inhaler. And I don't even have asthma" (97). Adam and Amal become fast friends after that point, and begin hanging out. He obviously begins to develop a crush on her. Adam tells her that when he first saw her with the hijab he thought she was a fanatic, but then realized she was not; however, "[y]ou made for a pretty good-looking fanatic!" (148). It is clear that the appropriation of the hijab in her social context awarded her a social distinction and recognition from those she wanted to impress. In retrospect, her "free" choice does not appear to have been motivated from some forces deep within her self, but rather was guided by a social logic of consumption according to which some forms of exotic cultural consumption award distinction and prestige.

In addition, the fact that some characters ridiculed Amal's hijab in itself awarded her exotic capital with Adam, about whose opinion she was most concerned—it proved to him that she had "more balls than any other girl." As Simmel notes, even the choices of those who reject mainstream fashion are determined in an inverse way to the field at hand:

This constitutes a most curious social-psychological complication, in which the tendency towards individual conspicuousness primarily rests content with a mere inversion of the social imitation and secondly draws in strength from approximation to a similarly characterized narrower circle. So the phenomenon of conscious departure from fashion illustrates how ready . . . human characters are . . . to show their strength and their attraction in the negation of the very thing. (Simmel 1971, 307)

By rejecting mainstream fashion and adopting a countercultural fashion, Amal knows that she's "sharing something with millions of other women around the world and it feels so exciting. . . . I'd never felt so free" (29). But such a freedom is determined, and Simmel is correct: "Fashion"—and even the rejection of fashion—"is merely a product of social demands" (297). This particular fashion choice appears, in retrospect, to have been determined by the social demand that one must distinguish oneself with difference, perhaps with exotic differences—as long as one's difference isn't *too* different (i.e., one cannot be different in a way that would challenge the state or the pursuit of education and career)—and that one way to distinguish oneself is to appear countercultural, and standing against dominant trends conspicuously demonstrates the strength to resist such trends—although color matching the hijab with other fashion accessories is a way to be countercultural while simultaneously abiding by dominant cultural standards.

Universal legitimation

In the novel readers also learn that good Islam is basically the same as all good religion (as one might expect from an author who has been involved in interfaith efforts). At one point Amal suggests that although she went to a Catholic elementary school, there was nothing wrong with that, as "all that 'love thy neighbor,' 'respect your parents,' and 'cleanliness is next to godliness' stuff was basically what I would have been taught in Religious Education in an Islamic school anyway" (10). She has a Jewish friend named Josh, and she expects that he won't be surprised or offended by her wearing the veil, as "Orthodox Jewish women also cover their hair and there are tons more things that are similar with our faiths" (62). Amal claims that the demand that men and women remain abstinent before marriage is universal: "'it's not just in Islam, you know,' I say. 'Christianity, Judaism, Hinduism, Buddhism'" (75). When a terrorist bombing is reported, Amal's school holds a peace vigil. Amal fondly recounts the event: "something builds up inside me as a priest and a rabbi and a sheikh and a monk stand together on the steps in front of Parliament House and prove to us that our labels mean nothing compared with what we have in common, which is the will and right to live" (252). The terrorists who carried out the event are not Muslims; what they did was "political" not "religious": "Muslim is just a label for them. In the end they're nutcases who exploded bombs and killed people. It's politics. How can religion preach something so horrific?" (257). As with the distinction between Islam and culture, this distinction between religion and politics is made on an ad hoc basis in different ways at different times, depending on the social agenda at hand. In this case we learn that no true religion would advocate violence or killing; religions are apparently unified in their nonviolent message. As we saw with Moore's rhetoric in *The Gospel According to Biff*, the apparent universality of the tenets of what Amal puts forward as authentic Islam lends additional legitimacy to them—if all great religions or spiritual traditions agree with Amal's norms or claims, then they must be true. As with Moore, Abdel-Fattah presents this story as true fiction.

A bourgeois lifestyle for everyone

[L]iberty can be made into a powerful instrument of domination.

HERBERT MARCUSE, 1991, 7

"Choices are always determined by social contexts that limit, reward, or punish particular paths." Ideologies that sacralize freedom of choice, however, tend to obscure the social forces that determine the paths that individuals take, thereby mystifying or naturalizing them. *Does My Head Look Big in This?* is marked throughout by such an ideology. In the story, Amal and her parents justify her choices by appealing to the rhetoric of freedom of choice, yet the social forces that seem to direct her choices remain unidentified and unanalyzed—according to Amal, the motivation for her choices hits like lightning and cannot be explained.

An analysis of social fields reveals that wearing the hijab is a way of conferring distinction to the wearer in a capitalist society, as long as the difference is not too different—and Amal and her friends make sure that is the case by assuring that her hijab matches her hand bag and her shoes. The wearing of the hijab is turned into a cultural practice perfect for boutique multiculturalists: the hijab is a lifestyle marker that stands out as exotic and countercultural—and attracts boys—without interfering in any way with continual consumption, education, or career; all cultural choices are subordinated to economic demands. Ironically, the novel demands that readers choose choice, and—more specifically—one must choose fashionable choices of the very sort one's social field requires.[9] Ewan and Ewan are correct, "In a theater of perpetual quick judgment, one [is] encouraged to assemble an effective response to the judgment of others" (Ewan and Ewan 1992, 140). Amal makes herself a commodity with just the right countercultural accents, selling herself to her peers, especially Adam. Abdel-Fattah has therefore produced a form of Islam that dovetails perfectly with a middle-class consumer lifestyle. If capitalism requires for its maintenance the creation of subjects who pursue a career that provides disposable income that can be invested in the consumption of products that award distinction before the judgment of others, then Abdel-Fattah's novel is capitalist ideology *par excellence*.

In addition, *Does My Head Look Big in This?*, as a novel for young adults, is a tool for socializing youth, one that teaches them to internalize the rules of the game, that is, that to be successful in this field one must distinguish oneself fashionably, but in ways that don't seriously challenge the social order (for that would be extremist). Young adults learn that their inherited cultural traditions must be domesticated for consumer society, trimmed of all that might chafe with petty bourgeois lifestyle.

In the end, Amal's message turns out to be little different than Biff's: what all religions want is for one to enjoy oneself—perhaps by consuming products that make one happy and which award social distinction—as long as one doesn't interfere with the state or the economy. And, like Biff's tale, this story presents this message as a universal truth of all religions; Amal's message is not just for Muslims, nor just for "religious" people, but for everyone—as such, Abdel-Fattah's ideology claims a global rather than private legitimating scope. In addition, this ideology, where persuasive, likely has an unintended constitutive gerrymandering effect: the ideology of individual choice cedes most social power to the economy and mystifies the economy's constitutive role in the limits, shape, and direction of individual choice. This ideology encourages readers to internalize the behavioral demands of late capitalism—that one produce and consume—thereby making these demands seem like the expression of an autonomous self rather than what they are (i.e., demands or constraints). This myth therefore serves a constitutive function with respect to a comprehensive behavioral scope (i.e., encouraging individuals to consume in ways that garner social distinction), and—through the rhetoric of choice—legitimates the consumerism that results. Despite the dominant narrative about "spirituality" and "individual religion," there's nothing private or individual about Abdel-Fattah's emphasis on individual choice. It is, perhaps, the near-universal ideology of late capitalism.

6

Productivity: The new protestant work ethic

The government of work now passes through the psychological strivings of each and every one of us for what we want.
NIKOLAS ROSE, 1999, 119

In *The Protestant Work Ethic and the Spirit of Capitalism* (2002), Max Weber argued that John Calvin's doctrine of predestination produced existential anxieties that motivated Calvinists to work hard. According to Calvin, his god had chosen in advance who to extend grace to; some people were predestined for heaven—"the elect"—and the rest were predestined for hell. Individuals could not know for certain whether they were among the elect, but there would be signs; specifically, God would work through the lives of his chosen, awarding them gifts of good character and making them successful in their vocation. According to Weber, this doctrine motivated Calvinists to work hard in order to prove to themselves that God was working through them and that they were therefore among the elect. Success in one's vocation would ease fears about life in hell. The spread and success of Protestantism ended up providing motivated and competitive workers for the engine of capitalism. For Weber, however, once that engine was up and running, it no longer needed Protestant ideology to motivate workers; once the cycle of competition is in place, a form of economic selection—like natural selection—takes place: independently of their motivation, individuals have to adapt and compete or they are selected out. While Calvinists wanted to work hard, we have to. Weber goes so far as to suggest that we are, perhaps, locked into an iron cage from which we cannot escape.

Arguably, self-help and spirituality manuals serve an ideological function within this iron cage. If we cannot escape from it, perhaps we can consume ideologies that assist us in acclimating to our prison. In addition, perhaps the consumption of these ideologies can assist us in succeeding in competitions with our fellow prisoners; maybe we cannot escape, but we might be able to secure a competitive advantage over our peers.

In *Governing the Soul* (1999) and *Inventing Our Selves* (1998), Nikolas Rose argues that in the latter half of the twentieth century we see an explosion of self-help and psy discourses (psy discourses include psychological, psychiatric, therapeutic, and other discourses that encourage individuals to reflexively work on their selves) that function to align individual interests with corporate or business interests. These discourses substituted a new social ethic in place of the Protestant work ethic:

> It celebrated calm, order, and security within the organization, it thus directed the individual to fit harmoniously into the routines of work, to conform and to co-operate. The social ethic fostered adjustment without question, and redefined success in terms of a safe career, integration with one's peers, and dependence upon the company. (Rose 1999)

To some extent, this involved the presentation of autonomy and personal fulfillment as taking place through success in the workplace. Work was recast as an opportunity rather than an impediment, if only one rightly adjusted oneself to its demands: "work is no longer necessarily a constraint upon the freedom of the individual, . . . [but rather] an essential element in the path to self-fulfillment" (119).

Of course, the desires individuals are encouraged to pursue on the route to self-fulfillment are not arbitrary; these discourses normalize some desires over others and recommend reflexive disciplinary practices designed to align individual behaviors with normative corporate goals (see Rose 1998, 104ff). These discourses and their coordinated practices, however, do not operate through repression of subjectivity, but by inciting certain kinds of subjects rather than others: "Such practices . . . seek actively to produce subjects of a certain form, to mold, shape, and organize the psyche, to fabricate individuals with particular desires and aspirations" (Rose 1998, 114). In addition, as Eva Illouz points out in *Saving the Modern Soul*, these psychological discourses are designed "to manage disruptions of biography (e.g., divorce, bereavement)" (Illouz 2008, 157), in order to prevent such disruptions from interfering with work and productivity. Once disciplined and aligned, such subjects actively seek objectives that serve corporate interests and their newly formed individual interests.

Although dealing with very different social contexts, Bruce Lincoln discusses the alignment of individual and corporate interests via the processes of socialization in *Emerging from the Chrysalis: Rituals of Women's Initiation*.

There he discusses how, in the past, Navajo girls were transformed into women by an elaborate rite of passage. The rite of passage involved the use of a cosmological narrative that, according to Lincoln, was designed to socialize the girls into the social roles they would be expected to fulfill as women. While Lincoln recognizes that this may have made life more meaningful for women—filling their lives with a cosmological purpose—it did so in a way that served the interests of the community over the interests of the women themselves:

> Successful initiation . . . thus produces Navajo women who will put their abundant labor at the disposal of others . . . . It produces women who serve food, keep house, tend children, till the land, herd the animals, and what is more, who learn to derive satisfaction and pride from all this. (Lincoln 1991, 113)

These rituals therefore lead women "to desire for themselves . . . precisely what society desires of them" (112).

Lewis Richmond's *Work as Spiritual Practice* and Matthew Fox's *The Reinvention of Work* recommend ideologies that do just the same: they teach individuals to seek self-fulfillment through the alignment of their individual desires with corporate interests, and they encourage reflexive practices designed to help individuals accommodate themselves to those parts of corporate life that might chafe. In summary, they encourage petty bourgeois workers to desire and achieve precisely what corporations desire of them. They provide an ideology that perhaps serves as the new Protestant work ethic.[1]

Work as a Spiritual Practice

Buddhist entrepreneur Lewis Richmond's *Work as a Spiritual Practice: A Practical Buddhist Approach to Inner Growth and Satisfaction on the Job* intends to bring the principles of Buddhism to the workplace, in order to help middle- and upper-middle-class workers succeed in their career ambitions, people dealing with "all the usual pressures and problems of a start-up—cash flow, meeting payroll, and competition, not to mention long hours" (122)—or people who shop at Saks or drive BMWs (117–118; only rarely does he discuss examples of people at work in blue collar or working-class jobs). One key theme is reiterated in a quote—attributed to Harry Roberts—that Richmond cites several times throughout the book: "To find joy in work is the greatest thing for a human being" (5). The other main theme involves accommodating oneself to the challenges of the workplace; when one cannot change the system, one can transform one's inner self to accommodate the system as it exists.

For Richmond, "spiritual practice" is something that happens not only in one's "inner life"; rather, "it can be alive and active all the time, even in the workplace" (18–19). Spiritual practice in the workplace can be a means of job satisfaction:

> [W]hether you love your job or hate it, you can be awake and aware in your work. I want to redefine the term *job satisfaction* to mean not a job where everything goes well and we rise quickly to the top but a job where we can grow, develop, and mature as human beings, regardless of what happens. (19)

Thus difficulties at work are not an impediment to spirituality, but an opportunity to exercise reflexive meditation or awareness practices; challenges we face are redemptive: "So it is with these painful emotions. Their job is to warn us, to rouse us, to help us to act and to move" (32).[2] We respond to challenges by accommodating ourselves to the existing conditions at work, not working to alter the conditions. The inner self can be satisfied independently of the outer circumstances. At one point, Richmond suggests that the "inner" is more real than the "outer" in any case:

> A Buddhist would say that, if anything, the thought is more real, because it is the source of the action. So we must pay attention to our thoughts, and our feelings, and the whole of our inner life. It is the source of how we choose to act and to live. (121)

Most of the book offers practical advice for transforming one's inner self in order to navigate white collar work life, which Richmond takes for granted as natural. "If we want to be paid well, have good benefits, and keep climbing our career path, we must put up with a fast-paced, stressful work environment. There seems to be no help for it" (31). There are chapters, therefore, on how to deal with stress, anger, failure, ambition, control, and so on.

One example of Richmond's accommodationism comes when he discusses the advice he gave to a nurse who was having a difficult time with stress at her job, in part because she was so busy that she did not have time to take the scheduled breaks she was promised. Rather than, for instance, suggest that she demand the break she had been promised, he suggests that she meditate while she's walking from one patient's room to the next (35). The nurse tries the exercise, and adopts it to her circumstances (she hums rather than recites the mantra he suggests; 39). The new exercise is a success because it calms her down amidst a stressful and busy day. In this case, spiritual exercise amounts to altering one's mental habits in order to increase one's productivity without negative side effects or consequences.

In the same chapter on stress, Richmond discusses a Buddhist practitioner he was advising who was meditating while working; the problem with this man was that his mindfulness meditation was making his work too slow. "He looked as though he were carefully calculating every movement, trying to be 'mindful'" (41). Richmond's response is to point to the young man on the same job with the best "scorecard," that is, the person who was most productive. Richmond suggests that this young man was doing better because he had "a balance between paying attention and letting attention go" (41). In summary, awareness meditation at work is useful if it helps defray stress, but not useful if it slows one down. The implicit lesson: the expectations of the job are paramount, and meditation is useful if it helps one achieve those expectations but not if it interferes with them.

The spirituality Richmond recommends may help with one's personal integrity, but it might not. He points out that sometimes it's not possible to maintain integrity in business:

> Once at the end of a lecture at a Buddhist center, a woman asked me, "How do you work in the corporate world and hang on to your personal integrity?"
>
> "I don't!" I reflexively responded.
>
> "Oh, thank you!" she said, laughing. I think she was both surprised and relieved at my answer.
>
> I was being a bit facile. I do try to hang on to as much of my personal integrity as a I can, but I don't always succeed, and I am careful to pick and choose my battles. The arts of compromise and tactical retreat are as important as standing your ground. I learned a long time ago that there is no purity in the world of work. (54)

Richmond does not define what counts as "integrity," so it's unclear what this means exactly. However, what is clear from this exchange is that the world of work is a force to which we must adjust ourselves, independently of concerns about integrity or morality. Similarly, when he discusses anger at work, he notes that anger may often be justified as the result of what we might perceive as injustice (again, like integrity, undefined), but that is just the way business works: "in the workplace, because of the power imbalance and the emphasis on money and profit, there are many small and not-so-small injustices" (63). However, these injustices again are *opportunities* for us reflexively to work on our selves. When we experience injustice, "our motivation should not so much be to protect ourselves as to feel compassion for the perpetrator" (62). Anger is egotistical, it focuses on "Me! Me! Me!" (67). In such cases we should attempt to be aware of our selfish focus on the ego, breathe deeply in order to calm ourselves, and visualize our "adversary" doing something kind or generous, such as apologizing (70). Even if the visualization is far-fetched, it can serve to separate one from one's anger. In this case, as with stress, the reflexive practices are designed to help subjects accommodate themselves to whatever social conditions exist.

When it comes to stagnation, Richmond defines the problem thusly: "In Stagnation we don't want to get up in the morning. We dawdle on the job; we don't put our all into it. The work we do pays the rent, but it isn't satisfying" (89). These are all problems because, presumably, we *should* want to get up in the morning, we *shouldn't* dawdle, and we *should* "put our all" into our work. The solution, again, is not to transform the conditions of work but to transform ourselves so that work becomes satisfying for us. Various problems and solutions related to stagnation are addressed:

1 Boring commute: a commute is actually an opportunity to meditate and enjoy ourselves; it's not something we're subjected to but rather a moment of "autonomy" where we are free from the forces of work (93).

2 Boring job: make it less boring by transforming oneself into someone cheery and funny, as one toll-booth man did by joking with those he was collecting money from; "to keep it up, day after day, the way he did, with that cheery grin on his face, is much more than humor . . . . [He] was giving something of himself to each driver who passed through and engaging the world at a spiritual rather than material level" (98).

3 Dealing with failure on the job: create an "energy shrine" with items or photographs that have a positive association; the shrine "uplifts you and gives you energy and a sense of purpose" (107).

4 Laid off: being laid off is an opportunity to find new work; failure in this case may actually lead to new success (109).

In each case things that we might think are bad or undesirable about our career are presented as good for us; if we do not see them as good, then they are an opportunity for reflexively working on ourselves such that we begin to see them as good.

Richmond provides readers with a telling metaphor for the relationship between the individual and work in the chapter on control:

Think of how you "control" a kite. The wind moves the kite, but you hold the string. You don't let go of the kite, but you don't hold it close to your chest either. You let it soar. . . . Controlling by Paying Attention means throwing yourself all the way into the situation and trusting yourself and others enough to let the wind do most of the work. (189)

The message seems to be: don't fight the forces of the wind or business; doing so will only hurt. Rather, let oneself be carried by the wind—that is the way to success. What is key here is that one cannot and should not challenge the wind or the forces of business. Such a metaphor naturalizes the structures of the business world by presenting them as forces of nature.

When we come to the chapter on ambition, Richmond presents capitalism as a positive force. "One of the strong points of our capitalist system is that it encourages and rewards ambition. The desire to do better for yourself, your children, and your family, the urge to invent, to innovate, to explore, and to create, can be a positive force for good in the world" (130).[3] He qualifies this claim by saying that it can also promote greed, which is bad if it becomes "addictive" (130). As with Stephen Mitchell's *The Gospel According to Jesus*, wealth or the accumulation thereof is only bad if one becomes attached to the wealth. "Now, 'more' [i.e., desire for more money] is not in itself bad. It is legitimate to want more. In fact, the workplace is one of the prime areas in our lives where our search can bear fruit" (131). Richmond draws the line not at desire for wealth but at the line where that desire turns into greed (another term that is not explicitly defined). Even desire for consumer goods is natural: "Consumer economies run on the principle that the more people want, the better" (132), and that is presented as just the way things are. While Buddhist monks might prefer to segregate themselves from this sort of consumer life, "most of us, not being monks, don't really live that way" (132). Many desires "are not only legitimate but spiritually rewarding," as even the monks would admit, according to Richmond (133).[4]

Near the conclusion of the chapter on ambition, Richmond suggests that if we reflexively approach ambition as a spiritual practice, with a cheerful attitude, "[a]mbition is no longer a goal to be achieved; rather, it brings a quality of joy, even love, that needs no goal" (141). As such, with the right conscious or mindful efforts, pursuing a career ambition is a joyful journey, independently of the results of one's success.

In the chapter on money and time, we learn that we should work not for money but for the sheer joy of work. We should work for the sake of work itself: "find small ways to work not for pay but for the sake of work itself" (152). Even little things, like cleaning up a dirty break room, can make work joyful:

When you do something to satisfy your own state of mind, it is not just for yourself. Your state of mind is real, it is tangible, it affects others. It is nice for the next person to visit a clean snack kitchen, but what is even more important is for that person to feel your shining mind. (154)

Richmond is recommending us even to go so far as to volunteer for uncompensated labor, in order to exercise an opportunity for finding joy. Similarly, in the chapter on accomplishment he argues that "True Accomplishment is not about winning, acquiring, or being on top. It is about sharing, giving, and including" (184). Success in the conventional sense—acquiring money, for instance—is fleeting, but true accomplishment—that sense of "making a difference"—will stay with one (185).

In the chapter on generosity, Richmond explicitly naturalizes generosity: "Generosity is not a spiritual add-on; it is fundamental. . . . It is something we all instinctively know how to do" (201). I would argue, however, that presenting generosity as natural ironically does not encourage it but rather the opposite; teaching that it is natural implies that we should go with our gut, so to speak. If one's gut rarely prompts one to be generous, then rarely showing generosity is just natural, and one need do nothing more. And when it comes to specific examples of generosity throughout the chapter, it typically amounts to merely being kind to one's coworkers. In addition, despite the fact that he's said that generosity is something done without hope of reward, he actually encourages it as something that is, in fact, rewarding. If one is kind to those in one's field of business, that will be remembered if one is laid off—prior acts of kindness might help one get a new job (204; 218). Similarly, while bosses might struggle with providing negative performance evaluations to a subordinate, being kind when delivering negative feedback can make the process easier (205). Also, there are limits to how generous one should be: "Generosity in the workplace does not mean giving up all sense of strategy about how to survive and protect ourselves on the job. But it does mean that when the choice presents itself . . . we can choose the path of the heart" (212–213). Thus generosity amounts to little more than interpersonal friendliness, something that should come natural, and something that's only required when necessary—since it is natural, it should be self-evident to one when to be generous and when not to be. In summary, given the vagaries of the recommendations at hand, it appears that one should be nice whenever one feels like it.

Near the end of the book Richmond discusses what Buddhists typically call the need for "right livelihood," which means having a job or career that is not harmful to others. He points out that working in a slaughterhouse, for example, might be undesirable for a Buddhist (227). A modern example might be the "chairman of an oil company," as oil spills could harm the environment (227). However, he makes it clear that it is too much to expect individuals to take this seriously: "in reality, we all participate in harm to other beings to one degree or another . . . . There is no escape from this Interdependence" (227). He points out that some people might try to recycle more, or try to purchase products from "green" companies, but there is no right or wrong here. Because these things are so complex, we should do what we can, but we can't be perfect and we shouldn't try. Rather than focus on whether or not a practice or livelihood is right or wrong, instead focus on transforming one's job into a place where one can find fulfillment:

> When your job is to process credit applications for a multi-national financial conglomerate, where is that pride? Where is that accomplishment? . . . You have to create it out of your own resources, effort, and sense of self-respect.
>
> *The primary purpose of this book is not to change the world. It is not to transform the workplace, or commerce, or the nature of work. It is not even to transform organizations. Its primary purpose is to transform individuals.* (emphasis mine; 230)

As such, it is clear that *any* livelihood can be the "right livelihood," independent of one's job. If one is kind to one's coworkers, finds fulfillment and joy, and sees challenges as opportunities for growth, then one "has already achieved Right Livelihood" (230).

It is worth noting that in the conclusion to the book, Richmond suggests that despite its many benefits, there might be some negative aspects to the free market, such as the fact that where there are winners there are also losers (247). However, his criticisms are overshadowed by the praise he offers. The benefits of capitalism include the fact that the free market "produce[s] wealth and generate[s] profit" (246); in addition, the market is an apparently natural "collective expression of all those individual wants and needs" of human nature (249). Therefore, despite the drawbacks, we needn't worry too much about the negative things.

Additionally, employing the miracle motif, Richmond argues that we can create the outward world we want with our inner thoughts:

> The marketplace begins in the mind.
>
> To put it another way: The marketplace does not control us, we control the marketplace—at least to the extent that our inner values and character are stronger than the lure of advertisements and possessions. If we truly want our system of commerce and the conditions of our employment to change, then the place to start is with ourselves. (250)

Unfortunately, it is unclear how business or the market might be transformed, even if we transform ourselves. It seems that, if anything, business might get fiercer as we get better at our jobs through the employment of the reflexive strategies he's recommended. We will be working harder, with fewer breaks, offering uncompensated labor, and although we'll be kinder to one another, that kindness apparently does not require us to break with any expectations of business or the pursuit of profit, which clearly remain paramount throughout the book. If anything, transforming ourselves will make the free market *more competitive*, which will mean more "losers," to use Richmond's term.

In summary, for Richmond "spirituality" is useful for acclimating to or accommodating the business world, which functions as a natural force that blows like the wind: we should be ambitious for success, we needn't hang on to integrity (which is likely impossible in any case); we shouldn't get too angry at injustices at work but rather transform our angry reactions into sympathy for the perpetrator of the injustice; we should know that being laid off is a good thing rather than a bad thing; we must remember that boredom is to be managed by transforming our inner selves rather than the conditions of the workplace; we should prepare to offer uncompensated labor; we must be generous, where generosity is reduced to social niceties; there is no *wrong* way to do business as long as one conducts business in a way one personally finds fulfilling; and all the negative effects of capitalism can be mitigated if we approach the outer world with the right inner world. It's clear that Richmond very much naturalizes the capitalist mode of production, encourages individuals to align their goals with the goals of business, and to accommodate themselves to the latter whenever there might be a discrepancy of interests; when capitalism chafes against individuals, it is the individuals who must transform themselves so that chafing no longer takes place. Ambition is naturalized and personal fulfillment is completely aligned with corporate interests, as fulfillment comes *through* one's success in the workplace. Richmond's book very much attempts to teach individuals to desire precisely what corporations might desire of them.

The Reinvention of Work

Matthew Fox is the author of a number of popular books in the "spirituality" genre; in *The Reinvention of Work: A New Vision of Livelihood for Our Time*, Fox turns his attention specifically to the question of work and career. Fox's central claim is that we must transform our inner selves so that we begin to see work as having a cosmological significance, thereby making it meaningful for ourselves, rather than dull or dehumanizing.

Like many of the authors considered in the earlier chapters, Fox makes appeals to a wide variety of "religious" or "spiritual" traditions, especially the "mystics." In the introduction, he writes:

The reader will hear not only from Western mystics such as Hildegard, Eckhart, Aquinas, Rilke, Heschel, and others, but from mystics of Eastern and Middle Eastern traditions as well, including the Hindu Scriptures known as the Bhagavad Gita, the Chinese Scriptures known as the Tao Te Ching, and individual mystics such as Rumi (a Muslim Sufi) and Kabir of India. (Fox 1994, 12)

As with the other authors discussed earlier, appeals to such a wide variety of "sacred" and "authoritative" voices is a legitimating move; Fox presents his view as merely a summation of the universal teaching of all great mystics.

Fox assumes a pantheist view: a noncorporeal "Spirit" (with a capital "S") pervades our world and acts or expresses itself through us as individuals. One of the fundamental ways Spirit manifests itself is through work. We are fulfilled, it seems, when Spirit manifests itself rightly. How can that happen? From the very beginning, Fox insists that "[g]ood living and good working go together" (1). To be fulfilled is necessarily to be fulfilled in part through work or career. When Spirit, work, and life are aligned, our lives are infused "with meaning, purpose, joy, and a sense of contributing to the greater community" (2).

Fox additionally draws upon the cosmology specific to the Bhagavad Gita, which he quotes repeatedly throughout the book. The Gita is an Indian philosophical poem written around the first-century CE, give or take a few centuries, and part of a larger epic called the Mahabharata. It teaches that humans are continually reincarnated in samsara—the wheel of birth and death—until they are liberated, at which point they can rejoin the divine substance that underlies the universe. The Gita allows that there are several paths to liberation, but Fox's emphasis is on what the Gita calls karma yoga, the discipline of action. According to the Gita, one of the ways for men to achieve liberation from samsara is to act according to their class-specific dharma (i.e., class duty). There are four classes: priests; warriors; farmers, artisans, and merchants; and servants. Krishna—the god who delivers the teaching in the Gita—insists to Arjuna that as a warrior he must act according to his warrior dharma, and must fight in an incipient battle despite whatever misgivings he might have. Krishna promises Arjuna that if he acts according to his dharma, he can escape samsara. One of the central threads of the Gita is the claim that "discipline in action surpasses renunciation of action" (Miller 1986, 59), and that liberation comes through the path of disciplined action. Therefore "Look to your own duty; do not tremble before it; nothing is better for a warrior than a battle of sacred duty" (36). Indeed, "Your own duty done imperfectly is better than another man's done well" (48). Fox adapts this emphasis on duty, except that he changes "dharma" to the words "work" or "role":[5] "work is about a role we play in the unfolding drama of the universe. . . . How readily the idea of work as a role fits a new cosmology, that of work playing a role in making the cosmic wheel go around" (6). Work is necessary, and we must surrender to it:

> Holiness does not consist in non-action. It consists in the appropriate action undertaken with a purity of intention. The reinvention of work requires first discerning which actions are appropriate today . . . . As the Gita puts it, "One who does holy work . . . because it ought to be done, and surrenders selfishness and thought of reward, that person's work is pure, and is peace. This person sees and has no doubts: he surrenders, is pure and has peace. Work, pleasant or painful, is for him a joy." (138–139)

Fox makes a key distinction between "work" and just a "job"—the latter lacks the cosmological significance he suggests that the former should have. Working for an extrinsic reward such as pay is a "job," but "[w]ork comes from the inside out; work is the expression of our soul, our inner being" (5). Work must be meaningful, as "[w]ork without meaning is deadly" (14). "[W]ork is sacred," or at least it should be; the problem is that in the modern "secular" world we have "desacralized" work (12). For Fox, our task is to resacralize work, in order to make it meaningful.

As with Richmond, transformation must begin with "inner" work. The antistructural miracle motif is hard at work here: "All the sources of injustice are not to be found in systems alone. Within our psyches lies the clue to our resistance to justice" (22). In addition, "much of our work can be transformed when we ourselves are transformed in our attitude toward work or toward the people or situations that make work a burden" (40). This might slightly involve a transformation of the social structures in which we're embedded; we can make work less of a burden if we "change the structures at work that render us bored" (42). Thus it seems that while transformation must begin with our inner selves, it should not necessarily stop there; inner transformation will lead to outer transformation (46). Despite this, it is clear that Fox emphasizes the former over the latter: "Our work takes on cosmic significance when it is inner work, a work connected to the origins of the universe. Therein lies its dignity" (54). Our *outer work* must . . . flow from our *inner work*" (134).

The central chapters are "From Machine to Green: How a New Cosmology Helps Us Revision Work" and "Exploring Our Inner Work: Work as Enchantment." It is in these chapters that Fox elaborates most thoroughly on how a reconceptualization of the cosmos and our work's place in it will make work more meaningful. He writes, "[t]he lack of a cosmology creates violence in people's lives. This is especially true of young people, for the young have an intrinsic sense that they are citizens of a universe, of the entire home of God" (60). We must therefore emphasize that we are all interconnected and interdependent, and that our work is, in fact, God's work (64). Once we realize that our work is God's work, we will have "a wonder-filled world in which to live. Work would be a joy, a pleasure, a celebration, even an enchantment. . . . Work can be ecstasy" (67). Because our world is a construction of our minds—"psyche and cosmos are essentially the same thing in the human person" (74)—transforming our view of the world will simultaneously transform the world itself: "If we think we live in an interconnected universe, an organism unfolding the one Great Work of a trillion galaxies, all of it in motion and expanding, then we will start living in such a world as well" (75). When work is properly harmonized with Spirit, the world, and our inner selves, work ceases to be work. On this point Fox cites the Gita: "'I am not doing any work,' thinks the person who is in harmony, who sees the truth. . . . 'It is the servants of my soul that are working'" (39). Once we transform ourselves— and thereby the world—we will enjoy work for work's sake; "we love it for its own goodness, virtue, and nature" (79). Following such a transformation, we will no longer work for extrinsic rewards such as pay, but for intrinsic ones; that is, we will work just for the sake of allowing Spirit joyfully to work through us in the great organism that is the universe (80–81). Fox claims that his own work is joyful in just this way (96).

Because Fox makes work fundamental to Spirit and fulfillment, one of the worst things—by contrast—is *lack of work*. "The results of lack of work are spiritually devastating" (9), in part because people feel like they lack control over their lives (10). It's implied, then, that we control our lives in part through work—work is an expression of our autonomy. It is no surprise, then, that Fox centers on unemployment as an evil that must be overcome if we are to set our cosmology aright again. Full employment would be necessary for Spirit to achieve perfection (220). This includes, notably, the employment of children (181ff). Life would be more meaningful for youth if they could participate in the joys or ecstasies of work, and there would be extrinsic rewards as well: "How much would our insurance rates and medical costs tumble if we were to train young people in basic nursing skills so they could care for the ailing and visit with the aged?" (182)

It is important to note the Fox criticizes both consumerism and "workaholism." When life is "reduced to a hunt for consumer goods," at that point "freedom becomes trivialized" (8). Fox cites evidence that Americans consume much more than they did a half of a century ago, yet have far less free time because of how much they tend to work (39). While Fox wants us to transform ourselves in order to resacralize work, he does not intend to promote a "work-and-spend" cycle (37). In addition, he criticizes the prioritization of profit (231) and criticizes businesses for producing detrimental effects on the environment. However, as with Richmond, Fox's emphasis on the positive aspects of work overrides his criticisms. While he sees room for reform regarding what he sees as the excesses on the margins, capitalism remains the order of the day.

In summary, for Fox we must work: fulfillment is impossible without work; if we transform our view of the world and see our work as an expression of a cosmological spirit, our work will be more meaningful and, consequently, fulfilling; transformation of our inner life is prioritized over transformation of the social world; and a complete fulfillment of ourselves and the world's spirit requires full employment, even for children. Although more critical of the social world than Richmond, the ideology is the same. Work within the capitalist system is naturalized—the mode of production is, indeed, an expression of the world spirit. We are told that we can achieve autonomy and fulfillment by accommodating ourselves to the world of business and work. And, in addition, we must align or harmonize our interests with the regnant mode of production, and this can happen by reflexively working on our inner selves when our interests do not appear to align.

Conclusion

Arguably, "[t]he present production apparatus is . . . , on the one hand, a gigantic machine for psychic and physical mobilization . . . and, on the other hand, a sorting machine that allocates survival to compliant subjectivities and rejects all 'problem individuals,' all those who embody another use of life and, in this way, resist the machine" (The Invisible Committee 2009, 51). If so, it's necessary for workers to adjust themselves to the system or risk being expelled by it. As Rose suggests, self-help discourses may be useful for just such a purpose. They do not require repressing selves, but rather *managing* selves through reflexive practices that align the expression of individual autonomy with capitalism. As is clear, Richmond's and Fox's discourses do just that. For both, the order of the day is productivity and accommodationism. When one has the demands of productivity chafe against the individual, the individual must accommodate productivity. As Zygmunt Bauman puts it, "Conspicuously missing from [such] visions of new dawns is a change in the landscape: it is only the [individual's] position . . . that is expected to be changed and—most certainly—'improved'" (Bauman 2007, 49). Where such discourses operate successfully, capitalism would not require a Protestant work ethic or Calvinist existential anxieties, as the ethic of this alternate ideology encourages hard work through other means. By aligning individual autonomy, fulfillment in career, and business, individuals are encouraged to desire for themselves precisely what the economic system desires of them.

Who consumes this ideology? It is most likely consumed by people who are already relatively successful in the business world. Working-class laborers are unlikely to be attracted to an ideology that presents their daily frustrations and experiences of domination as things to be accepted, accommodated, or perhaps even praised as the work of the world spirit. However, those among the successful petty bourgeoisie might very much like an ideology that presents success in the business world as something encouraged by all great religions or sources of ancient wisdom. Successful businessmen who are already working hard may profit from a characterization of their hard work as divine in nature. In addition, orientalist assumptions about the "mystic East" might even award men who read such books a small psychological compensation, social distinction, or exotic capital. The reflexive practices recommended might even work as promised in some cases, helping businessmen adapt to the small frustrations they experience on the road to their success. This ideology is far more likely the opiate of the bourgeoisie than the masses.

As should be clear, there is nothing particularly private or individual about this "spirituality." Richmond and Fox both hope to produce a transformation both of individuals and, through individuals, the workplace in general. Both authors claim a global jurisdiction for their ideologies, and a comprehensive scope over the behavior of individuals. They hope that individuals will reflexively transform themselves in ways that will matter beyond the moments of meditation; rather, they hope that the reflexive practices will transform individuals throughout the entire work day. There is nothing particularly gerrymandering about this ideology, as it recognizes no boundaries for what it identifies as spiritual practices—they are to reach through business like blood flows through the body. In summary, the dominant scholarly narratives about "individual religion" or the religion in the "private sphere" absolutely fail—once again—to capture what is going on in this case. The rhetoric of individual autonomy also fails. The ideologies proposed by Richmond and Fox are neither "freely" constructed nor "autonomous"; rather, they are the handmaidens of the regnant mode of production.

7

Individualism: A capital theodicy

Tell me, please, whether God is not the cause of evil.
AUGUSTINE, 1964, 33

The attribution of causation is often a deeply contested matter. For instance, who or what is responsible for crime? Individuals who commit crimes, or poverty? Sociologists might point to the latter, but our system of jurisprudence does not, at present, allow us to send poverty to prison—although we send many of the impoverished. By contrast, according to some forms of Christian ideology, individuals have "free will," and therefore, we should not attribute the causes of crime to poverty or—more importantly—to the Christians' god. In this chapter I argue that just as appeals to "free will" in Christian theodicy are designed to protect the gods, so does the ideology of individualism protect social and economic structures from criticism. *Individualism is capitalism's theodicy.* I draw examples from Karen Berg's *God Wears Lipstick: Kabbalah for Women* and Eckhart Tolle's *The Power of Now: A Guide to Spiritual Enlightenment* and demonstrate, through a close reading, that both books advance an individualist ideology that attributes the cause for all suffering to individuals alone.

"Individualism" as capital theodicy

The problem of theodicy asks: if God is all powerful and all good, why is there so much suffering in the world? Is God somehow the cause of this suffering? Should God bear responsibility for it? For many Christians, "free will" provides the solution to the problem of theodicy: although their god is understood to have created the world, he is nevertheless not to be held responsible for the creation of suffering or evil, as humans have a special faculty—given to them by their god—called "free will." "Free will" interrupts the causal chain between the creation of the world and the existence of evil, relinquishing God from responsibility. In his treatise on free will, Augustine asks whether the human will is self-causal or determined by a prior cause: "what cause of the will could there be, except the will itself? It is either the will itself . . .; or else it is not the will, and there is no sin" (Augustine 1964, 126). The stakes of the argument are clear: either the will has no prior cause, meaning that it is its own origin of a chain of cause and effect, or it is the result of a prior cause, meaning that it cannot be held responsible for its actions—that is, we could not hold individuals responsible for sin if their behavior was determined by external causes. "Free will" is the rhetorical move designed to save God from criticism: causal explanation for suffering should only regress back to human "free will," a miniature prime mover that partially escapes the causal field originated by the true prime mover.

While it is self-evident to social theorists that the actions of humans are determined by causal conditions that extend beyond the "individuals" to whom we often attribute the causes of actions, a wide variety of popular ideologies arbitrarily halt explanatory causal accounts at individuals, or their "choices" or "decisions." As Stephan Fuchs notes, "Decisions are not simply acts occurring in the world, but attributions to agency, to halt causal regresses" (Fuchs 2001, 9). In many everyday contexts, attributing causes to agents is necessary for the social world to function; for example, for a college to function, professors have to assign grades to individual students, rather than, say, to their parents. "In this light, 'decision' is a schema for assigning organizational responsibilities and allocating praise and blame" (128).

The task of social theory, however, is precisely to dissolve "individuals" and their "decisions" or "choices" into a social field. In his short treatise on the ideology of individualism, Steven Lukes writes,

[a] sociological perspective differs from the individualist picture in revealing all the manifold ways in which individuals are dependent on, indeed *constituted by*, the operation of social forces, by all the agencies of socialization and social control, by ecological, institutional and cultural factors, by influences ranging from the primary family group to the value system of society as a whole. (Lukes 1973b, 86)

And, he notes, individuals "always turn out on inspection to be social, and indeed historically specific. 'Human nature' always in reality belongs to a particular kind of social man" (75).

According to the Marxist tradition—and here I call upon some of its least controversial elements—the fate of the working class has little to do with the individual choices or decision of laborers. In "Branches of English Industry without Legal Limits to Exploitation," Marx recounts the industrial conditions in England in the latter half of the nineteenth century. He describes children—as young as six years old—required to work 12- to 15-hour days, sometimes 6 or 7 days a week. Many worked without protection with chemicals that brought illness or otherwise incapacitated them. One parent reported, "That boy of mine . . . when he was 7 years old I used to carry him on my back to and fro through the snow, and he used to have 16 hours a day . . . I have often knelt down to feed him as he stood by the machine, for he could not leave it or stop" (Marx 1990, 356–357). One report suggests that at one factory children worked for 10 ½ hours without a meal break (257).

For Marx, the causal explanation for what most would consider unenviable working conditions did not lie with the "choices" of the individual children described, nor with their parents. Rather, no doubt these children and their parents were likely faced with the lesser of two evils, so to speak, as these miserable working conditions were perhaps preferable to homelessness or starvation. For Marx, the causal explanation of their "choices" regresses beyond these individuals to the infrastructure in which they were situated—an infrastructure with, for instance, certain technical and industrial conditions, a surplus of cheap labor, the practice of capital investments in pursuit of profit, an established structure of competition, and so on. These individuals' "choices" are inexplicable if we look at them in isolation from the broader structural conditions. The infrastructure directs the behaviors of laborers in ways that they did not create and which are beyond their control:

> In the social production of their life, men enter into definite relations that are indispensable and independent of their will, relations of production that correspond to a definite stage of development of their material productive forces. The sum total of these relations of production constitutes the economic structure of society, the real foundation, on which rises a legal and political superstructure and to which correspond definite forms of social consciousness. The mode of production of material life conditions the social, political and intellectual life in general. It is not the consciousness of men that determines their being, but, on the contrary, their social being that determines their consciousness. (Marx and Engels 1978, 4)

Not only does the system direct the behavior of the laborers, but the elites as well. As Pierre Bourdieu writes:

> It is, in fact, the managers of the big institutions, the pension funds, the big insurance companies, and, particularly in the United States, the money market funds or mutual funds who totally dominate the field of financial

capital, within which financial capital is both stake and weapon. . . . [However,] they are compelled by the logic of the system they dominate to improve the pursuit of ever higher profits . . . . In short, because the dominant in this game are dominated by the rules of the game they dominate (the rule of profit), this field functions as a kind of infernal machine without subject, which imposes its will on both states and firms. (Bourdieu 2003, 28)

To return to the question of theodicy: capitalist ideology, like Christian theology, halts explanatory causal regresses at individual agents in order to explain (or explain away) the fact that people suffer in a capitalist system. There is perhaps no clearer example of this capital theodicy than Christian minister Russell H. Conwell's "Acres of Diamonds."[1] In this lecture (which was later published as a small book), all individuals have acres of diamonds in their own backyards, if only they make the effort to dig for them. "[T]he opportunity to get rich, to attain great wealth, is . . . within the reach of almost every man and woman who hears me speak tonight" (Conwell 1915, 17). In addition, Conwell insists that it is a Christian duty to become wealthy:

I say that you ought to get rich, and it is your duty to get rich. How many of my pious brethren say to me, . . . "Isn't that awful! Why don't you preach the gospel instead of preaching about man's making money?" "Because to make money honestly is to preach the gospel." (18)

Throughout the lecture Conwell points out that if one is not rich, it is due to insufficient effort. He gives the example of a shop owner who has not made much money; Conwell's response is that this is only because the owner is not working to get to know his customers and neighbors or to find out what they want or need. "If you cared you would be a rich man. . . . But you go through the world saying, 'No opportunity to get rich,' and there is the fault right at your own door" (29). What are we to make of the poor?

Some men say, "Don't you sympathize with the poor people?" Of course I do, or else I would not have been lecturing all these years. I won't give in but what I sympathize with the poor, but the number of poor who are to be sympathized with is very small. To sympathize with a man whom God has punished for his sins, thus to help him when God would still continue a just punishment, is to do wrong, no doubt about it, and we do that more than we help those who are deserving. While we should sympathize with God's poor—that is, those who cannot help themselves—let us remember that there is not a poor person in the United States who was not made poor by his own shortcomings, or by the shortcomings of someone else. It is all wrong to be poor, anyhow. (21)

Because people have opportunity and merit is rewarded, the responsibility for poverty is one's own. As one reporter put it in a sarcastic commentary, on this view "[t]he reason unemployment goes up and down is because of fluctuating levels of self-reliance. In the 1930s, tens of millions across the world were out of work because they all suddenly ceased to be self-reliant. . . . [W]e shouldn't be fooled into thinking the banking crash and recession made people unemployed" (Steel 2013). The ideological function of the myth of opportunity and meritocracy is to shift sentiments of sympathy and antipathy: the poor are not to be sympathized with, since their poverty is their own fault.[2]

It is clear that, were we armed with an alternate social theory, we could assign responsibility in alternate ways. Marx, for instance, would assign responsibility for economic inequality to an infrastructure, rather than to individuals within an infrastructure. If causal accounts attributing inequality to infrastructural causes stand up under academic scrutiny, then it is arguable that this capital theodicy benefits the wealthy on the one hand by mystifying the causes of wealth—thereby protecting the existing infrastructure from criticism—and on the other hand by excoriating the poor—thereby producing antipathy for them and sympathy for the wealthy.

God Wears Lipstick

Located within the self-help or spirituality genre, Karen Berg's *God Wears Lipstick: Kabbalah for Women* provides readers with a reinvention of kabbalah that advances an individualist ideology that suggests women are entirely responsible for their own suffering. In addition, much like the work of Richmond and Fox, the form of kabbalah presented in the book promises to help women in late capitalism accommodate themselves to the so-called daily grind, "in restaurants and stores, at school or on the street, at home or at work" (Berg 2005, 209), so that they may lead "productive lives" (261).

The book begins by naturalizing consumer desire. In the introduction, Berg claims that pleasure "is the purpose of our existence here on earth" (14). The first chapter, titled "We Have Desires," explores what might pleasure women. What might make a woman happy are all the relationships and accoutrements of a petty bourgeois consumer lifestyle:

> All of us want to be happy. And in truth, most of us really want the same things out of life: We want to love and be loved; we want to have satisfying relationships; we want to enjoy financial security; we want full bellies and slim waistlines; we want our children to be safe.

We want success, we want to eat chocolate, we want to party, we want to sit and contemplate, we want sex, we want companionship, we want safety, we want babies, we want a great new novel to read, we want the perfect lipstick, we want a good man who is our soulmate, . . . we want those diamond earrings and Jimmy Choo shoes, we want to share, we want to love. (19)

However, women do not always find their desires fulfilled, and *God Wears Lipstick* is designed to teach them *how* to actualize their potential. The key to fulfillment requires understanding the origin and nature of the universe. "In fact, the whole purpose of the study of Kabbalah is to enlighten you about these nonphysical laws [of the universe] for the sake of your receiving fulfillment" (20). Consequently, the first half of the book focuses on the nature of reality and women's place in the cosmos as a whole.

According to Berg, God is an infinite force that existed before our universe began. This force, which she refers to as "The Light," wanted to give itself, but had nothing or no one to whom it could give. "The Light is pure sharing, but it needed something on which to bestow its beneficence" (24). The Light made a "Vessel" to receive the Light's power, and "for a while, there was complete harmony" (25). Unfortunately, the Vessel itself decided that it wanted to give rather than merely receive. The Vessel, however, could not give to the Light, as the Light itself was pure giving and could not receive (27). The Vessel attempted to resist the Light's giving (by somehow restricting itself [29]), but the Light gave to the Vessel anyway, thereby shattering the Vessel. That moment was apparently the big bang, and it created the universe "as we know it today" (29). From this quasi-pantheist cosmology it follows that we are all a part of God; as such, when a woman wears lipstick, God wears lipstick—hence the title.[3]

Berg insists on a strictly heteronormative homology between these forces and men and women. The Light is to man as the Vessel is to women. Men give; women receive, but also want to give. "These two parallel systems are represented by the egg and the sperm, the egg being a Vessel. The egg is the home where the sperm can grow and develop" (37). Heterosexuality is therefore presented as normative and built into the nature of the universe. Homosexuality does not seem to be possible in her cosmology except as a violation of nature; it is no surprise that homosexuality is never discussed or even raised as a possibility. Also homologous are soul and body; the soul is to man as the body is to woman. A number of consequences related to petty bourgeois life follow from women's closeness to bodies: "No wonder we have a need for massages, manicured nails, hairstyles, and lovely clothes. None of this is negative. One of the elements that determines how much Light you can receive is the quality of your Vessel, so as a woman, you have a need to beautify that Vessel" (38).

To further explore male–female relations, Berg makes an analogy between a woman and a light bulb (41ff). She points out that light bulbs receive energy; however, if energy simply passed through the filament without resistance, no light would be created. The resistance of the filament to the energy passing through it is what creates the light. This is a metaphor for male–female relations, as women must manage the energy of masculine forces in order to receive what they want—thereby satisfying their desires and fulfilling their potential—and in order to produce light of their own—as Vessels both want to receive and to give. It is clear that women cannot fulfill themselves without a relationship to this male power, and that fulfillment comes from receiving from this power *and* simultaneously giving back to it. In addition, the resistance of the filament that creates the Light is precisely the resistance of women to offer any negative responses to men (arguably, this rhetorically twists the meaning of "resistance"). "You generate Light when you 'restrict,' or hold back, your habitual negative, selfish restrictions and allow your proactive, sharing nature to emerge" (112).

Somewhat contradictorily, Berg also suggests that woman must *first* give to the man in order to receive something from him: "I want something, so first I have to give" (50). And it is on this point that the emphasis on individual responsibility starts to become a key theme of the book. Women must be proactive, and "[b]eing proactive means taking responsibility rather than living in a victim mentality and endlessly complaining that the world doesn't treat you right" (52–53). Victims blame men; proactive women—by contrast—can achieve fulfillment apparently through accommodating their husbands:

Imagine, for example, that you come home from work after a tough day, hungry and tired. The kids are crying for attention, and your husband is as exhausted as you are. His socks and underwear clutter the bedroom floor, and toys are strewn throughout the kitchen. The mail is piling up. The pot is boiling over in more ways than one.

. . . So you want a peaceful household when you come home? . . . If you don't have expectations that someone else will solve the problem—if you take responsibility for it and become proactive rather than reactive—you'll find 150 creative ways to make your life better. Maybe you'll bring in a nanny from 5 to 7 each evening to cook dinner and ease your transition. Or you'll eat out or call in Chinese food twice a week. Or you'll ask a neighbor to help out or hire a babysitter and take a breather with your honey. (53–54)

It is clear from this passage that Berg assumes a middle-class context, and from this passage it seems a rather wealthy middle-class family, if they can afford a part-time nanny. What is central here, however, is that the key to women's self-fulfillment is in personally taking responsibility for the frustrations of her family. To complain about it or expect others to take care of these frustrations would be to have a "victim mentality" (53).

For Berg, "[t]he moment you take responsibility, you realize that you've created a new reality. You can take control; you can change your life" (54). If these women have not yet done so, they have only themselves to blame. "We are the only ones who limit ourselves" (55). If women are not actualizing their potential, it is because they—as a filament to the male powers of the world—are not reacting to men in the proper way. By taking responsibility for their response to the Light around them they can correct for their failures and maximize their potential. As Vessels want to both receive from and give to the Light, women will be truly fulfilled only if they are giving. This means that women must always accommodate men, rather than the other way around: "A man can say, 'I go to work every day. That's what I know.' But a woman must adapt to a multifaceted lifestyle. We have to juggle because we must create some kind of balance between sharing and receiving" (59). In summary, "Women are endowed with a special responsibility. We are here to help our men" (83). And helping men is what will make women happy: "Where does [fulfillment] come from? Unconditional sharing" (145).

Women are encouraged to respond to men perfectly, to find a perfect balance between the female power and the male power. That perfect balance is the only way that women can be completely actualized or fulfilled (89). However, perfection is unlikely to happen in a single lifetime. As such, women will be continually reincarnated until such perfection is achieved. "Kabbalah teaches that our souls reincarnate time and time again until the job is done" (89). Berg claims that reincarnation cannot be forced on a woman; if she is reincarnated it is necessarily because of that woman's individual choice (90). Why choose a particular incarnation? "[I]n order to assist the male aspect" (91). She raises the apparently contradictory fact that some women never get married; Berg insists this because sometimes souls miss each other; they "do not necessarily come down to this planet at the same time, which is why there can be great age differences when they reunite" (91).

According to Berg, the challenges that a woman faces are always lessons from her god, designed to help her correct for prior errors—either from the present life or from former lives. "Most of us come into this world with at least some baggage from our previous lifetimes" (153). As such, challenges are always to be seen as opportunities for reflecting on oneself, one's negative energy, and—through effort—transformation from negative reaction to positive sharing with the male power. "To become a truly fulfilled person, be prepared to undergo every kind of trial. Without the pressure, the fight, the work, it is impossible to transform yourself" (120). And, as always, the responsibility for transformation and any failure to achieve fulfillment lies strictly with the individual woman in question. If a woman's man is difficult to live with—perhaps he is "messing around with other women" (133)—this is what Berg's god intended. "If the creator made someone a certain way, He did so in order to give that person an opportunity to change" (134). With respect to such frustrations, it is fundamental to remember that "there is something in *you* that needs to change" (emphasis original; 155). Women cannot expect their man to change. "What matters is that you take sole responsibility for stopping the conflict" (161). Indeed, the conflict was likely the woman's fault in the first place, because of prior bad karma. Men want to give, and women must receive without negatively reacting; if there is conflict in a relationship it is probably because the woman is not receiving properly. To fix the relationship, a woman must alter her response to him, thereby more properly drawing out the Light within him. "He contains a spark of the Creator . . . , and your genuine act of sharing will touch him, causing the situation to inevitably soften and allowing for the light to emerge" (161).

Berg goes so far as to say that a man cannot harm a woman:[4]

No one has harmed you, nor can they ever harm you. Everything is a reminder to let go and trust God. Other people never truly hurt you; you hurt yourself by disconnecting from the Life Force. Everything negative in our lives is designed to help us remember this fact. (187)

Because the "ever-present energy of the Creator is yours to tap into anytime you wish," failure to do so lies with you rather than the universe; "You need only go inside yourself and draw it out" (164). Once women learn all the lessons Berg's god is sending them, they will achieve a perfect balance and therefore perfect fulfillment. At that point, having "completed its process," the soul will "return to the Creator" (178).

Berg provides us with an answer to the problem of suffering in the world, at least regarding women's suffering. A woman suffers because of something she has done wrong and about which the Light wants to teach her a lesson. As such, the frustrations of a middle-class heterosexual marriage are to be welcomed as opportunities for women to reflect on themselves, to look within to find what part of themselves needs to be changed. Once women react positively rather than negatively to the individuals around them, they will—like a light bulb—draw on the positive energy freely available to all who know how to tap into it. This, then, is the mechanism for fulfillment. The details of the mechanism are unclear—essentially it is magical—but women who react positively to the world will draw positive energy to themselves, and with it will come the accoutrements of middle-class wealth: success, chocolate, sex, the perfect lipstick, diamond earrings, and Jimmy Choo shoes. If women do not have these things, it is their own fault.

As I noted in Chapter 2, Luckmann argued that with the division of labor and segmentation of society, individuals will have more freedom to experiment with their inherited cultural traditions. However, the experimentation is not haphazard; "it is more likely that individuals will legitimate the situation-bound (primarily emotional and affective) priorities arising in their 'private spheres' by deriving, *ad hoc*, more or less appropriate rhetorical elements from the sacred cosmos" (Luckmann 1967, 105). Their creations "will consist of a loose and rather unstable hierarchy of 'opinions' legitimating the affectively determined priorities of 'private' life" (105). It seems that this is precisely what Berg has done; she has cobbled together cultural elements—which she claims originated with Abraham—in order to legitimate a rather sexist petty bourgeois lifestyle. In addition, she has done so in a way that self-servingly justifies her material success; if she and her husband are wealthy it is because they personally deserve it, as she has mastered her reaction to the energy of the cosmos.

For those women who cannot afford a nanny or Chinese take-out twice a week, it is because they, as individuals, have not learned the lessons the Light is sending their way. Berg's recommendation to them? Stop their victim mentality and change themselves. They can draw as much wealth and success as they want—an infinite amount, apparently—if only they change their negative reaction to others. To achieve success perhaps women should find a man and accommodate him in all respects.[5]

The economic structures of our world, despite their apparent relevance to the production and distribution of wealth in capitalist society, have nothing to do with an individual's success on Berg's account. Women's wealth and ability to consume are based entirely on their own individual karma. As such, the economic structures are unchallenged. This ideology fundamentally mystifies the relationship between individuals and the mode of production just as thoroughly as did Conwell's "Acres of Diamonds," and it discourages readers from sympathizing with the poor.

The Power of Now

Much like Berg's book, Eckhart Tolle's very popular *The Power of Now: A Guide to Spiritual Enlightenment* advances an individualist ideology that places the responsibility for all suffering on the individual alone. In addition, much like Moore, Abdel-Fattah, and Fox, Tolle presents his message as a universal truth found in all ancient and authoritative religious traditions. According to Tolle, all great spiritual traditions teach that relief from suffering is available to everyone, if only individuals transform their consciousness;

rather than focus on the past and the present, one must inhabit the "now" moment.

Tolle begins the first chapter with a story that is remarkably similar to the one that began "Acres of Diamonds." "A beggar had been sitting by the side of the road for over thirty years," when a stranger points out to him that he'd been unknowingly sitting on a box filled with gold (Tolle 1999, 11). Like the beggar, we are all sitting on boxes filled with gold, and Tolle's book will tell us how to access it.

Tolle develops a cosmology reminiscent of the Upanishads: there is a force, which he calls Being, that pervades the universe (he also calls this Being "the Unmanifested"). He would rather not call it "God" because of the traditional associations that are hung on that concept, which makes this Being seem finite, when in fact it is infinite (14). We are made up of this Being and could become conscious of it at any time—which would end our suffering—but our mind and our thoughts get in the way. He instructs individuals to exercise a form of awareness meditation; rather than think about one's self, the present, or the future, one should attempt to become aware of one's body and consciousness in the present moment. Such awareness should be detached and nonjudgmental: "don't analyze; just watch" (27). Drawing on some themes derived from the Buddhist tradition, he recommends detachment, dissolving the ego, and letting go of desires, as these things get in the way of consciousness of Being in the now moment.

Tolle teaches that pain is produced from wrongful thinking, such as individual attachments, frustrated desires, regretting the past, and worry about the future. "All problems are illusions of the mind" (64), whether we are talking about paying the bills or even death (71). As such, individuals are responsible for their own pain, which is self-created:

> The pain that you create now is always some form of nonacceptance, some form of unconscious resistance to what *is*. On the level of thought, the resistance is some form of judgment. On the emotional level, it is some form of negativity. (33)

In order to reverse this state of affairs, one must meditate with detached awareness on the present moment: "it is impossible to have a problem when your attention is fully in the Now" (64). In addition, "[o]nly *you* can do this. Nobody can do it *for* you" (42).

Tolle's individualism is starkly conspicuous when he considers the possibility of a woman in a "physically abusive" relationship with her partner (226). Similar to Berg's ideology, Tolle insists that she has chosen this partner, presumably on the basis of "mental-emotional patterns" (227). As such, she is the cause of her own suffering. "Of course her situation is self-created" (227).

It appears that not only psychological pain but also bodily pain is in part linked to the inability to become conscious of the Unmanifested within oneself. Tolle makes the bold claim that when one becomes conscious of Being, one's body will no longer age (123). In addition:

> Another benefit of this practice in the physical realm is a great strengthening of the immune system, which occurs when you inhabit the body. The more consciousness you bring into the body, the stronger the immune system becomes. It is as if every cell awakens and rejoices. . . . It is also a potent form of self-healing. Most illnesses creep in when you are not present in the body. (123–124)

As such, individuals are responsible not only for psychological suffering but also much of their bodily suffering—such suffering would cease if only the individual would become properly conscious.

Like Richmond and Fox, Tolle employs an inward/outward distinction, coupled with the miracle motif, according to which all social or outward transformation begins with the individual: "If you get the inside right, the outside will fall into place. Primary reality is within, secondary reality without" (77). "True change happens within, not without" (203). In order to change the outer one must begin by changing the inner—and again, that can only be done by the individual alone. "When you reconnect with Being . . . you cease to create [collective evils]" (181). Tolle insists that all forms of what he calls evil are caused by individuals not being properly aware of Being. When we identify with our ego or with the collective groups we are a part of rather than Being, that is "collective insanity" (110). This collective insanity leads to "the fear, the despair, the greed, and the violence that are all-pervasive" in our society (110), as well as "war, genocide, and exploitation" (181). However, individuals *should not condemn* such things:

> See the heinous cruelty and suffering on an unimaginable scale that humans have inflicted and continue to inflict on each other as well as on other life forms on the planet. You don't need to condemn. Just observe. That is sin. That is insanity. That is unconsciousness. Above all, don't forget to observe your own mind. Seek out the root of insanity there. (110)

No collective solutions are recommended, only individual ones—the only thing one can do is root out the unconsciousness in one's own self and then, if one succeeds, lead others in the same (see also 201, 204).

Near the end of the book, he raises the question of compassion for the suffering of others, but reinforces the claim that their suffering is an illusion. Here he suggests that others' suffering is not the *result* of an illusion, it *is* an illusion:

> when confronted with someone else's suffering or unconscious behavior, you stay present and in touch with Being . . . At the level of Being, all suffering is recognized as an illusion. Suffering is due to identification with form. Miracles of healing sometimes occur through this realization, by awakening Being-consciousness in others—if they are ready. (196)

However, Tolle qualifies this in two ways. On the one hand, this sort of compassion is unlikely for most of us, as it "requires a high degree of consciousness" (197), which most of us will not achieve. Secondly, he goes on to say that were we to achieve consciousness fully, empathy with another would be empathy with Being itself, and as such it would be an experience of joy. "True compassion goes beyond empathy or sympathy. It does not happen until sadness merges with joy, the joy of Being beyond form, the joy of eternal life" (197). Thus it seems that most of us are not capable of compassion yet—in the mean time we should focus on ourselves—and that if we were able to achieve it, it will be a joyful event: the suffering of others will provide us joy. Notably, this stretches the use of the word "compassion" far beyond its ordinary use.

In addition to the fact that suffering is an illusion, Tolle also claims that when we see "a world of death and bodies fighting, killing, and devouring each other" (199), that is only because of our individual belief. We project our belief onto the world, and the world mirrors our projection. If we as individuals free ourselves from our delusions, we "will literally inhabit a new world" (200), presumably one no longer filled with killing and fighting but only Being. Like with compassion for suffering, perhaps what we first saw as fighting and killing will turn into an opportunity for us to experience joy. Because there is, from the perspective of Being, no suffering in the world, there is nothing in the world to change. This point is driven home: "Your primary task is not to seek salvation through creating a better world, but to awaken out of identification with form" (201).

Transformation can happen to anyone, independently of an individual's social context or social location, "no matter who or where you are" (8). In addition, consciousness doesn't happen apart from everyday life in a capitalist society; as with Richmond and Fox, it happens *within* this context. "[E]ven here, within the sphere of practical living, . . . the present moment remains the essential factor" (57). The usual "outer" purposes affiliated with petty bourgeois life are legitimate pastimes, as long one does not become attached to them. If one approaches daily life with detachment, focusing on the now, "the outer purpose is just a game that you may continue to play simply because you enjoy it" (89). Individuals are expected to go about their jobs (213) and to maintain their interpersonal, familial, and intimate relationships (147ff), and so on. "You can still be active and enjoy manifesting and creating new forms and circumstances" in "your life situation" (184).

In addition, like Berg, Tolle is both sexist and heterosexist. He claims that women are more bodily and as such enlightenment is easier for them (164).[6] In addition, Tolle employs a heteronormative dualism, according to which women and men are incomplete without one another:

> On the physical level, you are obviously not whole, nor will you ever be: You are either a man or a woman, which is to say, one-half of the whole. On this level, the longing for wholeness—the return to oneness—manifests as male-female attraction, man's need for a woman, woman's need for a man. (150)[7]

Tolle therefore presents us with a spirituality that will not upset daily middle-class life in a heteronormative capitalist society, but will help individuals accommodate themselves to it. We will continue to work, continue our heterosexual relationships, and so on. Those things he classifies as "outer" will not change, and nor should they. Indeed, consciousness of Being *requires* us to accept our partners as they are rather than attempt any structural or relationship changes (154). When one's partner is not fully conscious, one must "relinquish judgment" and be "totally free of reaction" (160).

Like Berg, frustrations in life are necessarily good rather than bad. Undesirable social conditions do not exist: "conditions *are* always positive" (178), and those ones that *seem* negative to the mind or the ego are merely opportunities for working on consciousness. "Even a brief illness or an accident can show you what is real and unreal in your life, what ultimately matters and what doesn't" (178). As such, suffering is always redemptive: "The ultimate effect of all the evil and suffering in the world is that it will force humans into realizing who they are . . . . Thus what we perceive as evil from our limited perspective is actually part of the higher good that has no opposite" (179–180). Difficulties we face are there to send us a "message" (191).

As far as problems at work go, Tolle is an accommodationist. When we face undesirable circumstances at work that we cannot change, our choice is between resisting and surrendering, and Tolle makes it clear that to surrender is the best option—resistance only leads to more illusions and suffering. "[Y]ou have two choices . . .: resistance or surrender. Bondage or inner freedom from external conditions. Suffering or inner peace" (213). Much like the inward freedom recommended by Moore's Jesus, Tolle suggests that "if you cannot accept what is outside, then accept what is *inside*. If you cannot accept the external condition, accept the internal condition. This means: *Do not resist the pain*" (emphasis mine; 221).

Like Moore, Abdel-Fattah, and Fox, Tolle presents his teaching as a single universal truth found in all religions. "All spiritual teachings originate from the same source" (115)—the Being within. Consequently:

> When I occasionally quote the words of Jesus or the Buddha, . . . I do so not in order to compare, but to draw your attention to the fact that in *essence* there is and always has been only one spiritual teaching, although it comes in many forms. Some of these forms, such as the ancient religions, have become so overlaid with extraneous matter that their spiritual essence has become almost completely obscured by it. (9)

Because the essence is often obscured, Tolle will "reveal" the "deeper meaning" of these traditions for the reader (9–10). Throughout, the reader finds references to Jesus, the Buddha, Zen, Hinduism, the Bhagavad Gita, Taoism, and so on. As with all the other writers covered earlier, this is designed to legitimate Tolle's claims—if all great religions teach this, how can it be wrong?

In summary, Tolle's book claims the following: suffering is caused by wrongful states of mind; the social world can never cause suffering; the solution to suffering involves transforming consciousness; once enlightened we can and should go about our daily work life and enjoy it from an enlightened perspective; the suffering of others does not require transformation of the social world; instead, other individuals need to transform their consciousness and surrender to the existing social conditions.

The mode of production, it turns out, can in principle have nothing to do with an individual's suffering. As with the doctrine of "free will," Tolle's causal regress—designed to account for suffering—stops where it begins: with the individual. Both the gods and the economic system are thereby protected from criticism. Tolle's ideology is a perfect capitalist theodicy, and one that also discourages readers from sympathizing with the poor. Not only do the poor create their own suffering with wrong consciousness, but, in addition, if we transform our own consciousness, we'll no longer see their suffering as suffering—"suffering" will become just "Being."

Conclusion

To twist the epigraph from Augustine's work on theodicy, "Tell me, please, whether an economic system can be the cause of suffering?" The answers provided by Berg and Tolle are clear: a priori, a social structure—explicitly including patriarchy and implicitly even slavery—cannot cause suffering. While Marx claimed that "In the social production of their life, men enter into definite relations that are indispensable and independent of their will," for Berg or Tolle the child laborers described in *Capital* suffer not because of the mode of production in industrial capitalism but because Berg's god is trying to teach them a lesson—perhaps because of something they did in a prior life—or because they don't have a proper consciousness of Tolle's Being. Berg and Tolle's individualism is, at bottom, little different from Conwell's in "Acres of Diamonds." And, as with Conwell, their ideology prevents us from seeing how social structures are constitutive of individuals and thereby protects such structures from criticism. Individualism is the theodicy of capitalism.

Despite the dominant scholarly narrative about individual spirituality, there is nothing "autonomous" about the ideology Berg and Tolle propose. While they may have appropriated various elements from the cultural traditions available to them in ways that suit their present purposes, they have done so in a way that functions—unintentionally, to be sure—to legitimate a certain relationship between individuals and the relations of production in a capitalist context. Despite their insistence that their teachings are both ancient and universal, they are saturated with concerns that appear to be specific to white collar workers and consumers in a capitalist system. In addition, there's nothing "private" about their ideology; Berg and Tolle propose a set of reflexive practices intended to transform not a private self, but, indirectly, a public world as well. They hope their ideology will have a comprehensive behavioral transformation, one that will transform individuals not only when meditating but also when dealing with family, career, and consumption. Last, Berg naturalizes consumer desire while her antistructuralism blocks any consideration of why we might have some desires rather than others. In summary, the traditional scholarly narrative about "spirituality" being private, individual, and autonomous fails yet again.

Afterword: Things at the disposal of society

I have argued that the opiate of the bourgeoisie encourages middle- and upper-middle-class workers to accommodate themselves to consumer life in late capitalism in four ways. First, through quietism: "religion" or "spirituality is presented as properly involving the enjoyment of one's life in ways that must not upset the state, the economy, or the empire, which take precedence over any "autonomy" afforded to individuals. Second, through consumerism: individual freedom of choice is sacralized, such that the pursuit of distinction via the consumption and display of consumer goods is naturalized or seen as divinely ordained. Third, through increased productivity: through the deft application of reflexive "spiritual" practices, labor can become the means by which one achieves not only material success but also personal or spiritual fulfillment; individual aspirations are aligned with corporate goals, and the individual is encouraged to adjust him or herself to the latter when conflicts arise. Fourth, through the assignment of responsibility to the individual: because individuals are presented as already having the resources for material, economic, or psychological success at hand, failure or suffering is assigned to individuals alone, never the social structure. The opiate of the bourgeoisie functions to ease chafing between the social structure and its inhabitants—primarily by encouraging the latter to accommodate themselves to the former—and perhaps eases suffering by providing reflexive practices that do in fact help individuals psychologically adjust to life in late capitalism. However, this ideology simultaneously obscures the constitutive role of social structures in the creation of individuals and their desires, as well as the structural causes of individual suffering.

Contrary to the dominant narrative in religious studies, according to which those forms of culture identified as "individual religion" or "spirituality" are becoming more individual, private, and autonomous, the evidence considered here points in the opposite direction. It is clear that individuals are picking and choosing from the cultural repertoires available to them in order to cobble together something personally meaningful on an ad hoc basis. However, Moore's text claims not a private but a global gerrymandering reach, presuming to delineate the universally proper relationship between "religion" and the forces of empire—and ceding most power to the latter. The ideologies of Moore, Abdel-Fattah, Fox, Berg, and Tolle claim not a private reach but rather a universal one, as their inventions are presented as the universal truth of all great teachings or, in Berg's case, the truth of the cosmos as a whole. Moore, Richmond, Fox, Berg, and Tolle proffer an ideology designed not to affect individuals in their so-called private lives alone; rather, their ideology and associated reflexive practices are designed to alter the life of the individual in all spheres of life, specifically including work life. In addition, in every case, the ideology of the authors discussed here made sense only against the horizon of capitalism, and every one of them provided a legitimation of some sort for capitalism—a legitimation for empire, consumerism, increased productivity, or the assignment of the causes of all forms of suffering to individuals rather than the social structure. Insofar as the cultural forms produced are startlingly uniform in many respects and conform to a type that fits so well in a capitalist social structure, there doesn't appear to be anything particularly "autonomous" about them. Individuals once again "turn out on inspection to be social, and indeed historically specific" (Lukes 1973b, 75).

According to Luckmann, a modern capitalist society with a high division of labor does not need a universal legitimation; for Luckmann, each organ of society has its own ideology, but there is no universal "sacred canopy" to legitimate the coordination of spheres or to legitimate the whole. All ideologies operate not from "above" the social system but "within" their own, individual jurisdiction (Luckmann 1967, 101). "The effective social basis of the modern sacred cosmos is to be found neither in the churches nor the state nor the economic system" (103). But it is possible, however, that the ideology of individualism *is* capitalism's "sacred canopy." Luckmann predicted that individuals would cobble together umbrellas rather than sacred canopies, designed to legitimate their situation-bound life circumstances; he was only half right: individuals do cobble together forms of culture to legitimate their situation-bound life circumstances, but they often present these ideologies not as individual umbrellas but as having a global reach. Arguably, the ideology of individualism that consistently manifests itself in their discourses does in fact have a near universal reach in modern capitalist societies. If the ideology of individualism is capitalism's sacred canopy, "individual religion" or "spirituality" is not autonomous, but rather capitalism's handmaiden.

In the "Introduction," I suggested that many of those forms of culture scholars identify as "individual religion" or "spirituality" collectively constitute individuals while simultaneously masking the extent to which "individuals" are collectively constituted, while specifically constituting them as subjects of capitalism. The opiate of the bourgeoisie appears to constitute subjects as quietist, as consumerist, as productive laborers, and as individuals willing to take responsibility for their own suffering. In *The Division of Labor in Society*, Durkheim wrote that "In societies where [mechanical] solidarity is highly developed the individual . . . does not belong to himself; he is literally a thing at the disposal of society" (85). By contrast, I would suggest that within industrialized society, subjects interpellated by the opiate of the bourgeoisie are literally things at the disposal of society, a thought that, if true—and depending on one's sympathies—might be disconcerting.

* * *

For Foucault, in *Discipline and Punish* (1977), a grid of classification—like an elementary school report card—is an application of power that permits action on a subject, perhaps making her a subject of disciplinary practices that nudge the subject toward conformity with an ideal posited within the grid at hand. The attribution of agency is a fiction that works in precisely the same way: attributing agency to a subject or a social structure permits operation on the agent identified as having causal power.

Consider a mechanic working on a broken motor. She knows that none of the parts have agency or free will, yet she might claim that one particular part is the "cause" of the malfunction. Attributing agency to that part—the one that's "causing" the problem—will permit her to work on the motor in such a way as to bring about a desired result. The attribution of agency in society works similarly. All social phenomena, for example, gun deaths, have a wide variety of necessary yet insufficient conditions; however, depending on where in particular one wants to operate on those conditions, one may attribute the "cause" of the phenomena to one necessary condition over another, for example, to subjects who pull triggers, or to the lack of structural impediments to the procurement of firearms. Identifying the "cause" allows an operation of power, and which cause is identified depends largely on the desired result of those making the identification.

Identifying the cause of my father's failures and depression in him alone would permit one type of operation of power. Specifically, it would encourage him as an individual to take on responsibility for his failures and to reflexively work on himself and accommodate himself to the social structure in which he was placed—which is precisely what he did, through the consumption, for instance, of self-help literature. Alternately identifying the cause of my father's suffering in the capitalist system that structurally rendered him a disposable laborer might permit, by contrast, an operation of power on the social structure itself.

The attribution of agency to either individuals or to social structures is therefore a fiction made possible by whichever grid of classification one employs. The choice of one over the other is never neutral, since the operation of power on the "causes" identified necessarily advances or retards specific agendas and interests. As Foucault suggests in "*Society Must Be Defended*," "Knowledge is never anything more than a weapon in a war, or a tactical deployment within that war" (2003, 173). If, in this book, I largely prefer to identify the causes of various phenomena in social structures or discourses rather than free individuals, this is not because social structures or discourses have a magical agency or escape chains of cause and effect—a social structure is not an unmoved mover—but because halting our causal regress at the social structure permits an operation of power that conforms to my sympathies. Of course, sympathies do not autonomously spring from deep within the self, but rather social circumstances; my sympathies no doubt derive in part from watching my father become a casualty of this war. The key question at the end is, perhaps, not "what is the cause?" but rather "whose interests are advanced by assigning causation in this way rather than that way?" Do we want to operate on those things at the disposal of society—or, perhaps, make them work on themselves—or do we want to operate on the social structure itself?

Notes

Chapter 1

1 On this point, see also Jennifer M. Lehmann's *Deconstructing Durkheim*, especially the chapter on "The social determination of 'individuals'" (Lehmann 1993).

2 Timothy Melley provides a brilliant analysis of these competing views of subjectivity in the introduction and first chapter of *Empire of Conspiracy: The Culture of Paranoia in Postwar America* (2000).

3 On individualism, see also Lukes' important book, *Individualism* (1973b) and Foucault's *Security, Territory, Population* (2007) and *The Birth of Biopower* (2008). Norbert Elias provides a valuable if dated analysis of how individualism is a product of the modern division of labor in *The Civilizing Process* (1994). For more on Althusser and Foucault and how power is constitutive of subjectivity, see Butler's *The Psychic Life of Power* (1997), especially chapters 3 and 4. Therborn provides a useful elaboration on Althusser's idea of the interpellation of subjectivity in *The Ideology of Power and the Power of Ideology* (Therborn 1980).

4 Lehmann draws attention to this tension better than anyone else in the secondary literature (see Lehmann 1993, especially 103ff), but doesn't draw the connections to Durkheim's European ethnocentrism.

5 See also Lehmann (1993, 80).

6 Lehmann explains how a plurality of social forces entails limits on any individual social force, in a manner not dissimilar from Althusser's concept of overdetermination: "This is another way of introducing the notion of complexity as the distinct property of social causality. Each social force encounters a multitude of individuals. It is able to 'have its way' with some of these individuals and not with others. Conversely, each person is subject to a multitude of forces. Some of these 'have their way,' and others do not" (Lehmann 1993, 62). As such, "No single force has the power of a determinant. But action is not thereby delivered over to freedom and spontaneity. It is complexly determined" (62).

7 Susan Stedman Jones' book, *Durkheim Reconsidered*, attempts to defend this problematic voluntarist or "spiritualist" side of Durkheim's thought against commentators, like Lehmann, who interpret Durkheim as a thoroughgoing determinist. Rejecting Althusserian and Foucauldian determinism, Jones writes, "Whilst Althusser's social formations are deterministic, Durkheim's conception of determinate law and structural causality is compatible with agency and freedom of will" (2001, 13). Jones does not, however, note how this side of Durkheim is tied to his ethnocentrism.

8 Ivan Strenski has a useful discussion of Durkheim's depiction of the individual as "sacred" in *The New Durkheim* (2006, see especially 21ff).

9 I should make it clear that in criticizing Durkheim my purpose is not to flatten all differences between kinship societies and capitalist societies, out of some warm-hearted, liberal relativism. On the contrary, it seems clear to me that some social conditions might be preferable to others. But I am unpersuaded that such preferences are best determined by attempting to judge relative degrees of freedom from constraint in a society.

10 James G. Crossley provides an interesting analysis of the communalism vs. individualism trope in studies of Christian origins; see Crossley (2008, 101–142).

11 By contrast, Heelas suggests—rather oddly—that we should just take insiders at their word. See Heelas (2008, 93ff).

12 This is not to say that individuals are determined in a straightforward manner. Individuals are socialized or conditioned by competing social institutions, and conditioning is likely never complete but a set of ongoing processes (see Elias 2001, 30). For this reason any particular individual's behavior may be determined yet nevertheless unpredictable. Consequently, when there are apparent tensions between individuals and society, "they are not tensions between the non-social, natural needs of the 'individual' and the unnatural demands of a 'society' outside him" (145), but rather tensions between internalized social norms and those norms that have not been internalized—these tensions "are actually the product of discrepancies within societies" (145).

Chapter 2

1 It appears that the only mainstream sociologist of religion familiar with this body of scholarship is James Beckford (2003), whose work I will discuss later. Bryan S. Turner (2011) offers a nod to a consideration of the question, and uses "religion" in scare quotes a few times, but his treatment of the matter depends on outdated and superficial scholarship from the 1960s and 1970s about whether Buddhism is really a religion—following which discussion he goes right back to using "the sacred" in an unreflective manner. While the work of Stark, Finke, and Iannaccone on religious markets, religious goods, religious capital, and so on (e.g., Iannoccone 1990, Iannaccone et al. 1997, Stark and Finke 2000) might seem obviously relevant to the concerns of this book, they assume from the outset that "religion" is a unique type of culture and insufficiently theorize what makes "religious" culture different from other forms of culture; as such their work is extremely weak—and usually uncritically empiricist—on what I consider one of the most crucial questions. In addition, despite the fact that Stark and Finke deny being rational choice theorists (see Stark and Finke 2000, 41), they fail to historicize "choice" or "individualism" in the same way that RCT does.

2 See Warner (2010) for a good survey of this account, especially chapters 2 and 4.

3 I suspect that we are unlikely to see an isomorphic organization in a society with a large scope; if Durkheim is right, large-scale societies *require* a complex organization and division of labor for their maintenance—with increasing urban density—from which would follow a proliferation of ideologies.

4 Winnifred Fallers Sullivan makes practically the same argument, using more recent evidence, in *The Impossibility of Religious Freedom* (see Sullivan 2005).

5 It is interesting that the sorts of conclusions reached by scholars often perceived as "radical," such as Russell McCutcheon or Tim Fitzgerald, have also been reached by what are fairly traditional social theorists.

6 Marshall Sahlins provides a similar analysis of consumption in his work on "bourgeois totemism" in *Culture and Practical Reason* (Sahlins 1976). In *Modernity and Self-Identity* (1991), Anthony Giddens has an interesting discussion of how individuals use consumer products to fashion an individual identity in late modernity, although his discussion is less critical.

Chapter 3

1 For an account of how these distinctions were put to use in liberal discourses following the Protestant Reformation, see Martin (2010), especially chapters 2 and 3. See Klippenstein (2005) and Wood (2007) for an account of how the use of these and related terms by scholars of the so-called New Age movement, as well as the characterization of this movement as "individualist," can stall critical analysis.

2 There is of course one exception: the author of this post associates *individual* interpretations of Muhammad with the second, derivative set of associations, presumably because some individuals interpret Muhammad's message or experience inauthentically.

3 Tim Murphy has a similar argument; "we should reject James' taxonomy because in his use of it he is naïve about the historicity of his categorical scheme in a way that we simply cannot be" (Murphy 2007, 47). See Murphy (2007, chapter 2).

4 He misses the irony that this claim is being used to advance a certain morality at the same time that he argues that listening to "others" about what is right and wrong is bound to be "wrong." That is, he calls for a universal moral individualism at the same time that he advances this as a moral imperative for other individuals.

5 So our poster to the Facebook SBNR page is not at all far from the discourse James too has incorporated. He insists that outward religion is responsible for Muslim internecine warfare ("Look at the Middle East where Muslim is killing Muslim over who the successor of Mohammed is, when ultimately that shouldn't really matter. The words of the Prophet and the spirit of Islam are what matters, not the personal interpretations of particular individuals"), that true religion is pure, unmediated ("Spiritualism, or faith, is something directly between you and your God or Gods"), and individual ("Spiritualism allows people to think for themselves and to make their own choices in faith, based off their own observations"), and outward religion is best judged by universal common sense ("Even the Bible will tell you we are self-guided, as we ate of the Tree of Knowledge of Good and Evil, whereby we are now born with the innate knowledge of both"; "You are your own judge").

6   Here is one example: a high-school student's PowerPoint slideshow on "The Dangers of Organized Religion," made available on the web, shows a picture of the World Trade Center towers burning, and the following bullet points lie in the foreground: "Today, modern theology differs greatly from its foundations"; "However, traditional interpretation of holy texts often leads to violent, terrorist behavior"; "Needless to say, this behavior is harmful to humanity, causing death, destruction, and terror"; "This is because organized religion today provides multiple justifications of murder and destruction" (Moran 2009).

7   Here the author says "supposedly because of religion," which might be interpreted to contradict my thesis; however, from the surrounding passage I take the author to mean something like this: it is supposedly because of religion, but it is *really* because of *organized* religion.

8   "The God Debate," part of the Gifford lecture series at Edinburg University (available at http://www.youtube.com/watch?v=QCqHnwIR1PY).

9   It is therefore not surprising to find one opponent of "organized religion" say, "If you devote serious time to the practice of religion, it's safe to say you practice *toilet-bowl time management*, flushing much of your precious life down the drain with little or nothing to show for it. . . . [Y]ou can expect to waste even more time on repetitive ritual and ceremony, such as attending mass, learning prayers, and practicing unproductive meditations. . . . If I add up the time I attended mass and Sunday school, studied religion in school as if it were a serious subject, and memorized various prayers, I count thousands of hours of my life I'd love to have back . . . . The more time you devote to religious practice, the more you waste your life on pointless, dead-end pursuits" (Pavlina 2008).

10 That people's account of what their gods think about social and political issues hangs on their own personal views has been demonstrated in scientific studies; see Epley et al. (2009).

11 Oddly, in *Capitalism and Christianity, American Style*, William E. Connolly favorably cites Mitchell's work precisely because of his presentation of Jesus as kind and antidoctrinal, suggesting that the portrait of Jesus is "noble, inspirational, and perhaps uncomplicated" (Connolly 2008, 2–3) and contrasting this Jesus's attitude with an "ethos of revenge" (4) seen in other portrayals of Jesus. As Connolly focuses narrowly on the affective dimension here, he's guilty of the same depoliticizing gesture as Mitchell. Also worth noting is that Connolly, in an endnote, even goes so far as to engage in the return to origins trope by suggesting that Mitchell's Jesus might be closer to the historical Jesus (165).

Part Two

1 All four of these themes were identified by Jeremy Carrette and Richard King in *Selling Spirituality* (2005); see especially 21–22, 106–107. All of the following is greatly indebted to their groundbreaking analysis.

Chapter 4

1 The reader learns throughout the book that this new gospel is necessary in part because the authors of the canonical gospels left so much important material out, and in any case it was time for Biff's story to be heard (no explanation is given for why the canonical gospels left out so much material, or why Biff's story needs to be heard *now*—the closest readers get is "it's some kind of anniversary in dirt-dweller time of the Son's birth, and he feels it's time the whole story is told" [2]).

2 Joshua bumps into him by accident and knocks him down: "'You idiot!' Jakan shouted, rising and dusting himself off. His three friends laughed and he spun on them like an angry tiger. 'This one needs to have his face washed in dung. Hold him'" (24). The group proceeds to hold Josh down and pummel him.

3 For instance, at a funeral at which Joshua attempts to raise the corpse from the dead (and, notably, failing at the attempt), the Romans "were gathered in groups of five at different points around the perimeter of the crowd looking bored" (33) until the corpse starts to move. At that point, Biff "could see that several of the Romans had drawn their swords" (33). They relax once the corpse collapses.

4 When Romans kill Zealots for tearing down Roman statues, they legally "crucify" them (47); by contrast when a Sicarii kills a Roman soldier, he's identified by Biff as a "murderer" (61). Josh tells the Sicarii, "That was wrong. . . . You are wrong to kill that man" (61). In addition, "You serve evil. . . . The Messiah didn't call for the blood of this Roman" (61). The Romans are positively depicted as legitimately attempting to solve the murder and rightly killing the murderer. Although they cruelly detain some of the friends and family of the murderer, they do eventually release them, "beaten, starving, and covered with filth, but very much alive" (79).

5 Bartholomew says, "Do you ever see me cry? I have nothing, so I am a slave to nothing. I have nothing to do, so nothing makes me its slave" (39). As a Cynic—which derives from the Greek word for dog—Bartholomew lives with the village dogs. In fact, he's learning from them: "I'm trying to learn to lick my own balls" (40). While Joshua claims, "I'm sure there's something in the Law that forbids that," he nevertheless thinks that Bartholomew is "much smarter than he looks" (41)—and, in fact, as the novel progresses Joshua comes to reject the Jewish Law and accept an increasingly wide variety of pursuits of sexual desire as legitimate.

6 At another point Hillel reveals a lack of reverence for the Ark of the
Covenant and the Holy of Holies: "It's a box. I saw it when I could still see,
and I can tell you that it's a box. And you know what else, if there were
tablets in it, they aren't there now. So if you want to . . . be executed for
trying to get into the chamber where it's kept, you go right ahead" (97).

7 Josh later decides that he can sell this idea to Israelites by calling that divine
spark the "Holy Ghost" (320).

8 When they meet Balthasar, he appears with "a bright flash and a great
column of red smoke," and "stood as tall as any two men" (143). However,
after he sufficiently scares them, he laughs at them and removes his robe,
revealing that he "had been standing on the shoulders of two young Asian
women who had been hiding beneath the very long robe"—"'Just fuckin'
with you,' he said" (144). At one point Biff uses "sleight of hand" to pretend
to kill someone so that later he can appear to bring the man back to life
(273), and at another point gives a woman a potion that makes her foam at
the mouth, in order to make it appear as if she is possessed by a demon
(357).

9 When one of Balthasar's concubines forces Biff to move furniture around
to fix a room's *Chi*, he suspects that "it had a lot to do with Joy's need to
make me move heavy things" (171). His suspicion is later confirmed, as
she later admits, "I've never understood it. . . . [T]his feng shui stuff is just,
just . . ." (172). She trails off, but Biff finishes her sentence: "Stupid?" She
disagrees with the assessment, saying she just meant "difficult." However,
she offers no evidence to counter Biff's assessment, and the sense that
this is all perhaps stupid hangs in the air.

10 When they are learning about Buddhism from Gaspar, the shocking and
profound statements and koans Buddhism is known for are revealed to
be the result of errors, misunderstanding, or just silliness. When one man
came down from a mountain, after nine years of meditation, the villagers at
the foot of the mountain ask him for what wisdom he had for them:
"'I really have to pee,' said the monk. And with that all of the villagers knew
he had indeed achieved the mind of the Buddhas" (220). At one point, when
Biff says that he wants to "beat the crap out of" someone, Joshua tells
him, "You must *be* the crap" (232).

11 Although not a Pharisee, John the Baptist is criticized for his asceticism,
which is apparently as petty and unreasonable as the Pharisees' practices.
Biff tells John, "You really need to rethink this no marriage, no sex, no fun,
ascetic thing" (322).

12 Even if God did condemn men for sin, humans shouldn't judge each other's
sin. At one point Biff and Josh quiz a gentile about sex, a man who claims
to have "fucked a thousand women, half again as many boys, some sheep,
pigs, a few chickens, and the odd turtle" (123). At one point Biff sarcastically
says, "Right, . . . I'm going to take spiritual advice from a guy who fucks
turtles" (124). Josh retorts, "You shouldn't be so judgmental Biff . . . . You're
not without sin yourself" (124).

What does Moore do with the criticism of lust in the Sermon on the
Mount? At one point Biff is lusting after Maggie, whom both Biff and Josh
love. They're writing the sermon, and Joshua says, "Put in 'If a man even

looks at a woman with lust in his heart, he has committed adultery'" (371). When Biff says, "Seems a little harsh. A little Pharisee-ish," Josh retorts, "I had some people in mind" (371). The saying is therefore accounted for: it is a harsh saying, too harsh actually, and was only included to keep Biff from hitting on Maggie.

13 While Joshua says that Biff should be comfortable with unclean lepers despite his upbringing, Biff says that he could never quite get it—lepers always gave him "the willies" (342). In addition, when Biff asks Judas why he had to give Joshua up to the authorities, Judas says, "He would have just reminded us of what we'll never be." Biff says "Yep" before throwing Judas off a cliff (435)—which he could do because as he is *not* the messiah he cannot be held to the same standard of nonviolence. Indeed, despite Josh's emphasis on nonviolence throughout the novel, Biff regularly commits violence, and is often thanked—at one point Maggie rewards Biff's violence with a kiss and says, "You did good" (387).

14 In *The Soul's Economy*, Jeffrey Sklansky has an excellent discussion of the increasing focus on interior autonomy in American thought, which he dates back to the work of Romantics such as Ralph Waldo Emerson, and including figures like William James. According to Sklansky, these Romantics traded "psychic freedom" for economic self-direction (Sklansky 2002, 8). "By identifying moral agency with the 'inner self' rather than with political and economic sovereignty, they effectively redefined the founding ideals of freedom and democracy in ways that did not directly conflict with the revolution in property relations" under industrialization (37). "They thereby provided ideological cover for class inequality even as they envisioned a society founded in spiritual rather than material relations" (72). Along similar lines, in *Empire of Conspiracy*, Timothy Melley suggests that anti-institutionalism and paranoia about social control can lead to social complacency; "the directive to *fight* [the system] is a declaration of war on a unified and reified 'system.' This directive has the effect of encouraging resistance to social commitments *in general*. While such resistance might be liberating for some, it also amounts to a defense of the liberal values undergirding free market capitalism—atomism, privacy, competitiveness, and *strict* opposition to the social order" (Melley 2000, 57).

Chapter 5

1 What follows in this section is primarily theoretical; by contrast, Ewan and Ewan's *Channels of Desire: Mass Images and the Shaping of American Consciousness* (1992) provide an excellent historical account of the development of consumerism in the United States.

2 While I've cited Simmel and Baudrillard on this point, the similar works of Thorston Veblen (1953), Marshall Sahlins (1976), and Pierre Bourdieu (1984) are equally relevant. See also Bauman (2007), Bocock (1993), Lee (1993), and Featherstone (2007).

3 Theorists such as Rose, Halter, and Lee provide historical accounts of the efforts to coordinate macroeconomic objectives with consumerism and advertising by state and private agencies in the twentieth century.

4 Kathryn Lofton has an excellent discussion of this in her book on Oprah, especially in the chapter titled "Practicing Purchase." Lofton writes, "Oprah's Muslims are 'just like any other American,' except with different accessories. Religious difference in Oprah's America is a fashion choice rather than a theological commitment, a translatable cultural context rather than an exclusivist worldview. . . . For Oprah, modern religious identity is an afterthought to middle-class life" (Lofton 2011, 49).

5 Although neither Halter nor Lau make this explicit, it is clear that whether something is costly or easily appropriated is *context specific*. Insisting on keeping with the tradition of arranged marriage may be costless if one lives in a setting where that is the dominant practice; by contrast, insisting on arranging a child's marriage may be very costly in a late capitalist society in which there is an ideological emphasis on individual choice and romantic love.

6 Although it is beyond the scope of this book, there is a great deal of interesting literature on the increasing *pace* of consumption in late capitalism. See Harvey (1989), Ewan and Ewan (1992), Lee (1993), and Featherstone (2007). Beck and Beck-Gernsheim (2001) is also of interest, although less sophisticated.

7 There is much that could be said about the social construction of gender in the book, but that is outside the scope of my purposes here.

8 The distinction between religion and culture is also invoked when female circumcision comes up. "[I]t's culture not religion" (172).

9 It is worth noting that culture is increasingly complicated, and these things are never determined in a simple or straightforward manner. "This model is not intended to suggest that everyone is determined to desire what their cultural group holds up in high social esteem as being highly desirable patterns of activities. Only that cultural values, patterns, beliefs, symbols, and practices do exert considerable influence; they set the main parameters within which adults choose on the basis of what they see as their best 'desires'" (Bocock 1993, 82).

Chapter 6

1 Lake Lambert III provides a similar analysis in *Spirituality, Inc.: Religion in the American Workplace* (2009), although his book comes from a normative Christian perspective that often sees spirituality as inauthentic. His book is nevertheless useful insofar as he considers a wider range of data than I do in this chapter.

2 He later says that stress can be a good thing (34), and that worry is a "gift" (47).

3 In the conclusion Richmond further presents capitalism as a positive force: "Our system of free-market capitalism creates jobs and defines their purpose, which Is to produce wealth and generate profit. . . . The free market

is flexible. It empowers individuals, encourages innovation and risk taking, and brings out the best in people" (246).

4   Richmond reiterates the naturalness of consumer desire in the conclusion: "We are all, to one degree or another, prisoners of such desires. That is our human nature, and commerce is simply the collective expression of all those individual wants and needs" (249).

5   Fox quotes from Juan Mascaro's translation of the Gita, which—arguably very anachronistically—translates dharma as "work."

Chapter 7

1   Kathryn Lofton has a useful discussion of "Acres of Diamonds" in Lofton (2011, 45ff).

2   Bourdieu argues that the intelligence of the impoverished is also called into question. "Sociodicy here takes the form of a *racism of intelligence*: today's poor are not poor, as they were thought to be in the nineteenth century, because they are improvident, spendthrift, intemperate, etc.—by opposition to the 'deserving poor'—but because they are dumb, intellectually incapable, idiotic. In short, in academic terms, 'they got their just deserts'" (Bourdieu 2003, 33). See also Bourdieu (1998, 42ff). In her concluding remarks to *Saving the Modern Soul*, Eva Illouz similarly criticizes therapeutic or psychological individualism as theodicy: "Psychology resuscitates such forms of theodicy with a vengeance. In the therapeutic ethos there is no such thing as senseless suffering and chaos, and this is why, in the final analysis, its cultural impact should worry us" (Illouz 2008, 247). See also Zygmunt Bauman's *Consuming Life* (2007), especially 138ff.

3   Berg claims to have learned this cosmology from her husband's teachings, as he is a scholar of kabbalah. He claims to get his views from the Zohar and other texts Berg claims are ancient. One source of this esoteric knowledge, *The Book of Formation*, she claims was written by Abraham four millennia ago (12). Presenting her knowledge as rooted in "ancient" sources is clearly designed to add legitimacy to her claims.

4   In addition, "[t]here are no negative husbands or lovers" (195).

5   That this ideology is patriarchal and antifeminist—perhaps to the extent of encouraging readers to overlook or accept what we might consider spousal abuse—I take as self-evident.

6   On the same page he also makes a somewhat confusing claim implying that some races are more bodily than others. The argument is compressed and unclear, but it seems to be that some races carry a bodily collective memory of violence, which makes them more prone to violent behavior. "[C]ertain races of countries in which extreme forms of strife and violence occur have a heavier collective pain-body than others . . . and may also easily become either the perpetrator or the victim of violence" (166).

7   He later, in contradiction with this claim, recognizes that some people are gay (173–174).

Bibliography

Abeel-Fatta, Randa. 2005. *Does My Head Look Big in This?* New York: Orchard Books.

Althusser, Louis. 2008. *On Ideology.* London: Verso.

Althusser, Louis and Étienne Balibar. 1997. *Reading Capital.* London: Verso.

Arnal, William and Russell T. McCutcheon. 2012. *The Sacred Is the Profane: The Political Nature of "Religion."* Oxford: Oxford University Press.

Asad, Talal. 1993. *Genealogies of Religion: Discipline and Reasons of Power in Christianity and Islam.* Baltimore, MD: Johns Hopkins University Press.

Augustine. 1964. *On Free Choice of the Will.* Trans. Anna Benjamin. Indianapolis, IN: Bobbs-Merrill.

Barthes, Roland. 1972. *Critical Essays.* Evanston, IL: Northwestern University Press.

Baudrillard, Jean. 1998. *The Consumer Society: Myths and Structures.* London: Sage.

Bauman, Zygmunt. 2007. *Consuming Life.* Cambridge: Polity Press.

Beck, Ulrich and Elisabeth Beck-Gernsheim. 2001. *Individualization.* London: Sage.

Beckford, James. 1989. *Religion and Advanced Industrial Society.* London: Routledge.

—. 2003. *Social Theory and Religion.* Cambridge: Cambridge University Press.

Bellah, Robert, Richard Madsen, William M. Sullivan, Ann Swidler, and Steven M. Tipton. 1996. *Habits of the Heart: Individualism and Commitment in American Life*, Updated Edition. Berkeley, CA: University of California Press.

Berg, Karen. 2005. *God Wears Lipstick: Kabbalah for Women.* Los Angeles, CA: Kabbalah Center International.

Berger, Bennett M. 1995. *An Essay on Culture: Symbolic Structure and Social Structure.* Berkeley, CA: University of California Press.

Bocock, Robert. 1993. *Consumption.* London: Routledge.

Bourdieu, Pierre. 1998. *Acts of Resistance: Against the Tyranny of the Market.* Trans. Richard Nice. New York: The New Press.

—. 1984. *Distinction: A Social Critique of the Judgment of Taste.* Trans. Richard Nice. Cambridge, MA: Harvard University Press.

—. 2003. *Firing Back: Against the Tyranny of the Market 2.* Trans. Loic Wacquant. New York: The New Press.

Brown, Wendy. 2001. *Politics Out of History.* Princeton, NJ: Princeton University Press.

—. 2006. *Regulating Aversion: Tolerance in the Age of Identity and Empire.* Princeton, NJ: Princeton University Press.

Butler, Judith. 1997. *The Psychic Life of Power: Theories in Subjection.* Stanford, CA: Stanford University Press.

Carrette, Jeremy and Richard King. 2005. *Selling Spirituality: The Silent Takeover of Religion*. London: Routledge.

Cavanaugh, William T. 2009. *The Myth of Religious Violence: Secular Ideology and the Roots of Modern Conflict*. Oxford: Oxford University Press.

Connolly, William E. 2008. *Capitalism and Christianity, American Style*. Durham, NC: Duke University Press.

Conwell, Russell H. 1915. *Acres of Diamonds*. New York: Harper & Brothers.

Crossley, James G. 2008. *Jesus in an Age of Terror: Scholarly Projects for a New American Century*. London: Equinox Publishing.

Douglas, Mary and Baron Isherwood. 1996. *The World of Goods: Towards an Anthropology of Consumption*. London: Routledge.

Dubuisson, Daniel. 2003. *The Western Construction of Religion: Myths, Knowledge, and Ideology*. Trans. William Sayers. Baltimore, MD: Johns Hopkins University Press.

Durkheim, Emile. 1984. *The Division of Labor in Society*. New York: The Free Press.

—. 2001. *The Elementary Forms of Religious Life*. Trans. Carol Cosman. Oxford: Oxford University Press.

—. 1982. *The Rules of Sociological Method and Selected Texts on Sociology and Its Method*. Ed. Steven Lukes. Trans. W. D. Halls. New York: The Free Press.

Elias, Norbert. 1994. *The Civilizing Process: The History of Manners and State Formation and Civilization*. Trans. Edmund Jephcott. Oxford: Blackwell.

—. 2001. *The Society of Individuals*. Trans. Edmund Jephcott. New York: Continuum.

Emerson, Michael O. and Christian Smith. 2000. *Divided by Faith: Evangelical Religion and the Problem of Race in America*. Oxford: Oxford University Press.

Engberg-Pederson, Troels. 2010. *Cosmology and Self in the Apostle Paul: The Material Spirit*. Oxford: Oxford University Press.

Epley, Nicholas, Benjamin A. Converse, Alexa Delbosc, George A. Monteleone, and John T. Cacioppo. 2009. "Believers' estimates of god's beliefs are more egocentric than estimates of other people's beliefs." *Proceedings of the National Academy of Sciences of the United States of America* 106(51): 21533–21538. Available at: http://www.pnas.org/content/106/51/21533.

Erasmus. 1983. *The Essential Erasmus*. Ed. John P. Dolan. New York: Meridian.

Ewan, Stuart and Elizabeth Ewan. 1992. *Channels of Desire: Mass Images and the Shaping of American Consciousness*, Second Edition. Minneapolis, MN: University of Minnesota Press.

Featherstone, Mike. *Consumer Culture and Postmodernism*, Second Edition. London: Sage Publications.

Fenn, Richard K. 1982. *Liturgies and Trials: The Secularization of Religious Language*. New York: The Pilgrim Press.

—. 1978. *Toward a Theory of Secularization*. Storrs, CT: Society for the Scientific Study of Religion.

Fish, Stanley. 1999. *The Trouble with Principle*. Cambridge, MA: Harvard University Press.

Fitzgerald, Timothy. 2007. *Discourse on Civility and Barbarity*. Oxford: Oxford University Press.

—. 2011. *Religion and Politics in International Relations: The Modern Myth*. London: Continuum.

—. 1999. *The Ideology of Religious Studies*. Oxford: Oxford University Press.

Foucault, Michel. 1977. *Discipline and Punish: The Birth of the Prison*. Trans. Alan Sheridan. New York: Vintage.

—. 1980. *Power/Knowledge: Selected Interviews and Other Writings 1972–1977*. Ed. Colin Gordon. New York: Pantheon Books.

—. 2007. *Security, Territory, Population: Lectures at the Collège de France, 1977–1978*. Trans. Graham Burchell. New York: Palgrave Macmillan.

—. 2003. *"Society Must Be Defended": Lectures at the Collège de France, 1975–76*. Trans. David Macey. New York: Picador.

—. 2008. *The Birth of Biopower: Lectures at the Collège de France, 1978–1979*. Trans. Graham Burchell. New York: Palgrave Macmillan.

Fox, Matthew. 1994. *The Reinvention of Work: A New Vision of Livelihood for Our Time*. San Francisco: HarperSanFrancisco.

Fuchs, Stephan. 2001. *Against Essentialism: A Theory of Culture and Society*. Cambridge, MA: Harvard University Press.

Fuller, Robert C. 2001. *Spiritual, But Not Religious: Understanding Unchurched America*. Oxford: Oxford University Press.

Ganly, Sarah. 2007. "The negative impact of organized religion." *Associated Content*. Available at: http://www.associatedcontent.com/article/372622/the_negative_impact_of_organized_religion.html.

Gans, Herbert J. 1979. "Symbolic ethnicity: The future of ethnic groups and cultures in America." In *On the Making of Americans: Essays in Honor of David Riesman*. Ed. Gans, Herbert J., Nathan Glazer, Joseph R. Gusfield, and Christopher Jencks. Philadelphia, PA: University of Pennsylvania Press.

Giddens, Anthony. 1991. *Modernity and Self-Identity: Self and Society in the Late Modern Age*. Stanford, CA: Stanford University Press.

Halter, Marilyn. 2000. *Shopping for Identity: The Marketing of Ethnicity*. New York: Schocken.

Hammond, Philip E. 1992. *Religion and Personal Autonomy: The Third Disestablishment in America*. Columbia, SC: University of South Carolina Press.

Hanh, Thich Nhat. 1995. *Living Buddha, Living Christ*. New York: Riverhead Books.

Harvey, David. 1989. *The Condition of Postmodernity: An Enquiry into the Origins of Cultural Change*. Oxford: Basil Blackwell.

Heelas, Paul. 2008. *Spiritualities of Life: Romantic Themes and Consumptive Capitalism*. Oxford: Blackwell.

Heelas, Paul and Linda Woodhead. 2005. *The Spiritual Revolution: Why Religion Is Giving Way to Spirituality*. Oxford: Blackwell.

Iannoccone, Lawrence R. 1990. "Religious practice: A human capital approach." *Journal for the Scientific Study of Religion* 29: 297–314.

Iannoccone, Lawrence R., Roger Finke, and Rodney Stark. 1997. "Deregulating religion: The economics of church and state." *Economic Inquiry* 35: 350–364.

Illouz, Eva. 2008. *Saving the Modern Soul: Therapy, Emotions, and The Culture of Self-Help*. Berkeley, CA: University of California Press.

James, William. 2004. *The Varieties of Religious Experience*. New York: Barnes & Noble Classics.

Jones, Susan Stedman. 2001. *Durkheim Reconsidered*. Cambridge: Polity Press.

Klippenstein, Janet M. 2005. "Imagine no religion: On defining 'New Age.'" *Studies in Religion/Sciences Religieuses* 34(3–4): 391–403.

Lambert, Lake, III. 2009. *Spirituality, Inc.: Religion in the American Workplace*. New York: New York University Press.

Lau, Kimberly J. 2000. *New Age Capitalism: Making Money East of Eden*. Philadelphia, PA: University of Pennsylvania Press.

Lawson, Jenny. 2012. *Let's Pretend This Never Happened: A Mostly True Memoire*. New York: Penguin.

Lee, Martyn J. 1993. *Consumer Culture Reborn: The Cultural Politics of Consumption*. London: Routledge.

Lehmann, Jennifer M. 1993. *Deconstructing Durkheim: A Post–Post-Structuralist Critique*. London: Routledge.

Lincoln, Bruce. 1991. *Emerging from the Chrysalis: Studies in Rituals of Women's Initiation*. Chicago: University of Chicago Press.

—. 2012. *Gods and Demons, Priests and Scholars: Critical Explorations in the History of Religions*. Chicago: University of Chicago Press.

—. 2006. *Holy Terrors: Thinking about Religion after September 11*, Second Edition. Chicago: University of Chicago Press.

Lofton, Kathryn. 2011. *Oprah: The Gospel of an Icon*. Berkeley, CA: University of California Press.

Lorber, Judith. 1994. *Paradoxes of Gender*. New Haven, CT: Yale University Press.

Lowenstein, Roger. 2008. *While America Aged: How Pension Debts Ruined General Motors, Stopped the NYC Subways, Bankrupted San Diego, and Loom as the Next Financial Crisis*. New York: Penguin.

Luckmann, Thomas. 1967. *The Invisible Religion: The Transformation of Symbols in Industrial Society*. New York: MacMillan.

Lukes, Steven. 1973a. *Emile Durkheim: His Life and Work: A Historical and Critical Study*. London: Penguin.

—. 1973b. *Individualism*. Oxford: Basil Blackwell.

Luther, Martin. 1991. "On secular authority." In *Luther and Calvin on Secular Authority*. Ed. Harro Höpfl. Cambridge: Cambridge University Press.

Lyon, David. 2000. *Jesus in Disneyland: Religion in Postmodern Times*. Cambridge: Polity Press.

Marcuse, Herbert. 1991. *One-Dimensional Man*, Second Edition. Boston, MA: Beacon Press.

Martin, Craig. 2010. *Masking Hegemony: A Genealogy of Liberalism, Religion, and the Private Sphere*. London: Equinox.

Marx, Karl. 1990. *Capital*, Volume 1. Trans. Ben Fowkes. New York: Penguin.

Marx, Marx and Friedrich Engels. 1978. *The Marx–Engels Reader*, Second Edition. Ed. Robert C. Tucker. New York: W.W. Norton & Company.

Masuzawa, Tomoko. 2005. *The Invention of World Religions: Or, How European Universalism Was Preserved in the Language of Pluralism*. Chicago: University of Chicago Press.

McCloud, Sean. 2007. *Divine Hierarchies: Class in American Religion & Religious Studies*. Chapel Hill, NC: University of North Carolina Press.

McCutcheon, Russell T. 2001. *Critics Not Caretakers: Redescribing the Public Study of Religion*. Albany, NY: State University of New York Press.

—. 1997. *Manufacturing Religion: The Discourse of Sui Generis Religion and the Politics of Nostalgia*. Oxford: Oxford University Press.

—. 2005. *Religion and the Domestication of Dissent: Or, How to Live in a Less than Perfect Nation*. London: Equinox Publishing.

—. 2003. *The Discipline of Religion: Structure, Meaning, Rhetoric*. London: Routledge.

Melley, Timothy. 2000. *Empire of Conspiracy: The Culture of Paranoia in Postwar America*. Ithaca, NY: Cornell University Press.

Miller, Barbara Stoler. 1986. *The Bhagavad-Gita: Krishna's Counsel in Time of War*. New York: Bantam Dell.

Miller, Peter. 1987. *Domination and Power*. London: Routledge & Kegan Paul.

Mitchell, Stephen. 1991. *The Gospel according to Jesus: A New Translation and Guide to His Essential Teachings for Believers and Unbelievers*. New York: HarperCollins.

Moore, Christopher. 2002. *Lamb: The Gospel according to Biff, Christ's Childhood Pal*. New York: HarperCollins.

Moran, Kenny. 2009. "The dangers of organized religion." Formerly available at: http://www.scribd.com/doc/15631116/The-Dangers-of-Organized-Religion. Archived at: http://fliiby.com/file/593834/7rkis1fxwj.html.

Murphy, Tim. 2007. *Representing Religion: Essays in History, Theory and Crisis*. London: Equinox Publishing.

Noll, Mark. 1994. *The Scandal of the Evangelical Mind*. Grand Rapids, MI: Wm. B. Eerdmans Publishing.

Nongbri, Brent. 2013. *Before Religion: A History of a Modern Concept*. New Haven, CT: Yale University Press.

Pavlina, Steve. 2008. "10 reasons you should never have a religion." *StevePavlina.com*. Available at: http://www.stevepavlina.com/blog/2008/05/10-reasons-you-should-never-have-a-religion/.

Prothero, Stephen. 2003. *American Jesus: How the Son of God became a National Icon*. New York: Farrar, Strauss, & Giroux.

Richmond, Lewis. 1999. *Work as Spiritual Practice: A Practical Buddhist Approach to Inner Growth and Satisfaction on the Job*. New York: Broadway Books.

Robbins, Anthony. 1986. *Unlimited Power: The New Science of Personal Achievement*. New York: The Free Press.

Roof, Wade Clark. 1999. *Spiritual Marketplace: Baby Boomers and the Remaking of American Religion*. Princeton, NJ: Princeton University Press.

Rose, Nikolas. 1999. *Governing the Soul: The Shaping of the Private Self*, Second Edition. London: Free Association Books.

—. 1998. *Inventing Our Selves: Psychology, Power, and Personhood*. Cambridge: Cambridge University Press.

Sahlins, Marshall. 1976. *Culture and Practical Reason*. Chicago: University of Chicago Press.

Sheldrake, Philip. 2013. *Spirituality: A Brief History*, Second Edition. Oxford: Wiley-Blackwell.

Simmel, Georg. 1971. *Georg Simmel on Individuality and Social Forms*. Ed. Donald M. Levine. Chicago: University of Chicago Press.

Sklansky, Jeffrey. 2002. *The Soul's Economy: Market Society and Selfhood in American Thought, 1820–1920*. Chapel Hill, NC: University of North Carolina Press.

Smith, Christian and Melinda Lundquist Denton. 2005. *Soul Searching: The Religious and Spiritual Lives of American Teenagers*. Oxford: Oxford University Press.

Smith, Jonathan Z. 1982. *Imagining Religion: From Babylon to Jonestown.*
    Chicago: University of Chicago Press.
—. 2004. *Relating Religion: Essays in the Study of Religion.* Chicago: University
    of Chicago Press.
Smith, Steve. 1989. "Preface" to *Everyday Zen: Love & Work,* by Charlotte Joko
    Beck. San Francisco: HarperSanFrancisco.
Stark, Rodney and Roger Finke. 2000. *Acts of Faith: Explaining the Human Side
    of Religion.* Berkeley, CA: University of California Press.
Steel, Mark. 2013. "You're not unemployed—You lack self-reliance." *The
    Independent* July 4. Available at: http://www.independent.co.uk/voices/
    comment/youre-not-unemployed–you-lack-selfreliance-8687753.html.
Strenski, Ivan. 2006. *The New Durkheim.* New Brunswick, NJ: Rutgers
    University Press.
Sullivan, Winnifred Fallers. 2005. *The Impossibility of Religious Freedom.*
    Princeton, NJ: Princeton University Press.
The Invisible Committee. 2009. *The Coming Insurrection.* Los Angeles, CA:
    Semiotext(e).
Therborn, Göran. 1980. *The Ideology of Power and the Power of Ideology.*
    London: Verso.
Tolle, Eckhart. 1999. *The Power of Now: A Guide to Spiritual Enlightenment.*
    Novato, CA: New World Library; Vancouver: Namaste Publishing.
Turner, Bryan S. 2011. *Religion and Modern Society: Citizenship, Secularisation
    and the State.* Cambridge: Cambridge University Press.
Veblen, Thorston. 1953. *The Theory of the Liesure Class: An Economic Study of
    Institutions.* New York: New American Library.
Verter, Bradford. 2003. "Spiritual capital: Theorizing religion with Bourdieu
    against Bourdieu." *Sociological Theory* 21(2): 150–174.
Warner, Rob. 2010. *Secularization and Its Discontents.* London: Bloomsbury.
Weber, Max. 2002. *The Protestant Ethic and the "Spirit" of Capitalism and Other
    Writings.* Ed. Peter Baehr Gordon C. Wells. New York: Penguin.
Williams, Raymond. 1977. *Marxism and Literature.* Oxford: Oxford University
    Press.
Wood, Matthew. 2007. *Possession, Power, and the New Age: Ambiguities of
    Authority in Neoliberal Societies.* Aldershot, England: Ashgate.

Index